Anymore

Edited by Cynthia C. Davidson
Anyone Corporation
New York, New York
The MIT Press
Cambridge, Massachusetts
London, England

Editor
Cynthia C. Davidson

Senior Editor
Thomas Weaver

Design
2x4

Anymore is the ninth in a series of ten planned volumes documenting the annual international, cross-disciplinary conferences being sponsored by the Anyone Corporation to investigate the condition of architecture at the end of the millennium.

Printed and bound in the United States of America.

Library of Congress Cataloging-in-Publication Data
Anymore / edited by Cynthia C. Davidson
  p. cm.
  "Anymore conference, held in Paris from June 23– 25, 1999. Anymore is the ninth in a planned series of ten volumes documenting the annual Any conferences" — Introd.
  Includes bibliographical references.
  ISBN 0-262-54110-6 (pbk.: alk. paper)
    1. Architecture, Modern— 19th century—Congresses.
  2. Architecture, Modern— 20th century—Congresses.
  3. Architecture—Philosophy— Congresses.
  I. Davidson, Cynthia C.
  II. Anymore Conference (1999: Paris, France)
  NA642.A59 2000
  724'.5—dc21   00-035159

Anyone Corporation is a not-for-profit corporation in the State of New York with editorial and business offices at 41 West 25th Street, 11th floor, New York, New York 10010.
Email: anyone@anycorp.com

Photo Credits
Group photos by Dominique Delaunay: pages 1, 6, 8–9, 294–95.

Images by Fiona Meadows and Frédéric Nantois: pages 16–22.

Photos by Hubert Damisch: pages 79–81.

Photos by Yoshio Takase: pages 92–94.

Photos courtesy of Arata Isozaki: pages 96–99.

Photos by Hisao Suzuki: pages 100–01.

Images courtesy of François Roche: pages 104–08.

Image © Office for Metropolitan Architecture: page 136.

Images courtesy of Rosalind E. Krauss: pages 146–52.

Images courtesy of Bernard Tschumi: pages 160–64.

Photos by Jean-Marie Monthiers: pages 198–202.

Photos by G. Fessy: pages 268–74.

Image courtesy of ADAGP: pages 276.

Cet ouvrage publié dans le cadre du programme d'aide à la publication bénéficie du soutien du Ministère des Affaires Etrangères et du Service Culturel de l'Ambassade de France représenté aux Etats-Unis.

This work, published as part of the program of aid for publication, received support from the French Ministry of Foreign Affairs and the Cultural Service of the French Embassy in the United States.

Translated from the French.
Rosalind E. Krauss:
"On Paper."
Julie Rose:
"Architecture Between Reflections and Plans," "High-Tech in Architecture: Of Disenchanted Technology."
Mortimer Schiff:
"Melange of Articles and Reflections," "The Offense of Wandering," "Gradations," "Practice[3]: Theory, History, Architecture," "A Strategy for Action," "The Architectural Project: A Real Virtuality," "Any Alternative?," "No More Context," "It Will Be Nice Tomorrow."

Translated from the Italian.
Matteo Cainer:
"Letter from Renato Rizzi."
Chiara Marchelli:
"The Scalpel and the Axe."

Translated from the Japanese.
Sabu Kohso:
"An Extra-Context."

Paris, June 23–25, 1999 As the capital of the 19th century prepared for the end of the 20th, a giant illuminated sign halfway up the Eiffel Tower counted down the days to the year 2000. Across the Seine, the Anymore conference convened in the old Cinémathèque française at the far end of the Palais de Chaillot. At this confluence of a 1960s brutalist movie theater (once haunted by the young Godard and Truffaut) and the curved galleries upstairs – future home of the Cité de l'architecture et du patrimoine – filled with shrouded and dusty examples of past architectural styles, Anymore? was a pointed and pertinent question. Anymore architecture? Anymore 20th century? The Eiffel Tower glittered a reply: Jour 192, Jour 191, Jour 190 . . .

It was around Jour 546 when Jean-Louis Cohen, the organizer par excellence, began talking with me about Anymore, not long after he became director of the Institut français d'architecture. François Barré, directeur de l'architecture et du patrimoine, Ministere de la Culture et de la communication, gave IFA the funds for Anymore, which, with the great organizational skills of IFA staff Marie-Hélène Contal, Brigitte Schoendoerffer, Eric Briat, Marie-Ange Bisseuil, and the staff at the Cinémathèque, brought some forty speakers onto the Anymore stage. Photographer Dominique Delaunay made wonderful group portraits at the rooftop lunch breaks, all while chanting "fromage." The evenings were equally memorable thanks to the generous hospitality of Monsieur and Madame Dominique Boudet and IFA President Dominique Perrault and his wife Aude, who graciously opened their homes for Parisian garden parties. And then, as if providing more, a perfect postconference architectural field trip to Bordeaux was beautifully choreographed by Francine Fort, director, and Nadine Gibault of Arc en Reve. Back in New York, editorial interns at the Anyone office helped to make both the conference and this book possible: Benjamin Prosky, Brad Samuels, Jaime Johnson, and Brainerd Taylor, all Vassar College students. The tapes of the conference were transcribed by the ever reliable Edwin Gunn and then expertly deciphered by Thomas Weaver, who also performed multiple editing tasks. Mortimer Schiff, Julie Rose, and Rosalind Krauss translated many essays from the French for publication here, a project made possible by a grant from the French Ministry of Foreign Affairs and the Cultural Service of the French Embassy in the United States. Then designers Katie Andresen and Alice Chung of 2x4 gave Anymore its final form. Ultimately, however, Anymore? could only be asked because of the important, ongoing support of Harusuke Imamura and the Shimizu Corporation in Tokyo, who, along with the many conference participants, have made the entire Anyone project possible. And so, yes, there is more, and there is Anymore. – CCD

Cynthia C. Davidson

No city has a more enduring, and more reproduced, image than Paris. In the shadow of this emblem, of the (real) Eiffel Tower, it was fitting that the Anymore conference posed the idea of "anymore" as a question about the continuity of architecture and its history, theory, and technology. The coincident near-end of the 20th century and even of the 10-year Any project itself lent a certain resonance to the question of Anymore, for technology is rapidly changing how architecture is thought and, ultimately, how it is seen. As Akira Asada pointed out, any question beginning with **anymore** could only be answered in one of two ways: "much more (to come)" or "no more (to go)."

Regardless of the answer, the mood at Anymore was clearly one that anticipated change in more than the calendar. Even the idea of undecidability that has been the Any password for the past nine years seemed challenged. Rosalind Krauss sounded the alarm: "The ebullient character of the 'anys,' with their theme of proliferation and promiscuity – anyone, anywhere, anytime, anyhow – announced a kind of deconstructionist hedonism, the joy of self-deferral, the pleasure of self-duplication, the thrill of self-abandonment. 'Anymore,' however . . . may in itself contain some kind of lesson about the specificity of the signifier. . . . After all, the question 'Anymore architecture?' is framed as a problem in specificity."

To inject specificity into undecidability is a sobering thought, but it is one problematized by the digital. The long-term effect of emerging digital technologies on image production – on, for example, drawing and photography and architecture – seems, for the moment, to be both endorsing and confounding Walter Benjamin's speculations on the reproduction of the image in the mechanical age. Just as mechanical reproduction, as Benjamin wrote, "emancipates the work of art from its parasitical dependence on ritual," today the digital seems to provide emancipation from the ritual, or tradition, of making architecture. At the same time, however, it also confounds this idea by setting in motion a new kind of ritual of making, one that ensnares the original, or the "real," in the digital. The consequences of this are a return to a privileging of the visual; in the digital, the image becomes the architecture.

By introducing the work of visual artists James Coleman and William Kentridge into a discussion of architecture, Krauss also introduced in the face of emerging technologies the idea of nearly forgotten, disappearing technologies, which in their obsolescence become available as an aesthetic medium. By seizing on outdated and dying modes of image projection, Krauss writes, Coleman and Kentridge created new, specific mediums in art: respectively, "projected images" and "drawings for projection," two forms of art that cause us to see images – in this case, photography and drawing – in ways that resist the mass proliferation and acceptance of the digital.

Architecture's "projected image," however, seems to embrace the possibilities of the digital rather than challenge them. "The old concept of the polis was constructed by architectural means," Lars Spuybroek says, "but with [the digital] you can never talk in terms of space or perspective again. So why use space or perspective again in a building?" How this liberation from traditional operations in architecture manifests itself becomes a crucial question. Krauss reminds us what it means for the medium of architecture when certain design practices yield to computerization, which is simply "a design alternative, one that, imitating its use in aeronautics, rocketry, and shipmaking, encourages architecture to slip off the shackles of gravity and thus out of a certain notion of tectonics and embodiedness." If the changes in space and perspective are being made through programs written not for architecture but for other disciplines, is this a loss of specificity? In the reductive language of the digital, Barbara Stafford has pointed out, in the on/off binary language of the computer, there are no distinct boundaries between disciplines, and therefore no specificity. Is this then an undecidable architecture?

In her previous writing on architecture, Krauss suggested that there will always be four walls to architecture's reality and, as Jacques Derrida has said, that these will always have meaning. If this is the case, then the discipline of architecture will remain more or less intact despite its capacity for digital imagery. But this is not the only problem posed by digital instrumentality. There is also the problem of the image, or the iconography, of architecture. For the question that seemed to linger, unanswered at Anymore, was, How does architecture want to be seen? This question emerged as two ideas were brought to the conference table: one about architecture's disappearance (no more) and one about its image, or spectacle (much more). Though at first the concepts of disappearance and image may seem to have little relationship, in fact they meet in the digital, where architecture is arguably both image and disappearance.

From Frank Gehry's shimmering Guggenheim Museum Bilbao – a building made "tectonic" by aeronautics software – to Spuybroek's fantastic computer renderings of seemingly endless and gravity-free space, architecture today is captured in and on a surface, disembodied, essentially made only to engage the eye. In the image-intensive media age, architecture's relationship to the image has overtaken its meaning. One important question is whether architecture can register through the image any kind of meaningful resistance to the loss of its specificity.

It would seem, however, that we understand the image to be today's reality, a condition that filmmaker Alain Fleischer believes has problematized architecture as it has been known. "Today architecture has stopped waiting for the images it might manage to provoke once it is built," Fleischer writes here. "It seeks itself in advance. It bases itself and thinks of itself in images, within images. . . . Architecture is no longer merely an object in search of images that it might permit photography, film, or video to capture; it is no longer merely a stage waiting for the role that might be conferred upon it in some story . . . it is no longer merely an object that may be large-scale but is nonetheless reducible to an object of design. . . . Architecture has become its own scenario . . . filmed and edited by itself – and this, from the outset, from its initial conception." Do these "pre-images" mean that architecture has lost its perception in real time and space?

This raises another question: Is the production of images a way for architecture to take control of its reception? Given our media age, Bernard Tschumi would seem to think so: "Architects should not be involved with the media of construction but with the construction of the media"; that is, of its reception in images – with how architecture is seen.

*   *   *   *

The day after the Anymore conference adjourned, a small group of us boarded the Paris-to-Bordeaux TGV for an architectural trip that, for all its weekend brevity, was rich in vineyards and in architecture, from Victor Louis to Le Corbusier to Rem Koolhaas and Jean Nouvel. The trip was a small but vivid reminder of the value of culture, especially the value of the real as embodied in wine and place and objects.

On the train, on the way for the first time to see buildings we felt we had all seen before, I began to feel conservatively old-fashioned. Given the saturation of images that shapes contemporary life, would I be able to see past images to real architecture?

In Bordeaux, the much photographed, hilltop Koolhaas villa was brilliantly overprinted with traces of Mies and Loos, but the mood was sharp and cool. What emerged, what was "outside" of the image, was a kind of tool, a very visceral prosthetic device that enables a man and his family to endure a life of physical and psychological pain. It contrasted starkly with Le Corbusier's Cité Frugés, the workers' housing at Pessac that features a series of closely placed, yet hardly machinelike multifamily dwellings with gardens and roof terraces; and then with Lacaton & Vassal's low-budget Maison Latapie, a house of corrugated metal and plastic that even in its ability to be shuttered down and "disappear" was palpably there.

As our group committed still more images to film, it was difficult not to feel nostalgic for the real meaning of Pessac. We ate fresh, briny oysters while overlooking the Bay of Arcachon, the very waters in which Le Corbusier drowned, and as the tide washed in, architecture too, and the images we had seen in Paris, seemed washed of certain cultural ambitions. There is, as Rosalind Krauss pointed out, a sense of the mournful in Anymore, which echoes with Poe's ravens calling, "Nevermore. Nevermore."

*   *   *   *

One hundred ninety days after the Anymore conference adjourned in Paris, the Eiffel Tower, seen on television screens around the world, appeared to attempt liftoff from the Jardins du Champ de Mars. For all its many manifestations — in paintings, on postcards, on silk scarves and souvenir plates — as a surge of fireworks sputtered like giant rocket engines at its base, the symbol of Paris launched the City of Light not only into the next millennium but, once again, into the human imagination. It was a spectacular image, one made all the more powerful by its reality. Here, suddenly, was a moment of real architecture **plus** image, and it seemed to say there will be "much more (to come)."

June 24, 1999

Akira Asada [5]
Jean-Louis Cohen [18]
Marie-Hélène Contal [24]
Hubert Damisch [27]
Cynthia C. Davidson [16]
Ignasi de Solà-Morales [12]
Peter Eisenman [25]
Kristin Feireiss [21]
Francine Fort [22]
Mark Goulthorpe [8]
Elizabeth Grosz [30]
Paul Henninger [34]
Dennis Hollier [29]
Rosalind E. Krauss [26]
Phyllis Lambert [15]
Greg Lynn [6]
Fiona Meadows [19]
Frédéric Migayrou [7]
Enric Miralles [23]
Frédéric Nantois [31]
Franco Purini [14]
Saskia Sassen [17]
Kazuyo Sejima [20]
Lars Spuybroek [4]
Benedetta Tagliabue [11]
Mark C. Taylor [32]
Laura Thermes [13]
Bruno Vayssière [10]
Teri Wehn-Damisch [28]
Riken Yamamoto [3]
Yoshiyuki Yamana [1]

1. Paris Prologue: Emerging French Architecture
Following the marginal experimentation in the 1970s and an extraordinary surge in public commissions from 1981 to the mid 1990s, French architecture today is characterized by diverse and contradictory production. Public funding has by no means led to a "state" architecture but to investigative, critical designs that challenge typology, context, and technology. Several of the most stimulating teams, which operate at scales ranging from single-family housing to major cultural institutions, will discuss their problematic.

Archimedia, An Unpredictable Process of Free Interactions

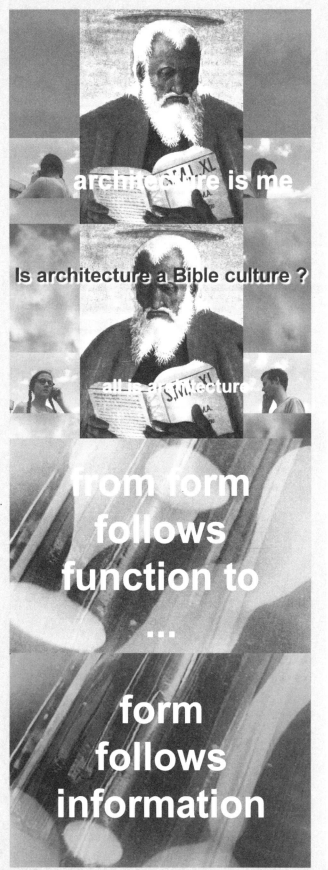

architecture is me

Is architecture a Bible culture ?

all is architecture

from form
follows
function to
...

form
follows
information

Fiona Meadows and Frédéric Nantois

Anymore is the ninth conference in the Any cycle, thus one cannot help thinking about another series of meetings on the topic of architecture in which the ninth one, also held in France, was essential. We are referring, of course, to CIAM IX, which took place in Aix-en-Provence in 1953. The parallel would surely stop there, were it not for the fact that one has the impression today that we are living in a period of questioning, that the present situation is also marked by a search for alternatives to the models already in place, and that many of us are quietly affirming a certain independence vis-à-vis the dominant tendencies.

Inasmuch as architecture is always facing situations that one can define by the constraints of program, context, client, need, and designer according to the conventional script, we must ask, do these categories alone describe and comprehend the preoccupations of architecture today? In order to extricate oneself from the established discourses, it is necessary to question these convenient categories as much in practice as in theory. And if in architecture a rupture or a renewal or a paradigm shift occurs, it is because now, in order to understand these alternatives, it is necessary to consider a more global situation – that of society in its entirety, and its transformations. Current thinking in architecture could then be approached beginning from other notions that better describe the intentions and objectives of that thinking. If architecture has regularly questioned the conditions of its actions, present society contributes in its own way to the renewal of that interrogation. Our concern is precisely to know how it is possible today to put forth the kinds of critical architectural thinking and practice that would engage the changes in society, that would implicate themselves anew in society, and that would question, as do other creative fields, the validity and legitimacy of those changes.

In the idea of change, of a kind of beginning, the first question that presents itself is that of the actual origin of architectural thinking and practice, that is to say, the search for an anchorage in society and its attendant realities. In fact, what is important to us is not to define precisely a point of departure that would provide us with a perfect model to follow, a paradigm from which we could deduce any Utopia whatever. Rather, we see that origin as expressing itself in the form of a condition that we would label an "informational condition." And if we refer to it by that name, it is not simply because of the technologies of information that participate in the definition but, more globally, because of the way society in its entirety is developing. In our approach, technologies are not an objective or a goal; rather, what interests us is their generalization, their banalization, their infiltration into every aspect of everyday life – and the fact that they are a product or an expression of the society that always participated in the definition of architecture. This condition persists today because daily reality can no longer conceive of itself without its informational double, that is, without a schematization, a modeling of its complexity in the various fluxes and interdependent networks of exchange. But even so, this viewpoint does not provide us with a coherent unifying theory of a situation that is far from being homogeneous, nor does it lead us to a certain techno-determinism or holistic conception of the world. Thus if one reflects on the existence of this condition at all, it is not to call upon ready-made solutions but, on the contrary, to problematize architecture. It is at once a theoretical tool to analyze the complexity of the situations that architecture faces and a conceptual tool to integrate new operational notions in particular projects. But even if this condition – one expression of which would be globalization – is something that cannot be ignored, it does not imply that one has to accept its rules and principles in tacit fashion. It rather seems evident that one must maintain a critical approach vis-à-vis these tools and ideas.

One of the questions related to the hypothesis of a new origin for architecture is whether there are functions, or at least particular practices, that would imply a new architecture. On the one hand, this question led us to concern ourselves with the techniques of the system of actual production and, on the other, with urban agglomeration and its ongoing development. What is unusual in all this is that one of the tools of production has also become the privileged medium of leisure activities. The computer, central to the work situation, has become more and more significant in numerous other activities, including familial ones. But its presence involves only a few direct implications with regard to space, compared to the number of eventual indirect implications that will effect a recomposition of social relations between the two extremes of perpetual nomadism and assisted cocooning. The urban scale is the other essential element, the other essential condition, since the urban space is the privileged space of the exchange – an exchange that integrates a new geography of communications that no longer requires direct contact or physical proximity. The consequence is certainly not the disappearance of work or the urban setting, but rather a different way of thinking about and conceiving space, and a relativization of the architectural object. Thus we are led not to reinforce the stature of the object in seeking for it an ever-greater autonomy, but

rather to relativize it all the more – indeed to destroy it and to rethink it (its content and its form) – in its diffusion, in its place in the network. Even though the object can claim a certain independence, it cannot be dissociated from the global complexity, and it is this double logic that is so interesting. Under these circumstances, it is no longer the identity imposed upon the object that counts, but rather the facilities that become available along with it. In fact, in a certain sense one might say that the architectural object tends to define itself as a service.

That is the nexus we have sought to explore in different projects over the last several years. With our 1992 project Virtual Bauhaus, we became interested in an institution and the question of architecture education; the problem continues to be relevant today. The upshot was the dematerialization of the institution and of education, and of their reconfiguration into a network of global communication – every point of connection being both a school and a tie-in with a teaching network. More recently, in a project for the Mies Foundation in Barcelona, we proposed a hypersite rather than a hyperobject – a space that exists concretely and in its functioning only by virtue of the physical and non-local interrelationship generated by architectural tourism. The ensemble ends up in what we refer to as a "foundation without foundations" – a kind of theme park of variable geometry whose existence looms over the theme parks derived from the universal exposition. There, it was not a matter of the substitution of one mode of communication for another, but rather a temporary accumulation of modes of exchange, an accumulation that had also passed through a physical regrouping.

For another project on housing, we sought to define a habitat in accordance with its environment and its informational reality. We came up with the idea of what we called the "post-primitive hut" – by analogy with the first habitations, a shelter, though this time a technological one, suggesting a commutation space among the different regimes of communication, starting from which a different conception of the community link could be developed. We chose to define the entire conception by starting from the notion of the "glocal" – the convergence of the global and the local, the belonging as much to the proximate community as to distinct interconnected networks beyond. What interests us in the relations among people, the community, and information technologies is not the hypothesis of a sort of double virtuality that would extend, in metaphoric fashion, human values to artificial systems. The liberation from chronological time and the interrogations on the qualities of physical space for social interrelationships do not introduce the domination of a unique time and the abandonment of existent forms of exchange; rather, they facilitate the multiplication of different space-times, and the search for their interfaces.

If indeed there is a new origin, a new condition by which one can rethink architecture, the second question to be asked concerns the possible expression of this condition. How does one express the fluxes, the processes of exchange? Does the new situation exercise a direct impact on architectural forms? Is the triumph of software over hardware to be understood in the first degree? Our approach is that the taking into account of this condition need not be the occasion for substituting information for the aesthetics of the mechanical, and for the metaphor of the machine, the simulated representation of exchange fluxes. We do not conceive the expression of this condition as starting from the idea of an "informational style." For this reason, we do not situate our work at the heart of the logic of the tool of production in the hopes of mastering its development. A major risk is that architecture would only transpose the domination of this system of production – and the history of architecture has shown just what that can lead to. It should instead be possible to find an alternative path that is neither a fallback to obsolete architectural values nor a track pursued with technique alone.

The information technologies introduce a mediation that is of their language. Rather than looking for a literal transposition of that language, we are interested in the implicit transformation of the environment and of architecture by virtue of its presence. Rather than thinking of the form as a metaphor of the fluxes, we attempt to understand the possible implications in the processing of daily space. Then we attempt to define the interfaces and intervals by which a dialogue between a person and his/her renewed environment can be established. That leads us concretely to pose certain questions concerning architectural expression, which in no way constitute a value judgment. For example, between the house of Bill Gates and some structure we'll call "blob" architecture, which has the greater chance of being propagated, of becoming a daily benchmark of the integration of technological progress in architecture and of the change in the relations between the individual and his/her environment? For us it is certainly not a question of supplying a theoretical alibi for an economy that seems to be doing pretty well all by itself. Nonetheless, it seems to us that the Gates house, along with others, addresses a certain number of pertinent questions for architects – especially in the scheme of this conference, the concerns of which are technology, context, and theory. Does a particular aesthetic expression exist for the new qualities that the architectural object would possess? Can one translate into architecture the notion of intelligence, the idea of dialogue? Why must these concepts take a form for which the architect is both the designer and the programmer? The question of the architectural pertinence of technologies underscores the relationship between form and information, and is notably expressed by the tran-

towards an informational style ?

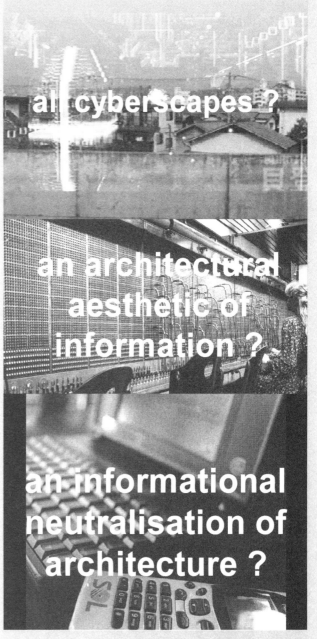

an cyberscapes ?

an architectural aesthetic of information ?

an informational neutralisation of architecture ?

sition from the logic of the finite object to that of the evolving process. But to the degree that the process is attached to a certain moment in time as it finally produces a static form, there is really nothing new in all of this. What interests us in the idea of process, however, is not the unique snapshot that one can take at a given moment but the notion of progressive programming. Also of interest is the idea that there exists a kind of supra-programming, in the sense of supra-information, resulting from a production of elements, which includes the analysis of a situation, the integration of different exterior constraints, and the initialization of evolutionary rules in time – all of these assured by a more complete and complex treatment of information. This supra-programming represents another approach to the question of expression. It also constitutes a way to oppose the neutralization of architecture. The idea of subordinating form to information produces an architecture of surfaces, pushing the envelope to the fore as a kind of interface of intelligent dialogue independent of the enclosed space. The destination of the construction no longer defines the rules of its occupation or the use of its space. Since architecture is evaluated by the services it renders, no specific typology is justifiable. Thus the architecture may be alternatively a tour de force that can symbolize by its form a capacity to react to information, or a neutral box decorated by information – the information becoming a kind of motif.

The question that concerns us is how to reinvest the space, how to differentiate it. If the information gathered from the environment and its treatment define the architecture, it would then be necessary to analyze the relationship between the individual and his/her context for acting in the world. For this reason we are interested in cases that are often left to the side, as much on the theoretical level as on the practical, but which could nonetheless be instructive. In particular, we work with clinical cases of persons with perceptual deficiencies or who have a specific handicap – people who, in their daily rounds, necessarily develop a unique sensibility vis-à-vis their environment, habits, and practices of alternative or marginal communication, and thus another kind of consciousness of the space in which they move. This is the problem we tackled in our Life Lines and City Lines projects regarding the presence of handicapped persons in the city. To define the equipment necessary for a city neighborhood to possess, we developed the idea of an evolving continuity of the environment, beginning with an analysis of the perceptions of handicapped persons. In supra-programming the environment, we introduced the possibility of permanent variations – the capability of the environment to respond actively by relying on the complementarity of the senses in perception and on their transformation, by recourse, to different processes. Space is thus managed by the time of interaction, not necessarily in a linear fashion but as a succession of nonlinear effects responding to an ever-changing instanta-

neous relationship – above all, one always initiated by the person who acts.

The third question, which follows directly from the preceding two, is that of authority. It is not a new question in art or literature, though architecture seems only recently to have discovered it. We do not believe in the disappearance of the author, and if anything, the present situation rather indicates the reappearance of authors.

What interests us here is the transformation of authority, its reification, its dispersion, its division as much among persons as among artificial systems. It is not a matter of notions of interactivity or of conviviality, both of which are the manifestation of the ancient notion – still invoked by architects – of "appropriation." Here as well, our interest lies in the daily rounds of the urban setting and in perceptions of it. On this point we put together several experiments. For example, in the interactive installation Dérives, the City as a Hypertext, we proposed that the spectator be the "liver," or actor, of his/her experience (to return to a Situationist term), the initiator of his/her navigations, of his/her wanderings. From that beginning a hypertextual construction of the urban setting appears, bringing into evidence the multiplicity of the spectator's readings and possible writings. In the project Spaces of Non Memory Places, we tackled the question of memorization and its relationship to lived-in space. We also treated its relationship to information technologies by elaborating the transition from traditional mnemonics to the total artificialization of memory, and to the dependence on the tools comprising the new mediation between it and the environment. The interest of this experiment lies in bringing to the fore certain notions that reveal the "dimension," or "informational depth," of the environment – the complexity and unpredictability of relationships and transactions between a person and his/her environment. In this domain the current developments in artificial intelligence and robotics research are fascinating to contemplate. In effect, we have moved from a centralizing concept of decision-making according to the hypothesis that one can model the complexity of the world and derive from it a base of given information, beginning from which an artificial system could act in a fashion equal to that of a human being. We have moved, in fact, from that concept to a totally decentralized, delocalized one, based on the cooperation of independent systems that share nothing in common and invent their language of communication, learn permanently, adapt themselves, and collaborate in making decisions in collective fashion. What can all this provide for architecture? The replacement of architects by these systems? The adoption of these principles by humans? Certainly neither one nor the other – despite the convergence of the human sciences and the information technologies, we do

le mythe organise un monde sans contradictions parce qu sans profondeur, un monde étalé dans l'évidence, il fonde une clarté heureuse

many more

end product

not believe in the hypothesis of a hybrid individual, which in architecture would end up as the adoption of a new ideal as abstract as Le Corbusier's Modulor.

On the contrary, what interests us is the relativization of the power of decision-making, in the sense of another kind of exercise of authority – research into specific methods for architectural reflection and conception – and, on the other hand, the possible re-equilibration between the environment and the individual, the two now being thought of on the same level of importance. Thus the question of authority is no longer simply limited to knowing who decides what. It introduces as well the question of authenticity, to the degree that authority is permanently carried forward in an evolving process in which no player dominates. We are actually developing around these questions a new project called The House of Divorce. The project does not refer to the problems of couples. The terms house and divorce are inseparable – their relationship expressing the condition we have just addressed – the search for more and more coherence, organization, and equilibrium, and, at the same time, the affirmation of ever more evident partings of the ways. In this dialectic, in which resides an image of society in its ensemble, everyone is propelled always in two directions – toward more individualism and toward more interaction. The home itself has forever been the place of dialogue and of parting – including, in architecture, the dialogue and separation between theoretical approaches and contradictory individual expectations. The project is now in the preproject, or rather project of the project, phase. It will consist of a video triptych that presents certain hypotheses concerning the relationships among domestic space, the inhabitant, and the environment we have referred to – that is to say, the fragility of the relations between the individual going about his/her daily rounds and the mediation of information technologies; the search for the ideal and the quotidian nature of that search with the inevitable slipping of the mythic object toward the mediatic one – and the foundational parting, namely, the catastrophe at the origin of the home. The next phase of the project will consist of an installation in situ – experienced – and then an architectural project constructed and conceived beginning from this particular dynamic.

Our work consists of an inquest into the complexity of the architectural act vis-à-vis the societal act. It is clear to us that every intervention must above all pass the gauntlet of an interrogation regarding the necessity of architecture. And it is notably for this reason that we have developed our approach not only by way of research but by way of artistic experiences, and also by instructive architectural projects – always with a particular interest in the urban setting and in technique, which are the two essential expressions of the transformations in every society. Today, rather than try to find a solution to the question presented by Anymore, with its implicit hints of an end to it all, it seems that we are continually faced with a situation of many more and its implications – which does not necessarily mean many more architectures, unless one chooses to recognize in architecture (or so we would hope) the value of alternative approaches to the conventional project.

Fiona Meadows and Frédéric Nantois are partners of Archimedia, an association in Paris, where they experiment with the architectural potential of computer technology.

Two Projects

Dominique Jakob and Brendan MacFarlane

Puzzle House

The Puzzle House is an alternative to the mass-produced individual home. We developed this project around the idea of both reinforcing private space and integrating it more viably into the landscape. The individual Puzzle House is organized around a patio that allows cross-axial movement and views inside, and encourages reflection and family life. The materials are generic: coated concrete and natural aluminum structural elements. There is no private garden outside the house but rather a continuous "fabric" that is common to and shared by different households. On the basis of this definition of public and private, house, nature, and individual access roads become like pieces of a jigsaw puzzle that is put together in a deformed and fractured space. The interlocking pieces of this puzzle offer a variable composition of places, but one that is invariably structured in relation to the connection made between public and private.

The house, its access, and the surrounding vegetation make an ideal environment where all functions overlap. The house becomes a part of a puzzle in which the right angle disappears, and the turfed slopes of the roofs become foothills worthy of a Georges Braque landscape.

On this principle of overlap, all sizes and configurations of the house can be imagined, like the various widths of paths or streets. One no longer knows which roadway system, house, piece, or frame determines the other. It is the total integration of the habitat and the landscape, the opposite of architecture as object.

Puzzle House, Paris, 1997.

Previous pages and this page: Restaurant proposal, Centre Georges Pompidou, Paris, 1998.

Centre Georges Pompidou Restaurant

The program brief was to create a restaurant for the fifth floor of the Centre Georges Pompidou. The space would need to contain all of the usual programmatic requirements of a restaurant as well as open out onto an exterior terrace.

The problem here was to create an appropriate response inside such a particular architectural context as the Pompidou. Through working with the space, we became interested in the notion of trying to create an architecture that was made from what existed — not to import or create by addition but to propose the lightest possible intervention. Our interest was to discover or insert a kind of nonexistent, background presence, maybe at the extreme of an almost nonarchitectural or nondesigned response. This led us to work with the floor and to propose this surface as a new field of intervention, deforming it in such a way that we could insert a series of volumes beneath it, thus creating a new landscape of both interior and exterior conditions — a hidden, maybe camouflaged, situation. We proposed to make this floor surface, or "skin," out of aluminum, a material that, when brushed, both absorbs and reflects light, thus also reinforcing this notion of background, of appearance and disappearance. A minimal presence with a strong personality — a kind of mask.

The series of volumes that we slide beneath this skin — kitchen, bar, coatroom, and private reception room — found their eventual form and position through the usual negotiation process of design. This skin also acted as a stretchable surface that eventually absorbed all sorts of program changes. Again, a kind of nondesign decision operated at a reduced scale here, where external forces could more freely impact on the eventual form due to the already deformed forms being further deformable in the larger part. The project then became fixed at some point, caught or frozen in a state of movement. This sense of potential movement was something we wanted to capture, creating an atmosphere in parallel with the envisioned dynamic of the program.

Another aspect of working with the site and the floor as developable form was in appropriating the building grid of the Pompidou. Every structural increment, down to all horizontal surfaces, is divisible into an 80-by-80 centimeter grid at the smallest up to the primary structure of 12.80. We appropriated this "real" grid as our "concept." The deformed volumes then deformed the grid, thus creating a continuity as it became a "real" wall. This grid line was deformed for the four volumes using the software, Mechanical Desktop.

Another way to confront the site was to work with the principle that all types of fluids arrive via the ceiling of the museum and then pour into each volume, with each of the four volumes having their own systems for air, water, electricity, and information — a life-support system of sorts. Again this became part of a larger intention to return to the building's system in order to have a dialogue with it, thereby validating or referencing part of a series of earlier ideas inherent in the architecture of the museum, such as changeability, flexible systems, spontaneous systems, performance, and moving systems.

Dominique Jakob and Brendan MacFarlane currently practice architecture in Paris. Their work was shown in the 1998 Biennale internationale in Buenos Aires. Their current projects include the Café-musique, Seine et Marne.

Florence Lipsky and Pascal Rollet

School of Engineers in Advanced Industrial Systems, Valence, France, 1998.

As Sanford Kwinter pointed out at the Anyhow conference in 1997, our generation has experienced the need to reexamine its intellectual predilections and to abandon voluntarily the field of pure theory in favor of the development of a more pragmatic strategy oriented toward action. That position, regrettably, has often been construed by the critics to mean a concern with "practice" alone, excluding all theoretical interest.

But we believe we are living in a period radically different from the one our predecessors knew — with its greater sense of encouragement developing the intellectual component of architecture. In the perpetually swinging pendulum that characterizes the world of ideas, we detect today a return to the material component of architecture. That return is taking place in the form of a groundswell not yet visible or identifiable by everyone. We see it, though, as the logical and inevitable backlash of the sensational technological revolution in the tools of information-processing and circulation, which have opened the doors to a near infinite domain drenched in "virtual architecture." This virtual architecture is in fact experiencing a novel development that seems, by simple mirror effect, to be prolonging the life of theoretical thinking beyond these past twenty years. As Boullée wrote, architecture will truly be itself only in the ideal world. The project at hand will be better realized in the mind of the architect, the actual building becoming but a pale copy of this ideal. Such an approach has met with formidable success among young architectural students, whose entire education, from high school to university, reinforces a distancing from the real and the prizing of abstract teachings — all this in a society strongly attuned to the power of images. Here we are, then, very likely embarked on a "virtual" decade whose synthetic images will thrill the trendy magazines even as its 3D animations flood our Internet sites.

Amid the multiple movements architecture passed through in the 20th century, and at the dawn of the 21st, the question raised at the Anymore conference regarding the theories and concepts that still appear to have validity for the architecture of tomorrow gives us the opportunity to put forth a hypothesis: that the virtual wave we are presently surfing is stirring up, according to the natural principle of homeostasis, a material current that is simultaneously its opposition and accord. Monopolized by the prevalent virtual worlds, we take the measure of the moat dug between them and the real. We are well aware that we will have to effect a spectacular turnaround in order to rediscover an efficacious intervention into the real before

the real is done in completely. The return to equilibrium is not only necessary, it is inevitable. Otherwise we would have to envision the eventuality of architecture's demise.

In order to rediscover at least a bit of that efficacy, it is increasingly necessary to "read" attentively, beyond mere analysis, the place and the situation in which one works. This means understanding a context in all of its historical, geographic, and social dimensions, the better to transform it. It means considering this context and its physical, cultural, and political program as the material basis of architecture and not as an external constraint weighing on one's art in its demand to be satisfied. It means making this reading a fundamental moment in the architectural project — a moment of initial production and of initiation beyond the simple taking note of a new situation. Through this analysis of people and things, the closely held conviction guiding the entire project will be forged.

Moreover, it means taking an interest in the gestures of the people who will be living in this architecture — as great an interest as in the gestures necessary to construct it. It means prioritizing the habitual over the visual. It means thinking of the possible and rendering possible the thinking.

It also means physically implicating oneself in the achievement of a project in which the architecture integrates the political and cultural dimensions one believes in. It means choosing to lean, however lightly, on the course of things in order to effect change.

Very simply, it means listening and working with that part of ourselves that is made of matter. It means learning by way of that formidable tool our intellect gratuitously abandons and too often mystifies — our bodies. In architecture that means being principally preoccupied with the relationship of the human body to space and to matter.

Lastly, it means teaching all of this, and passing on the connective tissue, to future generations by very early and very directly confronting students with the constraints inherent in the manipulation of matter. In this way we might transmit an enlarged understanding of the world surrounding us — from the ancestral gesture of the hand placing one brick on another to the sophisticated manufacture of synthetic materials.

True, in all of this there is nothing really new. But in a fair and equitable reordering of things, certain values dating from the beginning of the 20th century have once again become news. Therefore, it is time to entertain the idea of a partnership with the industrial world that is daily transforming our environment through the development of new technologies.

It is time to integrate scientific notions into our thinking that will allow us to consider the vacuum as something other than the absence of matter. And it is essential that the relationship with contemporary artists, who have explored the notions of landscape, nature, and artifact far more deeply than any architect, be strengthened.

More generally, the time has come for architects to participate actively in the creation and implementation of management and control systems for the ambiences of comfort as understood in the broadest sense. The time has come as well to pay our respects to those architects who assimilate thinking about our environment at a global scale, and who respond to strategic initiatives intended to aid people living in conditions we ourselves would refuse to live in.

Architects are people who know how to pass from one world into another: their feet on the ground, their heads in the clouds, as it is often said. Today one respectfully asks of architects that they lower their heads somewhat and that they listen. If there is a theory in any of this, it is that we must turn to a theory of action.

Theory of action?

European youth, we are committed to action.

Reading: Relationship to Context

We believe in an indispensable acuity in the observation of places, objects, and situations in their physical, sonorous, visual, historical, social, and symbolic "reading." The notion of "reading" developed by GianCarlo de Carlo during the ILAUD seminar constitutes in our eyes the basis for the process of architectural conception. The "anatomical reading" of a spatial configuration produces an exercise that we systematically practice. It permits us to understand and to try to transform a given situation in all its dimensions.

Matter and the Body: Gesture

In thought as in gesture, the relationship between our body and matter is the focal point on which everything else is built. We believe that every one of us possesses within ourselves a profound need for protection inherited from prehistoric times. The use of stone and fashion for massive materials comes from the depths of the ages — from the primitive cave, that first shelter coiled in the folds of the earth that carries us. In this concept of origins, man defined a small interior as a sanctuary cut off from the menacing exterior. That adversarial relationship with nature imbues the basic attitude of the Western world to space.

On the other side of ourselves exists the nomad, who adventured onto the savanna or steppes and constructed lighter shelters made of vegetable materials covered with animal skins. That side imparted to us a longing for freedom and detachment — a desire, mixed with fear, for vast horizons, together with an incredulous fascination for those who live in a symbiotic relationship with their environment. Tent, wagon, caravan, and simple tree house constitute the models of light habitats completing our spatial imagination.

We are molded by this double nature. And from that nature derives our interest in techniques and their history, and in the fundamental sciences that permit advances in our understanding in this domain. Our perception of the subject remains poetic, though — attaching itself as much to space, seen as the primary material of architecture, as to the materials and the means invented for transforming and assembling them. With regard to matter, Joseph Beuys remains our guide.

An Architecture of Prepositions

If the context of each project places us in a specific situation calling for architectural responses that are adapted and not predetermined — pragmatic and opportune ones, some would say — a constant theme emerges. We are committed to establishing a network of relationships and exchanges among the personified elements. An encounter with Lars Lerup at the University of California at Berkeley firmly led to the development of this approach. Thus the architect, like a choreographer, talks about what takes place between individuals. Each project is a theater piece that places architectonic objects on the stage. Boxes on legs, black boxes, glass boxes, unfinished walls, protective roofing, spiderlike acoustic screens — each thing in itself tells part of a story in many voices. But more than the identity of the persona, what counts is the flux of energy exchanged between them. It is this localized deformation of the space-time continuum that creates the conditions for the phenomenon called Architecture.

Following Michel Serres, who evokes from his propositions a philosophy of relationships among the fields of knowledge, one might say that we are trying to build an architecture of prepositions: between, around, the length of, through, against, etc., are the key words of our quest.

Florence Lipsky and Pascal Rollet are partners at Lipsky + Rollet Architects in Grenoble. Their projects include the Artists' Workshop in San Francisco and an addition to the courthouse in Roanne.

Gradations
Finn Geipel

Aside from a few isolated, autonomous objects, architecture today is the result of the coming together of numerous actors, often with conflicting approaches and interests. Architectural debates that insist on maintaining the self-sufficiency of architecture as a "discipline" are, however, helping to turn it into a constricted and, to an extent, anachronistic field. By concentrating solely on the appearance of spatial forms, these debates reduce the very real, physical consequences of architecture to the level of mere packaging. In this scenario, it is only through the façade, rather than by way of any greater sense of depth, that a semblance of architectural meaning can be discerned.

In our view, this position is far removed from what makes up the "real life" of a building: appropriateness, adaptation, resistance, memory – more generally its structuring through use, as well as its impact on our "way of living in space." Today these issues are being neglected and are considered increasingly foreign to the very field of architecture itself. Consequently, the term structure in architecture no longer carries any significance beyond that of mere construction.

In addressing this issue, it is important to take up the discussion at the exact point where it left off with the arrival of postmodernism, and attempt to update these ideas[1] in order to go beyond the morphological study of components as if they were empty shells fixed in time. We must start thinking beyond spatial determinism about the interaction between spatial structures and the multiplicity of their uses.

In the face of this growing complexity, two changes in attitude seem essential: first, the repositioning of the architect in relation to professional experts dispersed throughout project management and to the myriad players involved in the construction process; and second, a conscious, deliberate commitment, which is often considered dangerous by architects because it affects current ideas of economic efficiency such as "programming flexibility" and the "radical mobilization of resources."

These topics, which architects feel are being imposed on them, could deliver architecture from its current aporia if they were integrated into the design process. Nevertheless, the economic system, which demands flexible, neutral, and economical architectural designs, seems unable to point to the most fertile areas of investigation. In other words, we have to get beyond the opposition between "pure appearances," completely detached from any social necessity, and "servile architecture," completely enslaved to political and economic demands.

Time Frames

In rapidly evolving societies, buildings – because of their relative rigidity – become anachronisms before they have barely managed to incorporate and signify change. Although some research was attempted during the 1960s and '70s with a view to responding to and generating mutations in program (we are thinking of the Team X theories, light structures such as those of Frei Otto, and user participation processes), this effort ultimately proved flawed and produced few concrete results. At the same time, the belief in stable, long-term, and universal programs that would allow scheduling/planning continuity has vanished today. It is precisely at this juncture that we see an opportunity to use the flexibility so much in demand, and so often misused,[2] by reinterpreting it as differentiated programming over time. To simplify, there are three different observable time frames:

The short-term, which is the length of a day, a week, or at most, a season. It describes the ability of a space to accommodate different activities simultaneously and in succession.

The mid-term represents the period of designing and building. By including the length of the development process itself, taking the mid-term into consideration could lead to new design methods introducing iteration and progress through successive stages.

The long-term refers to the ability of a building, a neighborhood, or a city to accept change, whether social, cultural, or economic, either by assimilating the change or by transforming itself.

These three time frames can coexist within a single project without being connected to each other. The variety and disjunction of the time-frames are key factors in understanding the thinking of urban planners who have worked on time-frame issues. To develop responses that interact with the short-term, mid-term, and long-term scales, three preliminary and closely intertwined questions must be answered:

Program: Which pillars should be fixed, what changes can be foreseen, which areas should remain undetermined?

Structure: What is the symbolic, technical, and spatial structure that accompanies current uses, which transformations are foreseeable, and which changes can be controlled?

Determination: What is the minimum degree of architectural, economic, and programmatic determination beyond which a building is reduced to a formless organization chart or a fixed – and therefore anachronistic – uniform framework?

Topologies

The relational approach allows us to shift the dualities of interior/exterior, location/connection, and foreground/background in the direction of questions that properly belong to the design process.

To the closed, isolationist model in which the break between the interior and the exterior in the sense of "feeling at home" vs. "feeling in danger" is reproduced by a string of

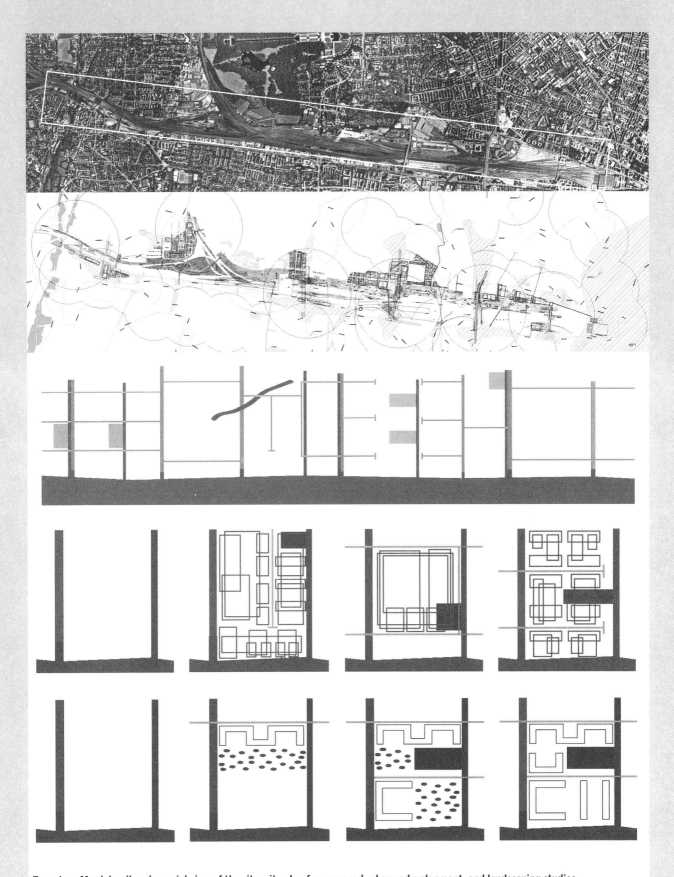

From top, Munich railyards: aerial view of the site; site plan for proposed urban redevelopment; and landscaping studies.

protected islands, hermetically sealed off from their environment, we can oppose the open, isotropic model in which the absence of any limit results in a uniform space from which difference has been eliminated. A topological approach restores thickness to transitional spaces or fringes by repeatedly shifting and alternating traditional boundaries. Within this approach, encountering and entering into dialogue can become the essential event in which moving along and remaining in place may require the use of a single system.

Iterations

In the last ten years, theoretical – and sometimes operational – research has called into question the practice of linear, deterministic planning, dissociating the phase of program and project design from its implementation in search of the possibility of readjustment over time through a confrontation of the various actors involved. Instead, it has called upon other fields such as geography or industry, or even other cultures. Several studies of the "chaotic" fabric of the city of Tokyo, a representation of disorder in contrast to the well-established top-down order of a city like Paris, have revealed a hidden order (see Maki and Shinohara). According to Augustin Berque, the contrast between the tendency to juxtapose and the tendency to create a hierarchy is what distinguishes Japan from France in a number of semantic systems, particularly language.[3]

In analyzing modes of production, the project terms top-down and bottom-up are used to oppose the industrial development methods (space, automotive, etc.) of the Anglo-Saxon countries (top-down projects) to those of Asia (bottom-up projects). Where the first type begins by drawing up a master plan with component parts to be developed later, the second develops by assembling component parts in succession without any ultimate design. The top-down project allows for radical innovation at the master-plan level, but remains closed to programmatic changes, otherwise the master plan would be called into question. The bottom-up project, on the other hand, only permits partial innovation at the master-plan level, but produces valid interim results within an iterative process.

Certain urban development phenomena or strategies can be compared to these project approaches. We can contrast the French zone d'aménagement concertée (ZAC), a mixed private and public housing zone that involves a linear, irreversible process from plan to completion, with the outlying suburban networks that seem to rise out of successive strings of autonomous islands. Though we may criticize these standard models for their exclusivity, we detect in them an opportunity to use an approach that would make it possible to manage the numerous actors, various time frames, and readability of the places and their relationships. This means confronting a top-down project with a bottom-up project. Thus at every moment the configuration of the positions taken by the actors (bottom-up) forms a space (top-down), while the taking of these positions (bottom-up) can/could only occur within a space of possibilities (top-down).

Gradations

In our view, these reflections help to explain why the current dynamics of economic and social processes require new models for programming and designing works. Above all, they help to explain why the chain that used to link the program to the project and to construction work, once linear in time and immediate in its effects, is no longer operative today.

The model that we are developing in our research and in our projects is based on a simple idea: gradation. The formal results of the phenomena just described (a multitude of players, varied time frames, the end of fixed programs) cannot be evenly determined. Instead they resemble a Saharan landscape where dunes, rocks, and peaks of intensity (formal, technical, functional, etc.) emerge in some areas, alternating with the relative neutrality of others. Obviously, the image of peaks and plateaus does not specify a topography but rather transfigures the term structure through a critical reading of the period from the 1960s to the 1980s. In this case, structure is not an anonymous, infinite network, which, by its very stability, ensures the possibility of connections at every point or the planned addition of cellular units. On the contrary, it is formed by distributing varying densities of content and form. The qualitative peaks (i.e., of maximum density) do not necessarily correspond to fixed, immutable areas, just as the vaguely defined areas are not necessarily the movable parts.

From Architectural Space to Urban Space

The building of the National School of Decorative Arts of Limoges (ENAD) is a large hall that defines a protective envelope in relation to the exterior, a rather unspecified skin. Inside this generic container can be found all the various programmatic entities: administrative offices, library, and cafeteria are seen as landscape plateaus, while the amphitheater and workshops are freely distributed as autonomous blocks. The blocks are the places for group work. Inside the first level of interlocking workshop blocks, mezzanine spaces are set up like small cellular units. The empty space always present between the skin of the hall and the workshop blocks is the area for circulating as well as for nonprogrammed activities. From the hall through the blocks to the mezzanines, the spatial scale diminishes, whereas the degree of detail, privacy, and climatic treatment increases. ENAD is thus a gradual structure, with spaces distinguished by successive degrees of envelopment and by a variable distance from the skin. Through this system, reminiscent of the Russian nesting dolls placed one inside the other, it becomes possible to move the place of work toward the emptiness of the interior space or toward the exterior. In the summer,

Métafort Multimedia Center in Aubervilles: monospace and roof studies.

activities move toward the outside to join the vegetation of the grounds, while in winter, they withdraw to the hall's interior, protected nuclei. In other words, users can lay claim to space by choosing to occupy one place rather than another, outside or inside.

The Munich Railway Axis project currently under study also works with the notion of gradation, but on an urban scale. The former railway area between the center of Munich and the western outlying area – an eight-kilometer-long strip – will be the focus of development intra-muros. Our project does not prefigure the form of the building but rather an initial topological structure based more on empty spaces than on full ones. The minimal definition of the six layered links – road, passageway, public transport, greenery, public program, visual and climatic opening – creates a matrix of relationships. The density and nature of the relationships bring about the first determination of various zones inside the strip. The zones pass from built-up areas to vegetation, from clear-cut links to barely linked areas, from public programming to private, etc. Our structure of links is rooted in the surrounding programmatic densities: the sites of business and trade in neighboring areas, underground stations, roads crossing the strip, types of soil, parks, leisure activities, and so forth. Far from being exhaustive, the networks of density and connections that we are proposing determine an initial matrix that guarantees both the coherence and open-ended possibilities of the whole. Construction and other relationships will slowly colonize the surface, alongside the growth of vegetation.

This gradual structure, which formulates peaks of strong definition in certain places, in addition to undetermined territories, has two objectives. First, it keeps the structure open to new developments, whether predictable or unpredictable (even though they will always have to be negotiated with a large number of players). Second, it provides validity and readability at each stage of development. Prefiguring the emptiness – which is both connected to and separate from the common space of the city – is the key to this structure. The structure, as the only constant constraint, allows for a multitude of configurations and rules out only a few. The project therefore does not focus on qualifying the empty part – which is for public relationships – since the full part – the private built-up part – will increasingly escape from all joint control.

The configuration of a gradational definition concerns not only the architectural elements but also programmatic and technical data. This approach gives the parts specific meaning in time, without hindering the changes to come. The process of defining in stages or by degrees should reveal essential nodes and at the same time authorize a rudimentary nonchalance in other areas. In this way, it prefigures future conversions while incorporating the diversity of current practices.

1 The opposition between structure and form no longer seems relevant, if the first term refers only to interior relations and the second only to the limit between two environments. From our point of view, structure includes both interior and exterior relations as well as their point of juncture: the contours, the envelope, the form.

2 There were projects prompted by such considerations in the early 1960s. It is remarkable, however, that in the name of flexibility (which was often merely technical and concerned all constructed elements without distinction) a large number of these buildings developed technically complex responses to ensure infinite variations that remain, in fact, highly improbable.

3 See **La qualité de la ville: Urbanité française, urbanité nippone** (Tokyo: Maison franco-japonaise, 1987), 321.

Finn Geipel cofounded **LABFAC** with Nicolas Michelin in 1987. Their projects include the **Métafort Multimedia Center in Aubervilles and the National School of Decorative Arts in Limoges.**

National School of Decorative Arts, Limoges.

It Will Be Nice Tomorrow

Anne Lacaton and
Jean-Philippe Vassal

Arts and Human Sciences Building, University of Grenoble, 1995.

The beauty of the obvious: the civil engineering structure just before technical prowess, in the sense that engineers make it (machines, factories). There are not a thousand and one solutions. There are just one or two answers, and one of them will surely be the better one. No architecture. One solves a problem of installation, incorporation, and program mathematically, as one does a technical, economic, or social problem. This is enough, where relevant. It is already a lot. Self-construction: sheds, huts, factories, suburban shopping malls. A box, a sign which is clearly named – readability. It is up to phony images of speed – aircraft wings and horizontal cladding – and to buildings ready to take off, to make direct suggestions about the destination – beaches and coconut trees. Not pretending. Dwellings: too much comfort. We lack extraordinary architectures as a result of too much middle-class comfort. New ways of living in and living. The House: inventing something else, mobility, nomadism, getting rid of foundations. The box, the parallelepiped – what else is there to do? The Farnsworth House, and then? Dealing with transparency, filters, open buildings that are permeable to climate. Inventing machine-houses, flower-houses. Project: there is neither the obvious nor reference. Every time a new problem crops up, a concertina of restrictions, requirements, expectations. Raising good questions and making rigorous replies to them, one after the other. Always raising the issue of the necessary, the sufficient – what is important, and what is not? Avoiding accumulations, looking for simplicity and readability. Monitoring every slightly complicated detail like the consequence of an error of reflection. Shedding the idea of form other than the architectonic or stemming from context. Building from the interior. The precision of the installation. The perfect resolution of the functioning. Use – shifts, sensations, inner perception, appropriation. Sense – the evocation of a building, its contents, its life, its period. Cost – cost-cutting, the right means, as inexpensive as possible, to build more. The rigor of the plan. A certain passion for organizing, setting, calculating, compressing, pricing, starting all over again, reading and rereading the program, economizing, simplifying. And then, that magic moment when the images come back, when the two directions of thought are perfectly attuned, interlock, fuel one another, as if spellbound. A moment of euphoria and ease, as if miraculously and unconsciously the joyous, living part that gives the project its meaning had steered the laborious part to do with development. Born who knows where, experienced somewhere, far away, in Africa or elsewhere, in books of poetry and films, in smoke-filled bars, train compartments, airport concourses, an image, a persistent idea, that one waits for, that one delicately gathers up, that one protects, safeguards, forgets, and finds again. It stays there throughout the project and ends up being absolutely indispensable. Architecture will be straightforward, useful, precise, cheap, free, jovial, poetic, and cosmopolitan. It will be nice tomorrow.

Anne Lacaton and Jean-Philippe Vassal practice architecture in Bordeaux. Their work was included in the 1998 Premises show at the Guggenheim Museum in New York.

Latapie House, Floriac, 1993.

House, Lège Cap Ferret, France, 1999.

Discussion 1

SÉBASTIEN MAROT I would like to ask the assembled architects a collective question. What is the place in your work today of both theoretical and historical reflection? I'd like to start by addressing this to Finn Geipel and Nicolas Michelin, who developed the concept of a laboratory for architecture. There is a theoretical treatment here that might explain the relationship between the agency and the community.

FINN GEIPEL What do you mean by a quick reformulation of the relationship between the agency and the community? The community formed by LABFAC refers to a number of special consultants that we have in France and abroad who each bring a different kind of thinking to our work – there is a sociologist, a philosopher, an artist, a technician – all from different disciplines. Our laboratory develops answers to certain problems raised by a certain context. Progressively, project after project, there is indeed a growing data bank, so to speak, that affects the thought in all of our projects. In the agency some prototypes are developed and work is done on computers, and then there are discussions with these special consultants. There is a constant back-and-forth between these specialized people and the architects in the workshop.

JEAN-PHILIPPE VASSAL We involve ourselves with data that is outside architecture. We see architecture as able to exist without architects, and it is often very interesting without architects. For inspiration we can look to anyone, from surgeons, sociologists, and farmers to greenhouse builders and sailors. But only by removing ourselves from architecture are we able to work. A number of things trouble us when architecture is discussed. When people think of an architect, they typically imagine a head contractor. But in reality, the architect is not really in charge of anything. Architecture is rather a whole series of projects, one after the other, which contribute to a body of work. We create buildings in which people have to feel at ease, so these projects are developed in partnership with other people, and the more disparate the backgrounds of these people, the better.

MAROT Is the disappearance of an internal reference to the discipline and the growing importance of working with people outside of architecture a position with which you align yourselves?

PASCAL ROLLET Yes, absolutely. We also work with outside contributors and in collaboration with people who are not from architectural circles, and it is largely through these cross-disciplinary connections that we find inspiration. For example, we have had a long working relationship with a number of people involved with dance, as well as close contact with graphic designers, particularly in the development of the façade for the engineering school we designed. From a theoretical point of view, this is something very significant. Two different moments become apparent – the moment we read and discover other things, and the moment we develop and apply certain ideas. Our work is based essentially on a research and application model, but it is difficult to say exactly what things are connected to each other, and equally difficult to pinpoint where that research comes from. Research is a big bathtub in which a certain energy is developed – we just dip our toes in, sampling different ideas. We don't know exactly how it works.

MAROT Yes, but beyond these relationships in the design and development phases, are you concerned with sticking to a theoretical idea of architecture in which the history of architecture will serve as a reference?

ROLLET Obviously there are people who are references for the work we do, like Renzo Piano, for example, but if there were real stars to put forward, I would nominate Charles and Ray Eames – architects who through their very attitude and way of working, their curiosity and the way in which they looked at the world, are a model and an absolute reference in themselves.

BRENDAN MACFARLANE The Anymore conference program suggests that there is the possibility of seeing theory from a European or French point of view, as opposed to a North American point of view, or from a perspective that's outside of Europe or outside of France. This is intriguing and relates to the issue of hybridization. I am from Australasia and Dominique [Jakob] has traveled widely in Africa and Europe. We live and work in Paris, that is, out of a European, or French, context. I posed the question to Dominique last night, in fact – do you really believe there is an almost antitheoretical climate in France? I thought that for us as an office we tend to fuse our backgrounds. We jump across these questions through our work, and probably somewhere in the middle of all of that, we can take that as a kind of proposition. What is interesting this morning is that all of a sudden we sound rather theoretical for a European panel.

FRÉDÉRIC NANTOIS Well I don't think so. The theoretical dimension cannot be dissociated from the actual project of architecture, as we witnessed in the presentations this morning – architecture as a play of quotations and references. If there were no theory, there would be no possibility for architecture. It is interesting to see various approaches, of course, but there is not one moment for theory and another for the project. An architectural project in itself can be a theory. It can be an element of a demonstration that is totally theoretical. So it cannot be dissociated, and in this way the historical dimension is also integrated. The history of architectural culture is not only a matter of a constant self-reference to a culture that we quote all the time, it is history and theory in the broadest sense. All this is very theoretical, of course, but in our work it is an essential element.

AUDIENCE The question of history and the place of theory make me think of the notion of region. We have to consider the issue of locale, the place where the question is being asked, because it's revealing to say in Paris, versus in California, that you just launch a problem and discuss it at length. It would be very interesting to look at the nuances within the locations of history and theory.

MAROT It seems to me that there is a clear tendency here to stretch two ideas that are quite common and commonly used by architects. On the one hand, there is the site, the context, the field in which a project is determined. For example, in Jakob and MacFarlane's work, we see a major role given to the site itself, to the point where the architecture disappears in its contact with the site. In their work there is some value in starting from the site as expressed by an area, such as a technical area like the Beaubourg. To do architecture without changing the surface volume would be to change it into a thickness, to inhabit a surface that would be a symbol of a site. On the other hand, there is the program, another order of determination that is often in simple opposition to any architectural or landscaping project. Fiona Meadows and Frédéric Nantois used the term *over-programming*. Does it mean that there are architects today who take inspiration from an immediate confrontation with the given elements of a site? Or is there another trend worth considering: that the main thing is the will behind a project, one expressed through the program, and which is the actual material for creation? This is a question that I'd like to ask everybody here. What is the relative share of reflection on the program and the reflection on confrontation with the site? Do we have architects who seek to invent the program on the basis of their reading of the site? Or do we have architects who think they can invent site on the basis of program?

MACFARLANE These questions are a good synthesis of some of the points that have come up today. We do differentiate between program and site, certainly in an objective sense, but when it comes to dealing with this thing called context, or dealing with what we're given or what we find, I like this word *confrontation* a lot. We go in search of it. I think the issue of the program and the site are all in one; we don't differentiate at the conceptual level. The site in its natural, physical form is just as important as the issues that are going to take place in or around it. We're very interested in trying to bring site and program together into a kind of medium that we can play with, that we can analyze and rework. Florence Lipsky talked about the idea of taking something and working it until you know it, and then doing something really exciting with it. That's something that interests us very much.

MAROT Obviously the two concepts are quite elastic. It seems that everybody here is trying to establish a dialectic between program and site.

NANTOIS When we talk about over-programming, we are not referring to functions. In fact, we tend to think that the specificities of functions in architecture are being phased out, especially when we talk about the integration of certain techniques and technologies that erase, or iron out, the differences between these activities. So that's not what we have in mind when we speak about over-programming. It's not a dialectic between programming and context but an assimilation, a single complexity. What is the urban context? What about a generalized urban fabric? The idea of over-programming comes from the fact that there seems to be a reconciliation of specificities, some generative rules in architecture. This is also why we have adopted a diagrammatic approach in our projects, because we don't want to represent but rather to take stock of the complexity and see how it can be organized. A diagrammatic approach is very interesting in this regard because it portrays a certain complexity and also establishes a link between theory and practice.

GEIPEL When I hear about dialectics and the coupling of program and site, it seems that we're still left with commonplace architectural categories, very closed categories that are easy to identify. I think our work as architects, or town planners, is a multilayered construct made up of plans, politics, economics, and so on. It sounds commonplace, but we're confronted with these multiple layers that are difficult to map and turn into a project. This is why we often restrict ourselves to speaking about a program and a site. We speak a lot about programming, but it's the architect's power that is important. Programming remains secondary. Our architecture lab works much more as a network of specialists in different areas that publish or work on these different layers and cooperate with us to try and associate throughout these different layers. We work a lot with specialists in ecology and environmental sciences. It's something that is not easily integrated, and in a sense, these different people from other disciplines are no longer a source of inspiration to us. This is why we said it so clearly. It's not an architecture that is the creative work of an author, but the work of craftsmen who bring the project out gradually.

FLORENCE LIPSKY I believe that we all spoke of complexity because a site is not just something we inherit but rather is a material. It's a situation. The issue of programming is more complex now, too. It is a cultural concept. All programs have a cultural dimension that has to be carried along with the rest. This is why we refer to complexity so often.

MAROT On the basis of the positions developed by the architects here, at least theoretically, we have one position that speaks of programming in terms of data, site situation, and so on, and another, perhaps more flexible concept, that really encompasses the site itself essentially just like a program. The opposition between these two theories is important. I think a large part of the modern tradition was developed from projecting programming onto sites. The postmodernist and then post-postmodernist era can be defined as a reversal of this, leading to the narrow position, or extreme position of something almost ludicrous, of trying to decipher the programming and the site.

NICOLAS MICHELIN I disagree with you because, in essence, you've just described a caricature. Some architects indeed argue that with new software programs, new approaches to sites, and so on, the landscape actually "does" the project, but I think that what we said earlier about programming also applies to site. When you speak of a layer or an iteration of the programs, it's the complexity and multiplicity of the layers that actually make up the project. Programming is like when you dissect a mouse in biology class; you take out the soft tissue, and you find the hard tissues. Likewise, in architecture, these soft and hard areas must coexist. There are different densities for every project. These programming densities are superimposed upon the site data. We develop topological maps with programming data — hard, soft, and so on — and from all this you can actually develop a project. Your vision, Sébastien, is too much of a caricature. You might be right, but we should not stress this. Rather, we should try to think out how an office today can actually approach these different layers of complexity. Obvi-

ously, without being too reductive, we feel that diversities work in favor of the economy of a project, but I don't think you can actually separate landscape and project.

VASSAL Well, I don't feel that you're dealing each time with a different case. You don't choose programming, you don't choose the sites. You can refuse them at best, that's all. But then one particular piece of data might override the others. With every project you're walking a tightrope, and you have to strike the right balance and try to be as inventive as you can with whatever system you are given. For example, when we had to build a very inexpensive house for railway employees, the developer had already chosen a certain site and could only invest 430,000 francs. It was interesting to work with this type of economic constraint.

SASKIA SASSEN I'm not an architect, so I accept that the best you can do is reject a site, to say no to it. But there are rhetorical aspects and objective conditions of any site. One condition has changed: the fact of globalization at a rhetorical level (even though it's not always a reality) and the fact of globalization at the objective level. For you architects who are creating physical buildings, does this make a difference in your practice? As a theoretician, I'm encouraged to rethink what a site or a context means, because there are lots of built-up areas that escape any context. Though globalization is not the local context, what is local in fact changes. I know I'm being a bit provocative here, but I wonder whether the discussion of site might not have changed at a rhetorical and objective level, at least in part.

NANTOIS Oh, yes, we quite agree. That's exactly the kind of context we took into consideration in our project for the Nice Foundation in Barcelona. It includes part of the history of Barcelona and it's also part of something more global. We developed this idea of a hypersite, a kind of alternator between two conditions – the local and the global. We also tried to develop this for a housing development in a huge built-up area in the suburbs of The Hague. It was a place, but an area totally different from its local conditions. This is the defining feature of globalization, the hallmark of globalization.

SASSEN Complexity can't be read as simply what is local.

NANTOIS It's not a direct substitution. Globalization doesn't mean that the local will disappear. There is a movement toward greater regionalization, so the project interfaces between the two. That's also why it is more interesting for us to make the architectural object relative to its context.

IGNASI DE SOLÀ-MORALES The symptom diagnosed here is that the theoretical data most often present is site and programming – two ideas that are related to the practical and concrete definition of a project. This seems to cancel out a more general level of discussion. It even emphasizes that for architects there can be no other discussion than the practical definition of the architectural work. It's a kind of theoretical breakdown and I'm not sure it's of great interest, because in certain cases it's a naive type of realism. Programming is a kind of given. It's good or it's not so good, you have or you don't have money. The same applies for the site – it can be complex or not complex, but it's there. You receive it, you take it, and you do something with it. But from a theoretical point of view, you've not even started when you have this data because it's not clear. It's problematic. The difference between this and what you find in the end is the space of theory – the interpretation of work, the construction you have to put on theory in order to come up with something precise. One can read a historical building just by looking at it. You've followed this fallacious, naive reading of architecture for years, as though architecture were an open book, and without being told that learning the language is extremely complicated and deciphering the reading was a problem. The same applies to sites and programming. I recently discussed with Greg Lynn the idea that the program as encoded in the computer is almost an automatic machine for producing projects. This is extremely strong, but it's technological naivete to think that because you have information and a defined program that the outcome of the two is the particular definition of a project.

MARDT When I used the word *programming*, I was not touching upon reality but being more rhetorical. It's an element of perspective. The program as such is often given and needs to be developed by the architect. The site refers more to constraints that you have to read into both the project and the programming.

FRÉDÉRIC MIGAYROU It's interesting here in Europe to see how our friends in America understand these concepts. I think as this conference develops, these ideas will continue to be raised, particularly this issue of context. You don't want the idea of context simply to be an area of analysis – external, theoretical – onto which we stick labels. By context, I mean things we've seen in the last twenty years in Europe – history and sociology, for example. If you look at external reference systems as well, look at something that's immediate. What can be taken on board right away? These procedures are linked to an engineering of the everyday – a tree, a pavement, a side-

walk. Nature is no longer something natural. It's been denatured, and these architects in fact are making context a permanent, ongoing resource – technological, natural, physical, sociological, or historical. So they take these pieces of syntax and make a material out of it, as it were, and then they build. As I see it, the reference to Greg Lynn is very interesting. Greg Lynn's work is not hypertechnological. It's a pragmatic translation of programming tools to create a link, or gateway, to what is real. Do the other architects here share that approach?

MACFARLANE The question is about pragmatism. It's a difficult question, in a way. A certain idea of pragmatism comes out of this discussion and our interests, but we also come from varied backgrounds, so the presence of theory or the presence of the history of architecture vis-à-vis the work you've seen today and the culture of architecture might seem like a simplification here. I mean, hopefully we've come from enough material of history and theory. I think today we're interested in presenting some of the most spontaneous areas from which we get our biggest cues. I take your interpretation, Migayrou, to be an oversimplification in terms of the work here today. I think it's a little too easy. I don't think we're about simplifying it down into site or program anyway. Certain interests come out of the work, but the things within the work itself are just as important.

PHYLLIS LAMBERT Do we change the project in terms of what the context is and then look at the context and change the project accordingly? Every time you have a context that's different, then you have to draft a new project – a little bit like Eero Saarinen. But I think these are important underlying questions.

ROLLET Do we change the project every time the context is different? I think the answer should be yes.

LAMBERT But is there a general theory in that regard? Every time you see something, you react differently? It must be terrible having to work that way.

ROLLET I see it as being very important. I think it's the only thing we can do right now to have a little bit of control over what's real. Let's return to what Migayrou said. I feel this need to really stick to something. I mean, okay, the context is here so act in terms of the context. The context of the environment is there, and then you can peel away these layers and get into more depth – look at the very nature of the situation where we'll be building something. If we do that it's because we need to have some sort of impact – even if it is very small, as Jean-

Philippe said. But at least where there's some sort of leeway in our decision-making or some impact on what's real, we can delve into that in some way.

GEIPEL I'm having some problems following this discussion because people are talking about site and context as synonymous. Shouldn't we speak of site or context? It's always difficult in discussions such as this to all agree on definitions, but I think it is important to make the distinction. If we're talking about the site, then let's explain what we mean by the site. If we're talking about a site in a geographic sense, something well-delineated, a place which is here, with borders, it could be characterized by its shape, by its forms. Frédéric talked about site being global and local. This interpretation is something very complex, something that we have to focus on, because these pieces of information are in a constant state of flux. We must bear in mind these changes and our action must encompass them whenever and wherever possible, But we must also be modest. We must recognize the fact that once we've done our job, we can't say that this is our work sitting on this site. It's the site that has changed, and it will continue to change.

CYNTHIA DAVIDSON It's interesting to me that Brendan Mac-Farlane said that the panel today sounds positively theoretical compared to other European panels he has seen. As an American, it doesn't seem very theoretical to me at all. Sébastien Marot immediately introduced the idea of practice to the discussion, as if the one common ground that unites you all is how you practice. I'm sitting here listening to old ideas about material, light, program, site. Nobody has offered a new idea or compelling ideas about what any of these things mean. I want to ask whether practice is taking over the place that theory had in architecture? Not that theory was ever strong in France, but it seems to me that for a lot of the younger people I meet everywhere, including the States, methodology and practice are an increasingly interesting aspect of work in some sort of turn away from theory. But I find it sort of ironic that instead of having a real debate about the distinction between history and practice, or history and theory, or theory and practice, we're all talking about practice.

MAROT But don't you think that practice is actually an interesting theoretical question? Given the questions we have here for looking at practice, theory should creep into these matters. It's good that we're thinking about things; we're reflecting. I don't want to leave you with the feeling that I'm trying to reduce things down, extract the essence of everything that was said, boil it down to a debate regarding context and program or practice and site. No, that's not what I'm trying to do.

DAVIDSON I don't think there is any practice without theory, whether or not people say they have a theoretical position. But it seems to me that we're talking about practical aspects of practice. Maybe I missed it because of jet lag, but I didn't hear any real theoretical concerns, for example, about the piece at the Pompidou, which is very blobby and interesting. The things that dictated it were all very practical. Maybe that's where we are now. I'm not saying that's wrong. I just find it interesting that the common ground is practice.

JEAN-LOUIS COHEN I think this is the very crux of the discussion. Professionals and architects here in France have, to a certain extent, taken some distance – for different reasons, and reasons that we can respect – with regard to theoretical discussions. Or rather, we in France use references from the social sciences, not so much from theory or philosophy with a capital P. I want to return to the question of context. I see context as a raw material that we work with, a material that we'll work in the project. I think it's fundamental. This goes well beyond the practices of observation mentioned earlier, or the interpretation that we read into things, but I think it should give rise to the different practices, different patterns of consumption. I think this is very important. But it's also important to go a little bit further than just saying what we do.

AUDIENCE I think that we have mainly been discussing the theory of practice. I'm wondering if you were given instructions to talk about theory and practice, because that's what you've all done, really. You all spoke to a certain extent about the guiding principles underpinning practice. But, more significantly, what's missing is that nobody spoke about some of the internal references to the discipline. Why was this steered away from?

NANTOIS In our video there are many references, many quotes, texts, pictures, and plans and drawings. It wasn't just something superficial. This is something that feeds our work. Nothing alluded to what we do in our office, the things that go on, the way in which we work in our office as architects. The references to our own architectural culture were placed within a historical context that was symbolic. We're not tending toward a quest for utopia. We don't believe in this. We're not going to reinvent a utopia because we have certain antecedents – the Modern Movement, for example. What brings us together here at the table? I'm not exactly sure what the common thread is. It's true that we're all quite different in terms of our presentations and the tools we use – conceptual tools, design tools – but the residue for the audience is important. The significant thing is the variety in our approaches.

Brought together as "young architects," it's as if a stamp or a label has been stuck on us. Okay, you're young up to a certain age and after that you're an old architect, but how do you go from one to the other? And one should not judge French architecture in relation to American architecture – we're not interested in categories that distinguish things or look at things in terms of identity on the basis of our age or nationality or where we come from or other factors. We don't look at things in that way.

2. Anymore Theory or History?

Theoretical investigation has become part of the practice of architecture. Not always escaping schematicism or innocence, the assimilation of philosophy and the social sciences has changed architects' perceptions of their discipline. A certain rift between North America and Europe, between the United States and France in particular, can, however, be perceived. Where American architects have drawn from their knowledge of theory a certain conceptual strength, the denigration of vision, a dominant mode of architectural conceptualization practiced by French intellectuals, has found a symmetrical twin in the denigration of theory by French architects. How is it possible today to construct autonomous theoretical objects, or will they always be constrained by history? Will designed or built objects continue to address theoretical interrogations?

Temple of Bodhisattva and Vaisravana, from André Malraux, Le musée imaginaire.

Denis Hollier

From among the five or six semantic equivalents the dictionary offers for the adverb theoretically ("in theory," "in principle," etc.), the one I want to select is "on paper." If I am to believe the terms of Anymore's agenda – that "a certain rift between North America and Europe, France in particular," exists in architecture-in-theory – then the Americans apparently practice theory more cheerfully than their French colleagues, who, at least in theory, are not supposed to feel at home on paper.

Being neither an architect – be it on paper or elsewhere – nor a theoretician, but at the most a historian, or even metahistorian, of the literary field, I will start from an object closer to my world of reference, one that in many respects – some of them theoretical but others architectural in the most concrete sense – is not too distant from the premises (in whatever sense you want to take that word) that assemble us today in this very building and this very room: that is, the musée imaginaire, both the book to which André Malraux gave that title and the radically new concept it tries to shape.

For what distinguishes the musée imaginaire (rendered in English as the "museum without walls") from real museums is first of all the fact that it exists only on paper. In that sense it is a museum in theory, a virtual or conceptual museum that opens the field for the invention of what Malraux calls "fictive works of art."

Commentators on Malraux's book have in general focused on the enlargement of the museological field that resulted from the giant step in the dematerialization of supports and the delocalization of works performed on that occasion. Thanks to photography, thanks in particular to the techniques of enlargement, questions of size have stopped being relevant. Noncanonical art – be it for reasons of medium (minor arts: tapestry, giltware, stained glass, mosaic) or for historical and geographical ones (non-Western arts) – can now confront canonical mediums on an equal footing.

Such an opening, however, is far from limitless. The museum without walls is not a museum without borders, and it would be naive to identify the age of les immatériaux with the disappearance of segregation. There are new frontiers that, even though nonphysical, are all the more tightly sealed, and in this regard I would like to explore the gap between the space opened by the concept of the musée imaginaire and the space actually covered by Malraux's book.

It is hard to imagine that today's reader (especially if looking at the first, 1947 Skira edition) would fail to be struck by a double absence: that of architecture, and that of photography. As for architecture, it is more than a mere absence – it is

an exclusion. Even without a wall, the museum maintains an interior and continues to follow the logic according to which the container cannot be part of the content. The possibility of a musée imaginaire of world architecture never seems to have crossed Malraux's mind. And when, in the course of his book, he refers to the building in which we are gathered today, the Musée des Monuments Français, it is not in order to open the question of what a museum of architecture could be but to recall the astonishment of the painters to whom its inauguration in 1937 for the World's Fair revealed the colors of Romanesque frescos they only knew from black-and-white reproductions. French resistance to architecture on paper, so it seems, predates the age of theory. The same allergy to paper, however, does not work for photography.

At the end of the 1930s Walter Benjamin spent a good part of his summers at Bertolt Brecht's place in Denmark. There, on August 10, 1936, he wrote a letter to Max Horkheimer, which I will take as a point of departure. "The Work of Art in the Age of Mechanical Reproduction" had just come out in French, translated by (or with) Pierre Klossowski in the June issue of Zeitschrift für Sozialforschung, which was published in Paris at the time. On June 21, the Writers Congress in Defense of Culture, the second of its kind, convened in London (the first having met in Paris a year earlier). Benjamin did not attend, but due to his text, he was present in thought; Malraux, the keynote speaker of the plenary session, promoted it in his address titled "On Cultural Legacy." At the time he wrote his letter to Horkheimer, Benjamin had not managed to read Malraux's speech (Etiemble, the secretary of the Congress was supposed to give him a copy).[1] But he had met Malraux, with whom he had discussed it.

I quote here from Benjamin's letter to Horkheimer:

This meeting between Malraux and Benjamin has always left me bemused. I often wondered if, during their exchange in this spring of 1936, these two intellectuals had occasion to realize to what extent their shared interest in the cultural effects of the work of art's entry into the age of mechanical reproducibility would lead them in divergent directions. Malraux is one of the very few French intellectuals who not only perceived the importance of Benjamin's essay but publicly – be it orally or in writing – acknowledged his debt. One wonders, however, to which aspect of the essay Malraux was most sensitive. Was it the opening pages with their analysis of the mutation in the circulation of original works of art that resulted from photography (a popularization of the traditional museum)? Or was it the later ones, where Benjamin describes a mass culture of a totally different order, coextensive with the opening of a space of works of art without originals, such as film? For Malraux does not seem to have been sensitive to this alternative between museum and cinema at the heart of Benjamin's argument. And from the pieces Malraux published in Verve (the two installments of "The Psychology of Art" in 1937 and 1938 and the "Sketch for a Psychology of Cinema" in 1939), all of them equally placed by Malraux under the aegis of Benjamin, it is hard to say if the "manifestly theoretical book" that Malraux mentioned to Benjamin was leaning in one direction or the other.

But the irremediable divide had already occurred for Benjamin. In his dialectic of the forms of cultural consumption, museum and movie house belong to two diverging lines of evolution. Their current coexistence is a mere residue, an insignificant anachronism resulting from a certain randomness in uneven cultural development. But under the guise of "this will destroy that," sooner or later the movie theater would supersede the museum. Just as, according to Marx, the capitalist mode of production is a necessary, if transitory, structure required by the transformation of individual work into collective labor, so the museum represents, according to Benjamin, what one could call a transitory form of cultural consumption, one required by the shift from individual to collective experience, halfway, so to speak, between feudalism and socialism. As an aesthetic object, a painting is eidetically defined by its inaptitude for collective consumption. A painting – and this is its definition – cannot be consumed by more than one person at a time; and certainly not, to use the phrase of Isidore Ducasse that the Popular Front culture adopted as one of its slogans, "by all." This is why even when the museum is swept by history into the prevailing current of democratic good will and pretends to be able to open its collections to group consumption, it remains a historically condemned institution. For this is structurally contradictory: far from being the vehicle of its triumph, it is the final stage of the crisis of the pictorial medium. In other terms, the obsolescence of painting doesn't start, for Benjamin, with the birth of cinema; it starts with the museum itself. It begins at the very moment when the painting is no longer aimed at the singularity of one gaze, of one desire.

Benjamin writes:

Thus the laughter of the masses in front of industrially produced images has an opposite value according to whether their object belongs to the museum or to the repertoire of the movie theater; as Benjamin argues, "The reactionary attitude toward a Picasso painting changes into the progressive reaction toward a Chaplin movie."[3] Reaction here starts with the decision to apply the techniques of mechanical reproduction to a preexisting original painting. In this regard Benjamin and Theodor Adorno, despite the tension that the former's essay introduced into their intellectual exchange, would have shared the same opinion: a Picasso exposed to mass consumption by whatever form of mechanical reproduction – postcard, poster, and even art book – does not constitute in and of itself a more respectable hybrid, a less absurd aesthetic object than a Beethoven symphony "electrocuted on radio" (Adorno's phrase) in a Midwestern housewife's kitchen.

The idea of a competition between museum and movie house is thus totally foreign to Benjamin's view; Picasso and Chaplin do not belong to the same cultural age. The reader of the essay has the feeling that the first pages, where he addresses the status of the photographic reproduction of nonphotographic originals, is, if not pure lip service, at least not much more than a preliminary warm-up. He will not go back to it. Having left the museum for the movies once and for all, Benjamin would not go back to the former, a cultural dead end, a kind of wing for the quarantine of incurable cultural forms.

What about Malraux? Among the many reversals that punctuate his biography, Malraux's renunciation of the novel remains one of the most enigmatic. Why did this hugely successful young novelist leave fiction writing for a reflection on art? Gaëtan Picon, already close to him at the time, relates this mutation to the context of what he calls (in a variation on Lenin's New Economic Policy) the Popular Front's "New Cultural Politics": "Paintings and sculptures stand at the point where gazes converge, while books exist at the point where reveries diverge." In front of a book one is always alone, but one is never alone in front of a painting. While readings, like dreams, can never be shared, within visuality there is ingrained something like a collective vocation; optical perception contains the seed of togetherness, the plastic arts are the prop of a perceptual collectivization. One could find here a kind of aesthetic version of the French Revolution's Law of Suspects. Painting and sculpture must, and therefore can, be consumed à la Ducasse, by all and not by one, while the book becomes politically suspect by virtue of the essential solitude of the act of reading. This was the time when André Gide, a fellow traveler, was writing in his Les nouvelles nourritures : "So if I had to be alone to have access to the contemplation of a work of art, the more beautiful it was the more sadness would prevail over joy." Needless to say, such a will to nationalize cultural heritage by extending the social campaign for the collectivization of the means of production to that of cultural consumption is the antithesis of Benjamin's position.

However, does it accurately describe what is at stake in Malraux's project? One tends to confuse the author of Le musée imaginaire and the future minister of culture. No doubt the latter will have to deal with museums where gazes will indeed converge, but this is precisely because they are not imaginary, because they are not museums without walls. The major innovation of the musée imaginaire, however, lies precisely in the fact that it allows Malraux not to be trapped in Picon's alternative between the book and the museum, between the divergence of readings and the convergence of gazes. Malraux did not leave the book for the visual arts; he brought the plastic arts into the space of the book.

In any case, the gap between Malraux and Benjamin might not be as wide as one might think, for what inspired Malraux was not so much the democratization of the cultural consumption of traditional objects (Picasso for all and not for one) as it was the metamorphosis to which those objects are submitted by their reprocessing through the culture industry. What is new, as he said at the London Congress after having quoted Benjamin, is the fact that through its photographic dissemination, our cultural heritage "due to this very transmission changes its status."[4]

One could even say that what motivates Malraux in the best pages of Le musée imaginaire is when he takes up Benjamin's challenge. While according to Benjamin movie theaters were supposed to supplant museums irreversibly, Malraux tries here to think their connections not in diachronic but in synchronic terms. Constructing a space where instead of movie theaters replacing the museum, the museum itself would accommodate cinema, Malraux reopens the question that Benjamin's essay had closed.

In all events, in Le musée imaginaire, the reference to cinema is much more active than the reference to photography. One of the greatest paradoxes of this book – which happens to be the first sustained reflection on the transformation wrought on the space of the museum by photography – is the conspicuous absence of photography itself, whose status remains merely instrumental. It permits the introduction of various noncanonical mediums next to paintings and sculptures, but among the 172 illustrations there is not one reproduction of a photograph, no Félix Nadar or Eugène Atget, not to mention August Sander or Alexander Rodchenko. Photography, the support of the musée imaginaire, does not enter it.

With two exceptions: the two photographs of female ballet dancers – the hieratic La Castiglione and a wild modern one – which are meant to exemplify the mutation brought upon photographic practice by film. Thus the only two photographs in the book are asked to support an argument that concerns not photography but film. It is in those pages –

where a very Eisensteinian Malraux sketches the theory of his medium – that the porosity of the space of the musée imaginaire to that of film is the most perceptible. They happen to be themselves the result of a montage type of editing; they are cut out from the part of "Sketch for a Psychology of Cinema" where Malraux had proposed a striking archaeology of film that minimized its debt vis-à-vis the mechanical and photochemical techniques of reproduction in favor of the stylistic inventions of montage, framing, and camera movements, i.e., the specifically filmic means of producing fiction. He now uses these very same stylistic features to characterize his conception of the art book as a kind of storyboard. This passage, however, is not the only one where the cinematographic – and not photographic – model for the musée imaginaire appears. On various occasions Malraux returns to the assimilation of page layout to film editing; the plates follow each other in the guise of montage – as in a shot-reverse-shot editing sequence – allowing the art book to animate a style "the way stop-shoot film techniques animate a plant's growth." Malraux's concept of the fictive work of art is an outcome of this dialectic between the musée imaginaire and film, the former giving birth to the equivalent of "stars" in the strictly Hollywood sense of the term: just as film stars exist only on screen, the fictive works of art of the musée imaginaire belong "to an unreal world that exists only through photography." "A star," Malraux had already written in 1939, "in no way is an actress who is filmed"; similarly, what the musée imaginaire brings to the gazes or the reveries of its readers can in no way be reduced to the status of original works of art that have been photographed.

What about today's status of the museum/film dialectic? Clearly, Malraux's solution is no longer on the agenda. The art book no longer has the strategic importance he attributed to it. Nevertheless, the exchange between the two spaces that Benjamin had placed under the sign of incompatibility is flourishing under that which could be called a polymorphous promiscuity. I am not thinking here so much about the creation of film departments in every major museum, or about the way audio-visual technology has invaded the pedagogical sections of the institution (not to speak of the galleries themselves), or about the pictorial fantasies through which many aging film directors have been trying to compensate for their feeling of historical disaffection with regard to the dreams of authorial status they indulged in their youth (as if they were asking the museum for refuge from the emptiness of the movie theaters now playing their pictures). Rather, I am thinking about the astonishment that some of us have felt when, in the course of a museum visit, we found ourselves suddenly entering a dark room with a screen on which figures were moving, giving us the sudden feeling of having entered a movie house in midscreening.

Now what about architecture? It is easy to understand the logic that excludes it from a nonimaginary museum. Architecture resists mise en abyme. It takes place, but the place is already taken. One understands less easily why the museum, having become imaginary, maintains the exclusion, why a museum on paper does not lift the ban.

I will propose two explanations directly connected to the logic of the musée imaginaire. The first has to do with its iconographic rhetoric, the main figure of which is the blow-up, to the exclusion of reduction. Enlargement permits the emergence of the imperceptible, bringing to visibility what was too small to reach the naked eye. For this very reason it works one way; it has no counterpart. Malraux does not seem to be interested in producing invisibility. "It is of no interest," he writes, "that a big statue becomes small."

The first virtue of enlargement, however, is less that of blowing up objects than of destroying dimensional references. When looking at one of the illustrations of Le musée imaginaire, the reader does not know whether it is a blow-up and if so at what scale. The page setting introduces the works within a Gulliverian space where the largest have the same size as the smallest. Malraux, moreover, was careful to withdraw any measurement from the captions. Deprived of any anchoring in the real, the works on paper float in a space with no scale, no standard of comparison. Having become fictive works of art, they escape the sensory-motor space of perception and gravity. Architecture does not lend itself, however, to such photographic decontextualization.

In the later editions of Le musée imaginaire, starting with the one Gallimard published in 1965, Malraux added to the illustrations a series of reproductions of monuments. These additional plate sections remain strangely unassimilated within the whole; they feel out of place, not belonging to the same ontological family of the other illustrations. For the monument cannot be detached from its geographical surrounding, from its Grund. The picture, with "the patches of forest, desert, or mountain" that it was unable totally to eliminate, insistently refers to a nonimaginary topographic space outside the book. Thus resisting photographic deterritorialization, architecture does not let itself be caught on paper.

The picture of the Temple of Bodhisattva and Vaisravana, half way between architecture and sculpture, with its colossal figures cut directly into the flank of a hill in China, includes two visitors (the only living beings present in the book) who, like two "scale figures," are there to remind us that architecture, even when extra large, is never out of scale; that it always needs to take place, and for that reason to measure itself against the earth. So, there is no architecture on paper.

On what condition could such an exclusion be lifted? Can architecture be framed? Be quoted? Following the logic of Malraux's project, it would require an architecture that would be able not to take place, that would be able both to happen and not to find a place, an architecture that would be able to be cut off from its premises. Such a requirement could be fulfilled in two ways. The first one, putting the burden on the side of the world, would require a delocalization of the buildable space so radical, in fact, that for want of a site, architecture could fantasize itself as not taking place. The second, putting the burden on architecture itself, would consist precisely in having it occur within the space of the museum. For the most literal way for an architectural work not to take place remains its failure to reach its destination, in other words, to exist only on paper, that is, "in theory." It is to let its double take its place and move to the museum.

1 Malraux's address to the Congress, "Sur l'héritage culturel," was to appear in the September 1936 issue of **Commune**. Reprinted in André Malraux, **La politique, la culture**, ed. Janine Mossuz-Lavau (Paris: Gallimard, 1996), 132–43.
2 Walter Benjamin, "The Work of Art in the Age of Mechanical Reproduction," in **Illuminations**, trans. Harry Zohn (New York: Shocken Books, 1969), 234–35. Translation modified.
3 Ibid.
4 **La politique, la culture**, 136–37.
5 "Marlene Dietrich is not an actress like Sarah Berhardt was, she is a myth like Phryne" (my translation). See "Esquisse d'une psychologie du cinéma," in André Malraux, **Scènes choisies** (Paris: Gallimard, 1946), 333.

Denis Hollier, a literary theorist and historian, is professor of French literature at New York University. His books include Against Architecture.

La Castiglione, from André Malraux,
Le musée imaginaire.

Practice³: Theory, History, Architecture

Ignasi de Solà-Morales

Modern architecture articulates a paradigm comprised, on the one hand, of rational technique and, on the other, of the expression of the attitudes and feelings of the architect as the interpreter of the hopes and desires of society at large.

The criteria of rational technique embrace a discipline based upon efficiency, an accord between the means and the necessities, the analytic recognition of those necessities, and the development of the material possibilities needed in order to accommodate them. Together these criteria are accompanied in varying degrees by the unopposed exigency that architecture, as with any art, is and has been, in all its dimensions, an expression of its own particular zeitgeist. As such it is in part a manifestation of the aspirations and objectives of justice, equality, and solidarity, as well as of the pursuit of harmony between individual life and collective life in the social agglomerations that constitute cities.

With Le Corbusier, Walter Gropius, Ludwig Mies van der Rohe, and Erich Mendelsohn (to name but a few modern masters), architectural discourse found its legitimacy in the broadest set of criteria, related both to rational technique and to psychological expression. Architectural theory adopted referents or paradigms that emerged out of social theory, and though history itself passed on to a secondary plane, theory remained present as a specialized narrative that the technical and psychological discourses served to reinforce.

Theory itself abandoned systematic intention and instead developed specialized discourses centered on problems of sanitation, transportation, land use, and the rationality of different types of urban construction. The interest in expressing technical efficiency, as well as the aspirations to create a more egalitarian society, also found justification in aesthetic theories derived from the psychology of form or from a certain symbolic sympathy — appropriated in each case to help establish meaning in architecture and a set of general evaluative criteria.

But with the new paradigm also came other changes. With the emergence of what is conventionally called modern architecture, the ideology of the "treatise" disappeared — that is, the effort to organize in an orderly fashion an ensemble of principles, upon which the practice of architecture was founded. In its place there appeared partial discourses, studies, manifestos, and historical narratives that were limited in scope, yet thanks to which the legitimacy of the new architecture was established.

In considering the role of history as the basis for theoretical principles, it is important to insist on the fact that either one of two versions of that history must hold. Either a history of architecture subsists within the history of the arts, posited by the great historiography written at the turn of the 19th century, or, in a similar manner, the more limited histories of new techniques and materials in the construction of houses and cities were compiled as a complementary discourse legitimizing the origins of those techniques and processes. The stories of Viollet-le-Duc, Hermann Muthesius, Adolf Plat, and Ludwig Hilberseimer were evidently salutary, constituting approximations of past phenomena by which one could literally illuminate the present, as well as narratives with which to explain various languages and techniques through their historical origins.

These limited histories not only played a supporting role in the overall epistemological picture, they also became, in the hands of their more ambitious authors, an instrument for comprehending the present in a narrative teleologically oriented from the past toward the present.

Sigfried Giedion, Nikolaus Pevsner, Bruno Zevi, Leonardo Benevolo, and many others constructed narratives all coinciding in a single assertion: that the historical trajectory variously initiated in the baroque, in the Industrial Revolution, and in the artistic avant-gardes, constituted a progressive process of bringing to light "a definitive truth" – the dawn, in fact, of a new civilization, of a new awareness of architecture qua architecture. If history was indeed an instrument tied to a new theory of architecture, then the relation between the two consisted in bringing to the fore credibility, certitude, respect for veracity, and the relevance of the psycho-technical principles on which today's architectural activity depends. Rather than introducing new techniques, the history of architecture contributed to rendering more credible what earlier theories had already proposed.

In a 1958 manuscript intended as the text for a BBC television documentary on Henry-Russell Hitchcock's book **Architecture: Nineteenth and Twentieth Centuries**, Colin Rowe, then on the faculty at Cambridge University, wrote:

The Modern architect, we might suspect, is accustomed to receive from the historian a thrill somewhat equivalent to that which the Victorian reader of novels was accustomed to receive from the contemporary novelist. He is accustomed in other words to expect a happy ending. Plots and subplots are to be resolved; punishments are to be received; rewards distributed; while the hero and heroine (could they be engineering an architecture, or are they architecture and sociology?), tried and proved by experience, are to be settled down to an extended life of infinite fecundity and unabated bliss. Is it in order in a discussion of architecture to introduce a theological concept and to speak of the eschatology of Modern architecture? Or would it be simpler to propose that histories of architectural development since the industrial revolution have usually led up to the present with the inference that the present is the end of history?

This lengthy citation, evidently of a critical disposition vis-à-vis the traditional historiography of the Modern Movement and of its predetermined legitimizing function, seems to clearly define what occurred sometime around the 1960s – the shift of the architectural paradigm of the period.

Due to a number of factors, the techno-psychological paradigm entered a period of crisis during the 1950s. One witnessed, in the name of phenomenology, humanism, anthropology, and critical history, the dismemberment of the rational-techno-social construction that structured what is called (to repeat the notion) modern architecture. Rowe's ironic commentary merely further confirmed the fact of the demise of an episteme against which Team X fought as valiantly as the Nordic architects, the Brazilians as resolutely as Louis Kahn.

History itself found the quickest route to occupy a central position in the theoretical foundation of architecture. A new paradigm, this time historical, would now constitute the theoretical foundation of architecture for more than twenty years. Western architectural culture now lent itself to reliving a veritable neohistoricism, with many evident differences from what is called the historicism of the 19th century, though also with a significant number of points of similarity. Among the latter, and not the least relevant, is the reappearance of a new, gratifyingly attentive regard for the materials of history – "the past as friend," in the familiar phrase of Ernesto Rogers.

Two great currents would dispute the hegemony of the historical discourse of architecture. On the one hand came structural formalism, which derived from the great tradition of pure visibility at the beginning of the 20th century. Aby Warburg, Fritz Saxl, Irwin Panofsky, and Rudolf Wittkower are the principal figures in this historiography, in which the continual return of formal structures tends to offer the instruments for the decoding of the present as part of a structural analogy with the past. On the other hand came **critical history**, with its Hegelian roots, emerging out of the neohistoricism of Georg Lukács and dialectical materialism, as it was developed in the **global history** project of the Annales School.

In the formalist tradition, whether it is a question of a fragment, an index, or a residue, the historian tries to demonstrate the continuities and discontinuities of the present with the past, proposing the underlying possibilities of interpretation beyond that of simple outward appearance. Colin Rowe's entire work is a brilliant example of this type of approximation of architectural history, and also of a cultural history in search of deeper structures showing the internal nerve of the work, its decisive raison d'être – at the same time that formal invariables render it intangible.

Equally, the new formalism, with its strong structuralist resonances, gave rise to the discourse of disciplinary autonomy. That autonomy stood contrary to the traditional dependence of architectural theory on the theoretical paradigms of the mathematical, physical, social, and psychological sciences and, as a consequence, on the necessity of attributing to architecture interdisciplinary discourses. In its more recent incarnation – as was also the case in that rich and brilliant theoretical moment of 19th-century eclecticism – the historical-formal foundation of architecture is conceived as autonomous and independent. Disciplinary autonomy is a consequence of this autonomy of structural analysis, which the methodological and philosophical currents facilitated.

Autonomy does not signify that architecture cannot be compared to other cultural or technical phenomena, or that its sphere of activity has no rapport with other arenas of reality. Disciplinary autonomy signifies not only that more specific instruments exist for architectural analysis and that these critical instruments can be the object of a theoretical elaboration, but also that they would be the starting points for new contemporary architectural practices.

The imposing weight of Rowe's historical analyses on culture and on the architects of the English-speaking world until the end of the 1980s, together with the occasionally implicit, but mostly explicit, theoretical work of Aldo Rossi, allows us to understand the absolutely central position of history – of a certain kind of history: formal, structuralist – between the 1960s and the 1980s in architectural theory.

No less decisive – first in Europe and then, curiously, after a gap of more than ten years, in the United States – is the fact that history is at the very center of the architectural theory elaborated by Manfredo Tafuri and his collaborators, beginning in the mid-1960s. Tafuri's project comprised a critical history – a discourse that starts from historiographic techniques and hypotheses derived from the critique of ideologies, which the discourse external to architectural practice and to its autonomous reflection imposes as the sole legitimizing agent capable of explaining, discerning, and evaluating architecture itself.

"By this standard, architectural history will always seem the fruit of an unresolved dialectic," Tafuri wrote in his essay, "The Historical Project," published as the introduction to his last great work of synthesis, **The Sphere and the Labyrinth**. He continued:

The interweaving of intellectual models, modes of production, and modes of consumption ought to lead to the "explosion" of the synthesis contained in the work. Wherever this synthesis is presented as a completed whole, it is necessary to introduce a disintegration, a fragmentation, a "dissemination" of its constitutive units. It will then be necessary to submit the disintegrated components to a separate analysis. Client reactions, symbolic horizons, avant-garde hypotheses, linguistic structures, methods of reorganizing production, technological inventions will all be seen thus stripped of the ambiguity ingrained in the synthesis "displayed" by the work.

Clearly no specific methodology, when applied to such isolated components, can take into account the "totality" of the work. Iconology, the history of political economics, the history of thought, of religions, of the sciences, of popular traditions will each be able to appropriate fragments of the broken-up work. The work will have something to say for each of these histories. By taking apart a work of Alberti, for instance, I can illuminate the foundations of bourgeois intellectual ethics in formation, the crisis of humanist historicism, the structure of the fifteenth century's world of symbols, the structure of a particular patronage system, the consolidation of a new division of labor in the building trades. But none of these components will serve to demonstrate the validity of that work. The critical act will consist of a recomposition of the fragments once they are historicized: in their own "remontage."

A fundamental paradox in Tafuri's thinking and of his decisive influence on architectural thought over the past thirty years resides in the double attitude of both rejection and acceptance. The internal discourse of the architectural discipline is ideologically contaminated. The architect is nothing more than the interpreter, brilliant or mediocre, of the dominant ideology. But he is not in a position to understand what he is doing or to understand **himself**. The history that nourishes architectural practice is not legitimate either. It lacks distance, it is instrumental, it is what Tafuri labeled **operative**. On the other hand, the reliable discourse, consistent and revealing of the true condition of architecture present and past, is the discourse of critical history, a theoretical practice that, starting from a negative position, assumes the sole possibility of a true interpretative discourse.

A critical theory of architecture exists. It is not an isolated intellectual activity, not an exclusively disciplinary instrument. It is, though, the discourse that best understands the ideological activity called architecture, and it aspires to replace every other regional or partially historical debate that can be constructed as an autonomous discourse.

With Lukács, whose influence on Tafuri and on his early mentors such as Giulio Carlo Argan, Alberto Asor Rosa, and Mario Tronti was considerable, the point was fundamental. But these ideas also found something in common in the immense work of Marc Bloch, Lucien Fèvre, and Ferdinand Braudel, by way of the journal and the studies of the Annales: the development of a history with material foundations such as geography, demography, and economy, which permitted a later opening into the history of ideas, ideological constructions, and social formations.

The specific form of structuralism discussed is also a matter of concern – elaborated in the writings of Marx in distinguishing between the structural and the superstructural, and understood in such a way that the task of history becomes to trace the path in reverse. The effect is to introduce superstructural phenomena, such as ideologies – for example, architecture – and to look for structural explanations for them and for the material bases for those explanations.

The neo-Marxist Tafurian history is not, though, teleologically predestined, as one might suppose, to revealing a sense of progression, and corruption of every avant-garde innovation is reproduced in practice with the same structure, whether it be Brunelleschi, Borromini, Piranesi, Le Corbusier, or Peter Eisenman. A tragic, irreconcilable fate destroys the permanent existence of a limitless passion for the cultures, since it ends by being on the contrary a cyclic history – a kind of eternal Nietzschean return through which the ideo-architectural objects become recognized as **pure futility or infinite diversion**.

Is history the proper paradigm for architectural theory? Whether answered from the side of history or that of architectural theory, the answer will be decisively **no**. If contemporary theoreticians agree about anything, it is over the exhaustion of the Hegelian model of explanation. Marx and Freud both endorsed, from different perspectives, the idea that beneath the bare facts lay a deep structure that had to be decoded and revealed. This epistemological detection was driven by a desire to go beyond appearance and image and the phenomenological world in order to dive into the depths where it would be possible to discover the true structures, the true nature of things.

Since Michel Foucault, we at least know that things exist only in terms of the multiple interconnections of their relationships, and that the knowledge we can access will depend, in any event, on our capacity to detect the greatest number of related lines intersecting in a particular event. Contemporary theory appropriates, as its point of departure, this vision of disorder inherent in reality, multiplying the differences in any given condition. From this premise, by tracing back we can return to the origin of things, or at least be capable of reconstructing an original texture.

But the task of history is no longer that of creating grand narratives. As Paul Veyne declared in his 1971 polemical work on epistemology, history is written beginning from operations that depend on our own intentions, on the **plot** that guides our research.[4] Effected by that plot, depending on the conspiracy of facts we wish to decode, we organize our tools and the hierarchy of documents we have decided to use and the narrative we end up writing.

It is not a question of there being a general history or even regional histories, but rather the fact that histories are always constructed on the basis of hypotheses and by the predetermined concentration of a nucleus of relationships that one accords the privilege of historic attention. There is a hierarchy in the narrative of subjective elements – hazardous ones, fortuitous ones – but there is also an opening to the demonstrative capacity of every ensemble of bare facts not previously determined.

More than the quest for new models of complete understanding, what history aims to pursue are the transversal routes, the microhistories, the cuts across as yet unexplored fissures, the search for other, new meanings. This total deregulation logically produces a relativism of the narratives themselves, which enter into open competition with other narratives bearing opposing, or at least different, interpretations. In this climate, who could call upon history to be the **magister vitae**, the giver of life, the founder of the architectural discipline?

The condition of theoretical thought, however, is no more consistent. It is true that the sciences have opened the door to the complexity of all points of view. To begin with, the sciences accept the cohabitation of different theoretical models without the necessity of previous protocols pitting one against the other. The logic of scientific research allows for the development and acceptance of new scientific theories based on a pragmatic conception of their capacity to correctly interpret a given domain of phenomena. Be it chaos theory or quartz theory – two scientific discourses that have acquired a certain journalistic currency – the acceptance of emerging ideas is based not on some new access to the nature of things but rather on the statistical stability of certain phenomena. Does this mean that we are dealing with a theory without principles? On the contrary. The apparent détente of theory within the mathematical, physical, biological, and social sciences, relates to the demise of the rule of dogmatism, including scientific dogmatism, and the unitary, exclusive conception of so-called rational knowledge.

To the extent that rational knowledge progresses and, as a consequence, to the extent that one understands history and the sciences as diverse narratives in a veritable epistemological pluralism, the idea that architecture requires unshakable paradigms to guarantee it a permanent form and identity would seem to dissolve as well.

In a conversation between Foucault and Gilles Deleuze, published in issue 49 of the journal **L'arc**, Deleuze was asked about his relationship to politics and the impression he often gave of retreating when queried on those matters. Deleuze's response was quite enlightening.

I think we're in the process of experiencing the theory practice relationships in a new manner. In the past one sometimes conceived practice as the application of theory, as a consequence of theory, and sometimes, on the contrary, as inspiring theory, as though itself being the progenitor of a form of theory to come.

In any event, one conceived of their relationships in the form of a process of totality – in one direction or the other. For us the question presents itself perhaps differently. The theory practice relationships are so much more partial, more fragmentary.

For one thing, theory is always local, relative to a small domain, though it could be applied to another

domain, more or less distant. . . . Practice constitutes a set of stopovers from one theoretical point to another, and theory is a set of stopovers from one practice to another. No theory can be developed without encountering a kind of wall, of which point one needs the experience of practice in order to pierce the wall. . . . I recall the theoretician in the role of a box of tools, having nothing to do with representing or constructing subjects. Those who act or fight have stopped being represented, whether by a party or a union, and begin to speak for themselves; they acquire the right to do it every time . . . Who acts, who speaks? It's always a multiplicity, even within the one person who acts or who speaks. We are all "groupuscules." Representation no longer exists; representation. . . the action of theory, the action of practice in the relationship of stopovers and networks.

A few paragraphs later, Deleuze adds: "A theory is just like a box of tools. It has nothing to do with the signifier. . . . It has to **do** something, it has to function. And not just for itself."[6]

Doubtless these words are themselves an index of a way of thinking about theory and practice that is very different from what in these last years has produced an untenable division between theoreticians and practitioners in the discipline of architecture.

Our universities and our schools of architecture are filled with theory and history courses that, while claiming the privilege of being both the illuminating voice of reality and its critical conscience, generate a masochistic mechanism among those who practice architecture – much like the unhappy conscience, noted by Marx in his **Eighteenth Brumaire of Louis Bonaparte**, of those who "do what they know without knowing what they do." At the same time, the glossy architecture magazines and profusely illustrated architecture books attempt to show the work and practice of architects as things sufficient unto themselves, things that explain themselves, whose accessibility and comprehensibility are immediate, and whose worth is patently evident.

For years a kind of advanced academicism believed that the proof of intellectual honesty was that the architectural theoretician was not contaminated by contact with practice, even where practice could sully or influence the supposed intellectual independence of the theoretician. The situation in which we continue to find ourselves is unacceptable, even when the schizophrenic theory-practice relationship in architecture is enriched by the interdisciplinary contribution of those who come to architecture from other spheres of knowledge.

The Any conferences were organized by a group of people who believed in the need to move beyond the specialized divisions between theory and practice, between the purveyors of foundational paradigms and the more or less brilliant executors of the ideas of those theoretical cadres. Can one posit that we have progressed somewhat in the nine years of Any meetings and publications? To respond either positively or negatively to this question would be to fall into the trap of progressivism — as though the development or the maturation of ideas were tied to the idea of progress. That is not the issue. Like the sea of Paul Valéry, always **beginning again**, the relationship between theory and practice in architecture is itself an inexhaustible practice.

1 Colin Rowe, "Review of **Architecture: Nineteenth and Twentieth Centuries** by Henry-Russell Hitchcock," in **As I Was Saying**, Vol. I (Cambridge, Massachusetts: The MIT Press, 1996), 184.
2 Manfredo Tafuri, "The Historical Project," in **The Sphere and the Labyrinth**, trans. Pellegrino d'Acierno and Robert Connolly (Cambridge, Massachusetts: The MIT Press, 1990), 14.
3 Tafuri, ibid., Appendix, **L'architecture dans le boudoir**, 323–35.
4 Paul Veyne, **Writing History: Essay on Epistemology**, trans. Mina Moore-Rinvolucri (Middletown, Connecticut: Wesleyan University Press, 1984).
5 "Les intellectuels et le pouvoir," in Michel Foucault, **Dits et écrits**, vol. II, 1970–1975 (Paris: Gallimard, 1994), 307–08.
6 Ibid., 309.

Ignasi de Solà-Morales, an architect and professor of architectural theory and history at the Barcelona School of Architecture, recently completed the new Teatro del Liceo in Barcelona. His **Differences: Topographies of Contemporary Architecture** is published in the Writing Architecture series.

Melange of Articles and Reflections
Patrick Berger

UEFA Headquarters, Nyon, Switzerland, 1999.

We have the feeling that never before have we known so much about things architectural and about the city, yet never before have we understood so little of what is being thought, what is being planned, and what is being produced in our present-day spaces. The situation is all the more corrosive conceptually in that it implies the failure of a contemporary knowledge that has helped us to understand the world but not to direct it.

We find ourselves in a formidably paradoxical cultural situation. The more our archaeological and historical competencies have helped us understand the sensate, material world, the more we multiply the luminous discourses that propagate the idea of the irreversibility of formal languages. This renders useless even the history of those languages that we are striving to bring to life.

Two relatively symmetric positions thus continue to articulate, one by identification, the other by opposition, the same crisis as it confronts historical formulation. The first gives rise to the return of styles or models borrowed from ancient or recent history. The second favors the development of signs of innovation whereby the procedural instructions forbid seeing in the patrimony an earlier state of contemporary language but rather see only an ancient narrative told in a dead language. For the first, states of grace will exist corresponding to privileged periods of history. For the second, there can only be a singular vision of a time frame in which succeeding events are irreversible.

The upshot is that an issue that has validity today still remains in suspension – the question of its relation to history. There is the matter of accepting that alternatives exist, choices other than a history of the exceptional, a history of architecture that only accounts for the excellence of forms. There are paths, such as those based on an ideology founded on a principle of autonomy, that imply that architecture, as with other plastic forms of expression, can think itself into existence, can transform itself, can be innovative following the norms of its own history. In effect we are committed to reflect on a subject matter suited to our times – that of giving form to the environment we have constructed over the past thirty years. The incomprehensible reality of that environment has brought about a situation where it can no longer be a question of restoring or applying any other fictional model. Urban reality demands, as a priority, to be rendered permanently intelligible. Whatever the nature of urban confusion, it is only when one begins from the actual state of things that new points of view will appear.

It is possible to implement the perspective of this workplace only if the idea brings together the architect who invents, the historian who authenticates, and the citizen who interprets and legislates. The question and the responses related to the organization of urban space depend on a knowledge of the double face of history. Urban space has always been simultaneously built up over necessary demolitions and the conquest of new space. This double aspect, together with its history, particularizes each site. Whatever vocabulary one chooses, to render urban or to give rise to a landscape, what is at stake is a representation: the encounter between the geographical state of things and the desires of the moment, of history. The qualification on the encounter demands the implementation of punctual ties between the architect and the landscape in order to render the latter intelligible.

The architecture must also be conceived beyond itself, in the role that it plays in the formal organization or representation of the surroundings. These days architecture must also jointly take into account the emblematic nature of the program and the lineaments of the urban situation in which it will insinuate itself and which it should validate. This finality leads to several possible resolutions.

It is mandatory that the architectural act undergo a change of statute, and that the artistic predisposition that has led architects to the belief in total aesthetic freedom must be seriously questioned as a viable philosophy of inscription for urban development.

It is essential that every conception adjusts to the reality of duration: we must plan based upon where we are, with the means we possess today, yet always keep in mind what we will transmit to the future.

It is equally necessary to create a cultural vision other than that of today's conservation and accumulation without limit. It seems urgent to put in place a cultural plan to distinguish among the artifacts of history, between those that should be preserved and those that can be disposed of.

New points of view responding to these matters cannot be introduced without freedom in architecture's relation to history. What we do not understand today is what we have not mastered as yesterday's project.

Patrick Berger is a professor of architecture at L'École polytechnique fédérale in Lausanne and at L'École d'architecture in Paris Belleville. His projects include the Maison de l'Université de Bourgogne in Dijon. He wrote this article in conjunction with art historian Jean-Pierre Nouhaud.

Mark C. Taylor

"Anymore Theory or History?" is not, of course, one question but at least two: Anymore Theory? Anymore History? Neither question is answerable apart from the other. What is the historical significance of contemporary theory? What is the theoretical significance of our historical moment? While theory is inescapably historical, history is unavoidably theoretical. We must, then, begin where we are. But where are we, here and now?

We are, it seems, in the midst of social, economic, political, and cultural transformations that are creating a pervasive sense of overwhelming complexity. Indeed, the historical moment is the moment of complexity – or, more precisely, the moment of emergent complexity. As always, when change is so extensive and so rapid, it is difficult to assume a critical perspective from which to assess the significance of what is occurring. Far from discouraging analysis, the recognition of emerging complexity invites a wide variety of interpretations and prognostications. For some, our era is marked by the shift from industrialism to postindustrialism, for others by the movement from modernism to postmodernism, or post-postmodernism, and for still others, by the change from market to multinational, informational, or digital capitalism. Weaving together multiple lines of analysis, New York Times **Foreign Affairs columnist Thomas L. Friedman argues that during the past decade, a new "international system" has emerged, which is replacing the "Cold War" system that has governed the world for the last half century. He names this new system "globalization." Friedman explains:**

Whether considered in terms of social, economic, or political processes, globalization presupposes the development of increasingly sophisticated informatic and telematic technologies. What Friedman describes as globalization might be better understood as the emergence of network culture. Anticipating important aspects of Friedman's account of globalization, Manuel Castells develops an extensive analysis of the transformative effect of recent technological innovations. According to Castells:

> Information networking technology jumped to a quantum leap in the early 1990s, due to the convergence of three developments. First, the rapid diffusion of digital technology into telecommunications, building upon major breakthroughs in microelectronics... third, computer interactive systems and local area networks... so-called Area Networks, became operational...

Castells devotes his extensive three-volume study to an exploration of the economic, social, and cultural impact of information and telematic technologies. Though calling for a clarification of "networking logic," he does not develop a persuasive interpretation of the distinctive operational rules and principles of networks and the worlds they create. If our historical moment is characterized by the emergence of network culture, then we must ask where we can turn to find theoretical resources for understanding the changes that are occurring.

This question comes at a difficult moment for humanists, as well as for artists and architects who are interested in theoretical questions. The theoretical trajectories that have dominated thought and practice for the past 30 years have reached closure. Theory is at a dead end. More problematic, the theoretical positions that have been most influential for three decades are particularly ill-equipped to account for, and respond to, this specific historical moment. For purposes of discussion, I will identify three closely related but clearly distinguishable critical tendencies. My remarks must, of course, be brief and schematic; nonetheless, I hope they will begin to suggest a possible way out of the current theoretical impasse.

Naming, as we all know by now, is a constitutive act that creates as much as it describes. The socio-economic transition that Friedman analyzes has a counterpart in critical theory. Just as the epoch change that Friedman associates with 1989 was the culmination of the deregulation and privatization of the interrelated telecommunications industry and financial markets in the 1970s and 1980s, so the current crisis of criticism brings to closure the critique of various aspects of structuralism that developed during the 1970s and 1980s. Within this context, it is helpful to gather admittedly different critical strategies under the now familiar rubric of post-structuralism. From this perspective, developments in history and theory suggest important parallels. While deregulation and privatization have led to a relative decentralization and distribution of certain social, economic, and political processes, criticism of the totalizing

propensities of formal structures – be they dialectical, binary, or digital – discloses the inevitable open-endedness and thus incompletion of every system that claims to be whole. This general critical trajectory has, of course, been very influential both within the academy and in the world of architecture. If 1989 forms a turning point in the process of globalization, 1968 marks a crucial juncture for recent critical theory. The theory that has been decisive for the past 30 years emerged on the world stage here in Paris in May 1968. Ironically, in Paris, French theory has become something of an American import. While long decisive, this trajectory has now reached closure, which is not to say that it is over.

The three major strands in this trajectory are associated with three proper names, which identify different critical strategies: Michel Foucault – social constructivism; Jacques Derrida – deconstruction; and Jean Baudrillard – simulation. Without minimizing the important differences between and among these thinkers, it is important to recognize significant points of agreement. This is not always easy to do because these figures often are more interested in stressing their differences than in acknowledging their agreements. Moreover, they tend to attract followers with different interests and investments who exacerbate disagreements for the sake of self-definition.

One of the ironies of current academic culture in the United States is that what had been marginal now has become central. In different terms, what once defiantly announced itself as noncanonical has, in many quarters, become canonical, and those who were proudly on the periphery now find themselves in positions of power. Sadly, many of those who have moved to the center all too often forget their past and reinforce precisely the structures and hierarchies they once resisted. If there is an orthodoxy among many humanists today, it is surely what has come to be described as "social constructionism." While Foucault obviously is not solely responsible for this development, his multifaceted work has influenced many who claim this label. The reasons for the attractiveness of social constructionism is often more political than intellectual – if, indeed, such a distinction can be made. Foucault's inventive analyses of the micro-politics of power disclose the subtle ways in which social, political, economic, and psychological control is exercised. When technologies of surveillance and control are dissected, it begins to become clear that structures and powers, which once appeared objective, are, in fact, subjective constructions. This line of analysis is not limited to the domain of social structures but extends to processes once called natural. All nature, from this point of view, is culture. This does not, of course, imply that objectivity is the creation of individual subjectivity; on the contrary, subjectivity is itself a construction, which, in turn, constructs orders that constitute both objects, other subjects, and even itself. As might well have been expected, this social constructivist position has provoked strong reactions not only among humanists but increasingly among scientists. The growing attack on the arts and humanities by respected scientists like E.O. Wilson, Richard Dawkins, Steven Jay Gould, and others signals an important development that cannot be ignored. And yet, the position of social constructionism does not offer adequate theoretical means to respond effectively. We should not "forget Foucault," but we must move beyond him.

The differences between Derrida and Foucault are not as profound as they and their followers would have us believe. One way to understand their relationship is to say that Derrida provides critical analyses of philosophical, literary, and, increasingly, theological texts whose structures and logics inform the very social processes that Foucault theoretically dismantles. This is not to suggest, of course, that Derrida is uninterested in the social, economic, and political aspects of life any more than it is to insist that Foucault ignores texts in the more traditional sense of the term. Nevertheless, there is a different emphasis in Derrida's deconstruction and Foucault's genealogy. It is not too much to insist that no one has done more to expose the hegemonic machinations of classical systems and structures than Derrida. Though his writings are difficult and his texts involved, his argument always comes down to the same fundamental insight: every system or structure that claims to be complete presupposes, as a condition of its own possibility, precisely that which it is constructed to exclude. This outside that is inside disrupts, dislocates, and decenters the structure in a way that leaves it incomplete and therefore open. While acknowledging noteworthy differences among dialectical, binary, and digital systems, Derrida is more intent on exposing the logic of totalization they share. As with social constructivism, this deconstructive critique is necessary but not sufficient. In this context, further questions need to be posed. Most important, do Derrida and his followers have too monolithic a view of systems and structures? Is it possible to imagine systems and structures that function differently and thus are not subject to the critique Derrida so effectively advances? In attempting to answer these questions, we should not forget Derrida any more than we should forget Foucault; nor should we stop with him.

Finally, Baudrillard. More than Foucault or Derrida, Baudrillard is important for his association with current aspects of late-20th-century culture and less so for his theoretical account of the phenomena he identifies. One could argue that in the past 30 years, Guy Debord's society of the spectacle has morphed into the society of simulation. Informatics and telematics intersect in contemporary media culture to create a world in which the real appears virtual and the virtual is becoming increasingly real. Virtual reality, in other words, is not merely a specific technology but a cultural condition. The intermingling of reality and virtuality confounds classical oppositions like reality/image, matter/mind, materiality/immateriality, mental/physical, as well as interpretative distinctions like infrastructure/superstructure, objectivity/subjectivity, and, of course, nature/culture. While Baudrillard recognizes the importance of the cultural shifts that are occurring, his thinking remains structured by oppositions that are no longer workable. Accordingly, he tends to collapse the former term in the foregoing binaries into the latter. That is to say, Baudrillard reduces reality into image, matter into mind, materiality into immateriality, etc. He insists on this reduction because he does not realize that the virtual condition reconfigures every such opposition in a way that leaves neither term the same. If this is so, how can the developments Baudrillard describes be freed from the outdated grid through which he processes them?

With these questions in mind, let us return to the historical moment from which we departed. This moment, I have suggested, is characterized by the emergence of network culture. But what is network culture and what theoretical resources are necessary to understand it? As we have noted, Castells argues that the decisive development in the 1990s was that "information networking technology jumped by a quantum leap." In calling for an analysis of "networking logic," he notes the importance of the notion of complexity for understanding networks: "The morphology of the network," Castells maintains, "seems to be well adapted to increasing complexity of interaction and to unpredictable patterns of development arising from the creative power of such interaction."[3] With his overriding concern for rich historical description and careful sociological analysis, Castells leaves the task of developing an adequate theoretical account of networking logic to others. He does, however, indirectly suggest the direction such an analysis might take. In the effort to comprehend networking logic and thus to come to a better understanding of network culture, the rapidly developing field of complexity studies provides invaluable theoretical insights.

The difficult task of analyzing the implications of complexity theory for current cultural developments must await another occasion. In this context, I will conclude by suggesting ways in which complexity theory might help us move beyond what seems to be a theoretical impasse. Recent theoretical positions that have been exceedingly influential leave us with three important questions:

Is it possible to develop an understanding of the interrelationship between subjectivity and objectivity in which neither is reduced to the other, but each is constituted through complex feedback loops that are mutually constitutive?

Is it possible to imagine nontotalizing systems and structures that nonetheless act as a whole?

Can reality/image, matter/information, nature/culture be reconfigured in ways that maintain the distinction between each term but do not reinforce their opposition?

Complexity, of course, is not a new concern for architects. Indeed, the beginning of what came to be called postmodern architecture can be traced to the appearance of **Robert Venturi's** Complexity and Contradiction in Architecture. **In this work, Venturi's interest in complexity does not involve just anymore but centers on the very specific more of Mies van der Rohe – a more, in other words, that is less. For Venturi, less is not more, thus he seeks a more that complicates rather than simplifies. The complexity Venturi defines, however, is not the complexity of current complexity theory. While Venturi attempts to displace the disjunctive either-or of modernism with the synthetic both-and of postmodernism, complexity theory rejects this, as well as every other binary opposition. In their exhaustive study entitled** Darwinism Evolving: Systems Dynamics and the Genealogy of Natural Selection, **David Depew and Bruce Weber offer a concise description of what is at issue in complexity theory: "Complex systems have a large number of components that interact simultaneously in sufficiently rich number and parallel ways so that the system shows spontaneous self-organization and produces global, emergent structures."[4] By extending the analyses of nonlinear dynamic systems that have been developed by theoretical biologists to social, economic, and cultural processes, it becomes possible to formulate an account of systems and structures that responds to each of the questions I have posed. Subjectivity and objectivity, reality and image, and information and matter are recast through their interaction in complex adaptative systems that act as whole without totalizing. Worldwide webs, it seems, are not merely fiber optic; their architecture can be discerned in physical, chemical, biological, social, political, economic, and cultural systems. Webs within webs create networks of networks whose complex logic defines emerging network culture. If we can grasp this logic, we might be able to understand our peculiar historical moment.**

Closure, we have learned by now, does not mean the end. On the contrary, closure paradoxically presupposes the opening it nonetheless creates. When extended to the issues under consideration in this context, the opening that closure presupposes is the more that is the condition of the possibility and impossibility of any system or structure. To think the closure of theory that marks our time is to imagine almost inconceivable complexity. Anymore Theory or History? Yes, yes. Always more and always more complex.

1 Thomas L. Friedman, **The Lexus and the Olive Tree: Understanding Globalization** (New York: Farrar, Strauss, Giroux, 1999), 8.
2 Manuel Castells, **The Information Age: Economy, Society and Culture**, vol. I, **The Rise of Network Society** (Cambridge, Massachusetts: Blackwell Publishers, 1996), 170. See also: vol. II, **The Power of Identity** (Cambridge, Massachusetts: Blackwell Publishers, 1997), and vol. III, **End of the Millennium** (Cambridge, Massachusetts: Blackwell Publishers, 1998).
3 Ibid., 61.

4 David Depew and Bruce Weber, **Darwinism Evolving: Systems Dynamics and the Genealogy of Natural Selection** (Cambridge, Massachusetts: MIT Press, 1997), 437.

Mark C. Taylor **is the Cluett Professor of Humanities at Williams College, and author of** Disfiguring: Art, Architecture and Religion; Imagologies; **and, most recently,** Hiding.

The Offense of Wandering

Hubert Damisch

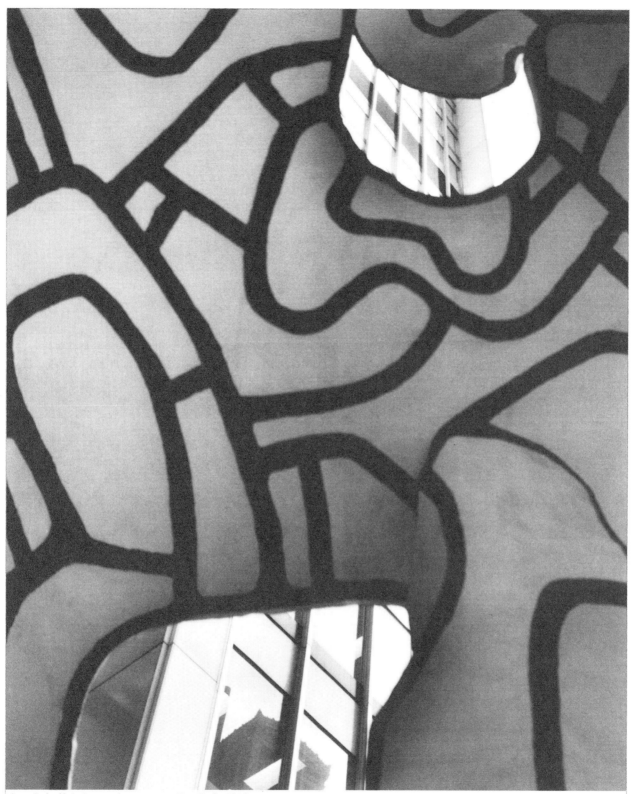

Jean Dubuffet, Group of Four Trees**, New York, 1972.**

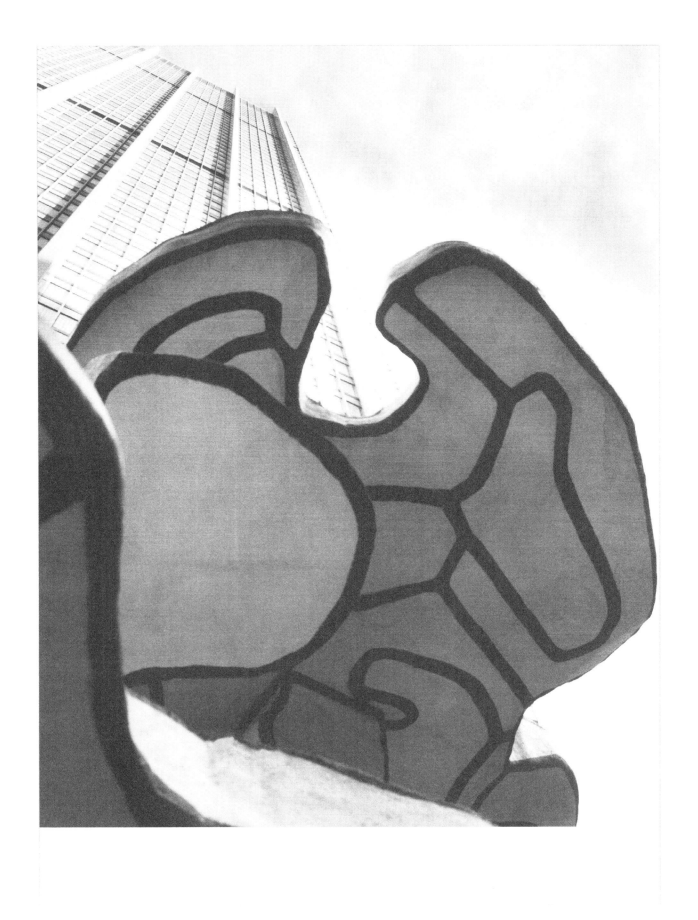

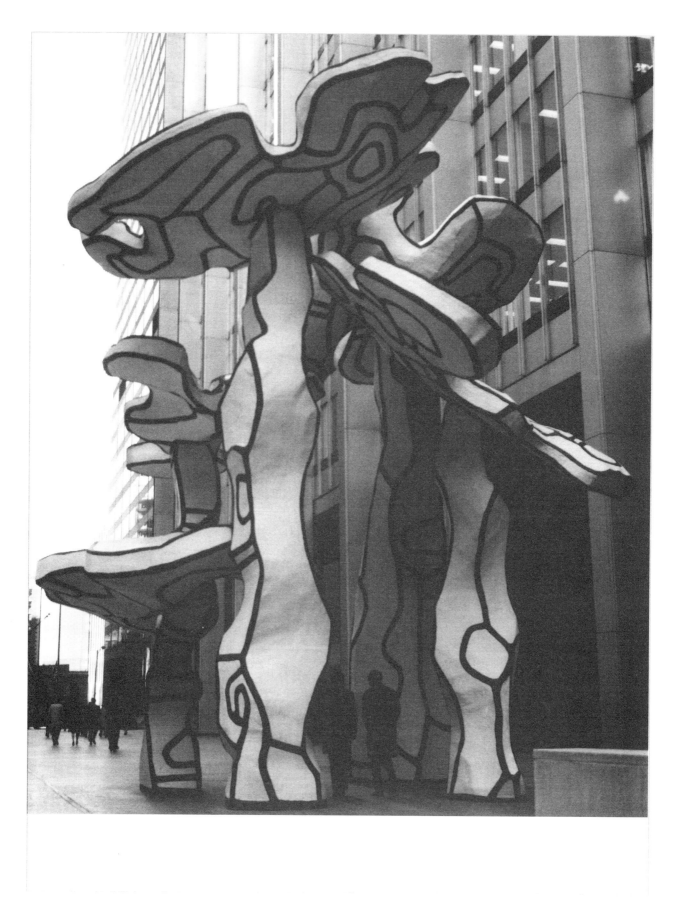

Not unlike the previous Any conferences – occurring each year at the same time but always in a different location – this Anymore conference, located (as the prefix any demands) under the sign of a generalized epistemological wandering, is subjected in 1999, the last year of the millennium, to a temporal horizon. Though taking place in Paris, it is also subject to an ideological and institutional horizon. An effort of accommodation imposes itself, accompanied by the invitation to deal with the absence or lack – a particularly sensitive matter in this building, situated as it is under the invocation of the author of Eupalinos – the absence or lack not so much of an "architectural culture" as of a clear notion of what the conjunction of those two words, culture and architecture, connotes, and what the implications of that conjunction are. What place does architecture occupy in what one might call the culture of our time? Under what species might one consider architecture as symptomatic of the state of that culture and its aims? If indeed there are aims, which would be architecture's own? What relationship does culture, or whatever it is that now takes culture's place, entertain in general vis-à-vis architecture? And, more profoundly, more secretly, what link, considered fundamental, can one discover between the very concept of culture and that of architecture?

I will address my remarks to this last question. Allow me to introduce it via the detour of an anecdote that for me possesses the quality of a moral fable. In June 1982, during its annual convention that year in Honolulu, the American Institute of Architects awarded the painter Jean Dubuffet a medal accompanied by a certificate with the following inscription:

Dubuffet did not make the trip to Honolulu to receive his medal. However, six months earlier, in a letter dated 22 December 1981, he thanked Robert Lawrence for the honor the AIA had conferred on him in the following terms: "I am especially moved to receive from the Institute the award mentioned in your letter, and I am truly happy that American architects have chosen in this way to demonstrate the interest they have in my work. I do believe, it is true, that my work points in a direction that can inspire architecture to explore rich possibilities, possibilities where we would begin to see new structures from which symmetry, rectilinear elements, and right angles would be excluded."[2]

The contradiction between the two discourses is patently obvious – that is, the contradiction between the words of the writers of the certificate conferred by the AIA (words that show every sign of having been carefully weighed) and those of the recipient, who takes exception to them in anticipation. The certificate makes implicit reference solely to the works – monumental sculptures of more or less huge dimensions – that well-known architects such as Gordon Bunshaft, I.M. Pei, and, more recently, Helmut Jahn, commissioned from the artist. These were works that those architects expected (the text leaves no mystery about it) would reinforce the effects of the structures with which they were associated. Whereas in his letter of thanks, written before he could have been aware of the wording of the certificate, Dubuffet stands rather distant from seeing his contribution to architecture as something like a complement – or should one say supplement? – something that, far from affecting it in its form, on the contrary merely emphasizes its worth, reaffirms its message, and (the AIA would express gratitude to him for this) helps in understanding the nature of the work. Instead, it is precisely on architectural terrain – in the very domain of architecture itself – that Dubuffet comes to intervene, and in quite another direction, and toward quite a different goal – as he had already done beginning in 1968, when he published his first "edifice" projects.

The entire affair is all the more edifying – the exact word – in that Dubuffet never made a secret of his feelings – likewise, never in the least mitigated – about the architecture said to be "modern." Nor did he hide the disquiet he felt seeing an out-and-out modernist such as Bunshaft interested in his works to the point of collecting them – indeed to the point of commissioning his Group of Four Trees, though you would have to say the work looks rather good at the foot of the vertical, rectilinear, glass tower that is the Chase Manhattan Bank of New York. (As does The Tree Stand, adjacent to the cement snows courtesy of Marcel Breuer, at the ski resort of Flaines.) In Paris, one might well think that Dubuffet's Tower of Figures is implanted on the Ile Saint-Germain, at Issy-les-Moulineaux, less in defiance than as a knowing wink of the eye on the edge of the contemporary metropolis. Located in the immediate surroundings of what young architects regard as "the city on the periphery" – that strange urban ensemble that (in introducing itself into the interspace) has come to despoil the binary play of oppositions between the city and its suburbs. Analogously, the Tower models the opposition between sculpture and architecture, and imposes itself as a kind of interrogation of what can become of architecture when it has neither the rights to the city nor, for that matter, the right to be cited.

I have chosen Dubuffet to introduce my remarks, less for his contribution, by itself resolutely peripheral, to the architecture of its time, than for the attack he never ceased to press against the general culture and the control it exercises on the arts. But when the time came for him actually to construct, necessity nevertheless compelled him to borrow knowledge from the domain that partook of what can only be called a technical culture, hereinafter pushed to the point of academicism. In this sense, there is no art more "cultural" than architecture. In fact, Dubuffet was the first to recognize that human beings were irremediably situated in a culture, and in particular could extricate themselves only partially – through art – from the cutoff from reality that language imposes. Let us begin, then, with regard to this concern, with the division that language imposes, at least in the West, between architecture and construction – a division that Dubuffet implicitly endorsed in his writings without really examining the matter more closely, and without excluding, as one will see, all culture seen as "technical."

What in fact does one read in Prospectus under the title "Edifices"? That the sculptor of the Tower of Figures was assisted in the interior design of the work by an architect, to whom we owe the general plans and the two models, the closest of which to the final configuration is named Le Gastrovolve, in reference to the involuted character of an apparatus whose exterior aspect of perfect compactness leaves no doubt that it defers to the constructive norms of the most advanced modernism. "The construction of the edifice shall be based on the principle of hanging the entire exterior envelope on the arborescent interior apparatus of the Gastrovolve, which, made as it is entirely out of concrete, will support the work. The floor boards will be cosmetic. The exterior envelope will be lightweight and thin, and simply attached in the manner of a curtain wall. It can also itself be made of concrete, but of small thickness, though preferably of stratified epoxy resin. In the latter case, a network of stiff materials, joining the meandering black tracings of the exterior decoration, can be used if needed – notably to strengthen the entire dome covering the highest room, which forms the cupola roof of the building, etc."[3]

The moral fable, one might say, begins to take shape. The same Dubuffet who denied that the creation of art was the business of specialists, did not hesitate to consult a professional when it came to erecting his Tower. This man who could not find words strong enough to denounce architecture that he judged lacking,[4] used techniques that were the very techniques of architecture itself. The moral that emerges from this story could take the form of a question. What does it signify for architecture that it is constructed and, perhaps even more significantly, that it is constructed in such a particular manner? What do all these facts and practices signify not only for architecture as a concept but also for architecture as a phenomenon of culture, through the prisms of which we can see something of culture's own architecture?

On the concept of architecture, Jacques Derrida has opportunely reminded us that it is itself a constructum, and whatever presents itself as an "architecture of architec-

ture" has a history, is itself historical from one part to the next. This remains very much the case even if we accept that it is a constructum that we inhabit, even as it inhabits us, and of a heritage that comprehends us even before we have made the effort to consider it.[5] One might object to the notion that every concept, beginning with the concept of culture, is more or less constructed – if the remark did not have the effect of obliterating the relationship (apparently a sensible but highly problematic one when you think of its history) that the concept of architecture clearly maintains to that of construction. A relationship of difference as much as of similarity. In this sense, Derrida is right to say that "from its ancient beginnings, the most basic concept of architecture has been constructed." But why would one not add (and why did Derrida not add) that this concept had been architectured, as is suggested by the lovely formula that insists that there is an "architecture of architecture"? It is not only because the verb architecturer – which entered the French language soon after the distinction was made between architects and engineers – has to be handled with caution, signifying, if I am to believe the Petit Robert dictionary, "construire avec rigueur." Rather, the reason should be sought on a deeper level, somewhere approaching the heading "architectural culture" – architecture as a fact of culture, culture as inhabited by architecture as much as it inhabits architecture, culture informed by architecture as much as it informs architecture.

This philosophy attributes to architecture the idea of construction – together with all its additional resonances, including even Kant's definition of architectonics as "the art of systems" – but does not necessarily signify that all there is to architecture is construction. Nor does it allow one to suppose that the two are equivalent in the sense that the concept suggests – whether it is the concept of architecture or that of construction. Conversely, the image of God as the Architect of the universe appeals beyond the idea of construction – the universe is not thought of purely in technical terms (in Kepler's time, the mathematics applicable to architecture were at a very rudimentary stage, and were almost entirely empirical), but also in aesthetic terms: regularity, symmetry, harmony, and even composition (harmony of the spheres, composition of forces, etc.), if not beauty itself. The dictionary distinction between construire and architecturer was justified by the rivalry that emerged in that constructive century par excellence, the nineteenth, between the professional groups heretofore constituted and which proclaimed for themselves disparate cultures – technology for the one, art for the other. But it all went contrary to reason in that the diverse functionalisms insisted there was no "truth" in the matter of architecture other than a constructive one, at a time when the use of new materials, particularly iron and concrete, went hand in hand with the development of methods of calculation, in the literal sense of the word. Beyond its obvious tautology, the formulation that architecture is architectured also abandoned the idea that architecture is constructed. The question that concerns us here – that of "architectural culture" in its ideological as well as institutional aspects – is essentially tied to the difference, indeed to the conceptual split, that exists between the verb architecturer and the verb construire, between art and technique.

In his writings on cinema, Roland Barthes was not afraid to assert that the dream of every critic was to be able to define an art by its technique.[6] This hope was paralleled by those linguists who laid claim to abstracting the condition of meaning so as to study language by its strictly technical, not to say constructive, aspects – in anticipation of recognizing an order that, in being presented as functional and therefore susceptible to entering into resonance with other morphological forms (mathematical, musical, etc.), can then take its place in the semantic order. So one could say a fortiori of architecture. Responding to this issue, I will allow myself to reproduce something I wrote more than twenty years ago as part of a research project, collectively undertaken, on the function of the sign in modern architecture; it was a period in France that was dominated by our readings of Manfredo Tafuri and the journal Oppositions. I refer to a text that for obscure reasons was never circulated but that, despite being somewhat dated, still has relevance today.

Architecture, then, is not simply a matter of supplement; a supplement of rigor (according to the dictionary), a supplement of meaning (with all the risks of failure we know these days), a supplement of beauty (architects are among the last

people in the world not to be afraid of the word) – beauty that it could flatter itself to have discovered in construction, as the functionalist aesthetic would have it. Schelling's definition of architecture as the "metaphor of construction" does not necessarily imply that the proper meaning of architecture, let alone its truth, is to be found in construction: note that Gothic architecture and its linear model of a constructive system possess in their details none of the rigor of the working drawing. But a whole aspect of architecture also derives from the category of the masque – and indeed the exterior envelope of Dubuffet's Tower acts as a masque, whose figures deny in dissimulation the constructive apparatus of modernity. A design, let us say in passing, that itself represents a challenge to the traditional norms of construction, be it the suppression of supporting walls replaced by suspended panels, the out-of-line floor planks, or the truly revolutionary constructive role subsequently assigned to pressed glass, etc. – in effect, all those things that are now part of the legacy, of the vulgate of architectural modernity. This, however, should not lead one to underestimate the work of deconstruction from which the vulgate derived. As Derrida insists, contrary to appearances, deconstruction is not an architectural metaphor:

It is a matter, then, of culture and of thought – if such things exist. The architecture we call modern did more than just instigate this project. It also precipitated a break with the principle of discontinuity, which construction had until then supported, by imposing new structural models in continuous veils – unthinkable until the invention of prestressed concrete – with the parallel demise of the distinction between the vertical and horizontal, upon which what Derrida called the ject of the project (le 'jet' du projet) had been grounded.[9] To say nothing of the montage of elements – girders and crossbeams, which Viollet-le-Duc's dictionary says nothing about, since they correspond to a level of structural articulation inferior to the formal and semantic units identified in the Raisonnè (column, base, capital, arc, vault, etc.) – the equivalents, in language, of what would be the level of articulation of phonemes in relation, semantically, to that of words.

Walter Benjamin did not fail to see in the precocious expression of architectural modernity that iron construction represented the first instance of the principle of montage – in a way that was neither metaphorical nor rhetorical, but strictly mechanical. "Never before in history," one reads in the notes of the Passagen-Werk, "did the scale of the 'very small' assume so much importance. Including the very smallest element, of minimal quantity. These scales imposed themselves in technical and architectural construction long before literature took notice and adapted them."[10] Montage as a modality of construction took quite another turn with iron: thus Marx, whom Benjamin quotes, writes, "One would require considerable practical experience and a more advanced science in order for form to arrive at the point where it is completely determined by mechanical principles, and as such completely emancipated from the traditional form of the tool, itself inspired by the human body." To which Benjamin adds, "In this sense, in architecture, for example, the load and the supports are also 'traditional forms inspired by the human body.'"[11]

But the principle of montage does not correspond simply to a new modality of construction as much as it does to one of form, emancipated in theory from every kind of anthropomorphism and every kind of organicism. As its corollary it appeals to the possibility of de-montage – not to be confused with deconstruction. Not that de-montage lacks theoretical, to say nothing of "deconstructive," instances, which suggests that a building is an object obeying a transitory principle, when in fact it demonstrates that it was built to last. For example, a clause was inserted into the land concession act related to the construction of the Crystal Palace that stipulated its demolition after the closing of the 1851 London Exposition (to the great consternation of the London public).[12] More extreme examples were those buildings that lacked foundations, quickly erected in their locations, as in the manner of the houses of Jean Prouvè, or even a structure dropped onto the ground by helicopter, as with the geodesic domes of Buckminster Fuller. The fact that architecture has come to the point of even repudiating the idea of a foundation is something that we should not accept without consequence, especially in what passes for "architectural culture." An architecture that will leave no trace of itself, not even ruins, spells a utopia that risks announcing itself to be as disastrous as its totalitarian antithesis. But in an architecture that, without ignoring the preeminence of living quarters, would, instead of looking for some foundation for them, rather expose them to every manner of variation and displacement, to every manner of transformation – an architecture of wandering, then, in its concept as in its realization – a thought, if not a culture, could there find a point of departure.[13]

1 Jean Dubuffet, **Prospectus et tous écrits suivants**, edited and presented by Hubert Damisch (Paris: Gallimard, 1995), 1: 636, note 176.

2 Ibid., 241.

3 Jean Dubuffet, "Edifices" (1968), in **Prospectus** 3: 342.

4 "The time has come for architects to respond to questions – notably the question of restoring to architecture its character of art, forgotten so long ago. Of art, and what that notion connotes of caprice and invention, the architecture of our time is dismaying – completely devoid of imagination, dependent on sordid considerations of economics and on the least effort, relying strictly on the rectilinear, on such a poor invention as the parallelepiped box." Letter to Marcel Cornu, 12 January 1969, in **Prospectus** 3: 497, note 51.

5 Jacques Derrida, "Point de Folie – Maintenant l'Architecture," in **Psyché: Inventions de l'autre**, (Paris: Galilée, 1987), 480.

6 Roland Barthes, "Sur le cinèma," interview with M. Delahaye and J. Rivette, **Cahiers du cinèma** 147 (September 1963). Reprinted in **Le grain de la voix, interviews** (Paris: Seuil, 1981), 22.

7 Hubert Damisch, "Le signe et la fonction," in **Modern'signe: Recherches sur le travail du signe dans l'architecture moderne**, a report on the research carried out by Le Cercle d'Histoire-Théorie de l'art de l'Ecole des Hautes Etudes en Sciences Sociales, in the account of the Département of Architecture (Paris: CORDA, 1977), 2: 13.

8 Derrida, op. cit., 517.

9 "[The question] of what it is that projects in front or in advance in the project (projection, program, prescription, promise, proposition) of everything that belongs, in the architectural process, to the movement of throwing, or of being thrown (jacere, jacio/jaceo). Horizontally or vertically: foundations for the erection of an edifice that always jumps toward the sky – there where, in an apparent sense of mimesis, there was nothing." Ibid., 514.

10 Walter Benjamin, **Das Passagen-Werk** (Frankfurt: Suhrkamp, 1982): French trans., **Paris, capitale du XIXe siècle, Le livre des pasages** (Paris, 1989), 182.

11 Ibid., 172.

12 Ibid., 183.

13 From **Tower with Figures**, Dubuffet continued to say that the work was not conceived "with a view to furnishing a lodging in the form actually in use in our homes," but as "an occasional home for retirement and reverie." **Prospectus** 3: 336.

Hubert Damisch is a historian of art and philosophy and the director of studies at L'École des Hautes Études en Sciences Sociales. His many books include Origin of Perspective.

Discussion 2

FRANCO PURINI I'd like to make a few comments concerning the problem of the history of architecture. In recent years we've moved from a written to a visual history. This move from writing to a visual dimension is a kind of condemnation of speech; a form of legitimation and delegitimation of writing. Ignasi de Solà-Morales referred earlier to a text by Manfredo Tafuri, who was one of the first historians silenced by this move of history toward a more visual dimension. But even history has seen another change, from in-depth history to surface history. It is not possible to analyze the phenomenon in terms of an in-depth structure. This situation, I think, is really important because it characterizes the production of history in our time. In Italy, for example, seven different histories of architecture of the century have been produced in recent years, and even a specific history of 20th-century Italian architecture. I think that this is a revolution proper; it is also very important for another reason – all the histories of architecture that I've read and that were written in this [20th] century, are the history of buildings or of building projects. The relationship between theory and history is very formal, very organic, but I think that the very idea of a project is an idea that no longer means anything. The histories of architecture that have been produced are the histories of a project, and since these ideas are dead it is impossible to write history. The most famous visual history is the book written by Kenneth Frampton, which is organized from a spatial point of view, like the inside of a supermarket. You walk in and you can look at different types of architecture – minimalist, contextual, and so on – and then actually look at what interests you and take it. But what we see today is the death of historical writing, which has its root in the Vasarian model – the history of architecture as the biography of architects. At the end of the 20th century, it would be interesting to be able to read a book on architecture where the dimension of personal histories, personal strategies and mythology, is not prioritized over the importance of the object itself. I think it is necessary to suppress once and for all the Vasarian model.

Criticism too no longer exists today, which is terrible. Nobody writes critical texts anymore. In light of Solà-Morales's reference, I would like to recall Tafurian Marxism as the last significant architectural criticism. Tafuri saw architecture through universal collapses, the idea that the history of architecture is the story of a fall: architecture in extinction at the end of the century. The only possible criticism or theory is a kind of a self-history, the architect as author writing his own history and his own criticism.

IGNASI DE SOLÀ-MORALES Both Tafuri and Colin Rowe had the feeling that history had in fact come to an end a long time ago, because when you look at things historically, there's always repetition. The processes in Brunelleschi are the same you see today in Peter Eisenman. There are always avant-garde movements and then there is a fall of avant-garde architecture into an expression of pure ideology. This is the way forward when it comes to interpretation. Colin Rowe looked at things in a geometric fashion – the analysis of formal structures – making it possible to state clearly that in the cities of Le Corbusier you can actually find the same schemes that you see in all cities today. In both cases, history is perceived as a series of endless repetitions. There are some people, perhaps, who get some kind of intellectual satisfaction from this sort of process. But I want to submit that history shouldn't be closed, or be an end in itself, or go full circle all of the time. I agree with you [Purini] when you say that the history of authors embodies a contribution that is worthy of interest. Patrick Berger's presentation was a personal history, and I better understand his project because I was able to understand his explanations. I would also like to discuss his idea of landscapes and why a horizontal plane seems to be better than a different type of formal approach – the decision, for example, that the trees be in a certain position with regard to the building. But I think that behind the decisions made within the scope of the project are reflected certain theoretical priorities that were not explained. We have the possibility, nonetheless, of explaining that within the framework of the history of landscapes – not only the places we saw on the edge of Lake Geneva, mentioned earlier – there is the idea that only the history of place explains the place, that the history of Spain, for example, can also provide us with some enlightenment. Reciprocally, the history of France also elucidates the situation in Spain. If you look at the conflicts between Le Corbusier and Mies van der Rohe, for example, we gain some understanding, as I see it, of contemporary architecture. It sheds some light.

RENATO RIZZI The theme of this panel is theory and history; perhaps I have misunderstood, but in one sense I heard a description of our age. I never heard an interpretation of our age. This age is based upon the notion of nihilism. Nihilism, I would argue, is the process of becoming, and on the basis of this nihilism we have technique. Technique for me has two meanings. Technique as what is available, the actual devices that we have to produce whatever we want, but technique also has the root *techne* – *techne* as art. It suggests that *techne* is also metaphysics – an indispensable condition if we want to rethink the meaning of the object. This is because theory is not the abstraction of rules but the supreme vision. In one sense I don't agree with Tafuri because he terrorized history. He said that history doesn't teach anything to architects. It was impossible in Venice to ask any historian what we can receive from history, because history was seen as a closed discipline. Croce said that history is the actual. Everything is actual because history is full of meaning. By way of this extended parenthesis I want to analyze briefly a paradox of the modern age. Mark Taylor spoke before about complexity and globalization – he proposed two oppositions – multiplicity and individuality. So yes, if we globalize it means that everything is connected, but when everything is connected, only a limited number of points have the power to control everything. In reality this means that unity and multiplicity play together in a very tough way. So why don't we think of theory today as the real unity of the multiplicity of meanings? I believe that if we were able to produce and think deeply again of theory as a *vision* and not theory as an *abstraction*, we could produce a greater plurality, because globalization is to reduce differences.

MARK TAYLOR I won't be able to address all the issues that you raise, but I want to try to focus on a few because they are important questions. First, the issue of nihilism. You correctly underscored its significance and relationship to *techne*, as you suggest, particularly as Heidegger works it out. But nihilism is a complicated phenomenon, and in some ways it has always seemed to me to be more multifarious than some readings of Heidegger suggest. It can be read in a certain way as the collapse of meaning in the absence of whatever, or it can also be read as an endless proliferation of meaning, which is not exactly the same thing, and its implications are different. Or it can be looked at in different cross-cultural contexts. If one looks at the phenomenon of nihilism from certain strands – Isozaki would be better here than I – from a Buddhist context, for example, and the whole notion of *mu*, it appears very different. So after saying that the age is characterized by nihilism, while I agree with you, we then have to try to articulate what it is that we mean by nihilism. There are different kinds of nihilism, as we know from Nietzsche himself, and it seems to me that there are both nonproductive and productive kinds of nihilism.

On the issue of globalization, the last point that you raise, and in many ways, the most crucial one – I would agree that the processes of globalization entail the kind of paradoxical coincidences of opposites that you suggest, but I would not want to associate globalization with unification, as you suggest. One of the things that I think needs to be thought through philosophically and critically is what's at stake with this notion of globalization that we use so readily, but I don't think has been thought through critically with sufficient

clarity. One of the presentations this morning was about the inextricable interrelationship between the global and the local, which is necessary, and which would be another way of looking at this. It's neither an opposition nor a synthesis, but that kind of coincidence, which gets at that logic of globalization, seems to me to be crucial.

BRUNO FORTIER Could you explain what you mean by this globalization that you're talking about, and how it ties into architecture? You see it in cooking, in medicine, and other areas, but how does it tie into architecture, and in what way is architecture concerned with globalization?

TAYLOR I probably can't do that very well because I'm not an architect. I don't mean that as an excuse, but part of the challenge of this session is to think through the conditions of theoretical reflection – where theory is at this particular moment and, correlatively, the problem of history – both history in relationship to the history of architecture and history in relationship to the peculiarities of the historical moment in which we find ourselves today. In trying to think through both of those issues, I was trying to suggest that the ways in which theoretical reflections have proved useful and productive for what seemed to me was the most interesting architecture in the past decade or two seem now to have been exhausted, which does not mean that they don't continue to contribute in certain ways. But then the question becomes, within current critical or theoretical reflections, what opens up other possibilities? One of the things that has informed a lot of the theoretical discussions in the States over the past few years has been a certain intersection among different fields, like literature, philosophy, and the arts. I would add to these disciplines those places where I sense that theoretical discussion will occur in the near future – Ignasi was suggesting this as well – like a relationship between the humanistic discourses and discourses opening up in certain of the so-called natural sciences. That's a different, but related, territory. Now, how all of that feeds back into the actual conditions of architectural practice I'm not in a position to say. That's up to Peter Eisenman.

PETER EISENMAN I'd like to provoke a discussion between Mark and Patrick because I think they presented two interesting viewpoints. I'd also like to suggest that two people present at this conference, Kazuyo Sejima and Rem Koolhaas, could also be on the Berger agenda, let's say, talking about complex adaptive systems, emergence, etc., because Sejima's and Rem's projects could be seen as a kind of less is less rather than more is more. Now is less-less a virtual less and therefore a more critical project because of its condition of double less-ness? In other words, does it have to be visually complex, i.e., Bilbao-like, to be complex? I wonder if Mark could take on Patrick's project in that context, or if Patrick would agree with Mark's theory, so that the two of them would come out on the same side of the fence? You could put Sejima and Koolhaas and Berger in the same basket with some others who practice a certain form of less is less. Is this complex theory in your terms, Mark, or would Patrick say that your theoretical strategy for today is overwrought?

TAYLOR The complexity that I'm trying to convey does not have to be literally, representationally complex. Complexity and simplicity are not opposites – this is an important point, and that's part of what's at stake with the notion of emergence. More or less simple rules can generate complex systems in ways that are aleatory; this is critical because it's part of what's at stake in the notion of system and structure – this is a quasi-metaphysical kind of reflection. Quasi in an effort to think of a structure that can act as whole, that is not an archaeo-teleological structure and can therefore act holistically, but instead allows for the possibility of chance. Now, what I don't want to promote is a notion of the simple as a monadic irreducibility; the simple is never an isolated momentary monad – there is nothing that is not always in some way networked in a more or less simple or adaptic system. This doesn't have to be literal, but in fact many of the most complex structures that inhabit us are at the same time simple.

PATRICK BERGER I feel there is some truth here. Hearing references to a number of the leading French intellectuals from many who are here, I am a bit taken aback. I remember what Gilles Deleuze said at A.F.E.M.I.S. [Paris' film school] on the meaning of cinema. It came across that every discipline, in studying cinema, has its own basic postulates. The first of these, which you heard earlier, was that construction is something that belongs, or is germane, to architecture. I don't see anything in history that could steer us away from this. Otherwise you could say that everything is in everything. The second thing I'd like to say is that Deleuze also once said that all of this work grows out of necessity and the spirit of the zeitgeist. As for theory, I think that what an architect wants, or needs, is that people think about the necessities, their priorities, and then consider how to go about obtaining these. Beyond that, what is usefulness? People asking us to build something that can serve a useful purpose?

SOLA MORALES Something is becoming clearer and taking shape in the history of architecture and in the materials of architecture. It's been commonplace to look beyond what is visible, because certain principles are concealed and must be revealed. Theories and histories of architecture have also argued this, but I think things must be turned around in a kind of metaphysical way. We would be better starting out with multiplicity in a given place. I mean, you don't necessarily have to look for the genius loci as some kind of god that's there because there is no god there. But many other things are there – an endless list of possibilities for understanding, many, many suggestions of different types of energy, and even beyond that the understanding of what we mean by an object, a square, a building, a place. Rather than something that's totally enclosed, we're talking about the convergence and the intersection of relations. The idea that we could have a theory of history is something totally different. As far as I'm concerned, the history by Kenneth Frampton is not a supermarket history. It's a history of architecture of the 20th-century that demonstrates this pluralism.

FREDERIC MIGAYROU I'd just like to go back to Peter Eisenman's basket of minimalists and people who use the concept of globalization. Is there not a metaphysics that is global, a type of identity that could shed light on the concept of complexity; or a metaphysics of space, also within the unity of form, that could provide us with diversity in appearance and expression? This goes back to something that I found very interesting when Franco Purini spoke, that is, the royal road, so to speak, of architecture and history. Panofsky, for example, wrote about sound and music giving rise to Gothic architecture. We find this relationship with space through all the histories of architecture. Take, for example, the early writings of Eisenman. His article on the Maison Dom-ino was very similar to Colin Rowe's "Mathematics of the Ideal Villa" essay. In Eisenman's essay there was an important attempt to break up this proto-space, and this enables us to understand why Eisenman was interested in Derrida and Deleuze. Architectural theory has developed from phenomenology, the theory of fields and space metaphors in French philosophy, and trying to break things up, breaking up this fundamental space. Whether it's successful I don't know, but with the nondialogue between architects and theoreticians it is impossible for the historians to leave the new occultism of the school of Panofsky – which characterizes all the thinking in schools of architecture with this idea of the fall, as Purini termed it. The notion of melancholia would be another example – you see this in Walter Benjamin and in the Marxist historian philosophers as well, and I think that we can look at the attempts of Eisenman in this way as an attempt to break up this initial space, this pristine, ancient space, that has slipped out of our hands. I'd like to ask historians about this closing-in of the history of architecture and the possibility, as Ignasi said, of the impossibility of being able to gain access to a methodology, a theory of history for looking at this complexity and diversity.

HUBERT DAMISCH I don't like the word *theory* or the word *history*. I didn't use them in my text. What I would be interested to hear would be a discussion about thought. Derrida looked at the history and philosophy of thought – how has thought been informed by architecture and vice versa, and how has thought been embodied in architecture? That's a question for Jacques Derrida; that's why we're interested in him. I mean, Derrida's not very interested in theory, nor am I, but we should be aware of what we mean by theory. Everybody's using the word *theory*, but what does it actually mean? I think it means trying to understand something, something that history has brought us. There is no history without theory and vice versa, so theory cannot work without history. It has to have some raw material, some grist to grind. What's great in history is that there are questions that emerge, questions to which history doesn't have the answer. But I think most histories of architecture that I've read, aside from Choisy on Viollet-le-Duc, talk about construction, histories that don't talk about that – nonthinking history. As Purini said, it's like going to the supermarket and you just go buy something – it's off the shelf. I love supermarkets. I like the work of Frampton, but it's not thought-provoking. When Frampton talks about tectonics, then it's more interesting.

But what could theory be? I truly don't know what it is. Well, it could provide us with concepts to try to better understand what is happening. Perhaps that's a role engaged in by theory. History doesn't give us concepts, or provide us with a rundown of concepts. It does not provide the concepts themselves. Usually when we historians talk about a concept, we talk about the history of a given concept. That's not what we need. Well, okay, we do need it. You could look at the history of the concept of construction, but what use or purpose is the history of a concept? Purini said earlier that we have to get rid of biographies. I'd say yes and no. Ignasi mentioned the battle between Corbu and Mies van der Rohe. Is that part of biography? But what does biography mean? Well, theory comes in and tells us that biography can be read as "construction" through the language of psychoanalysis. But what is this construction? This construction is the building together of theoretical ideas, the fitting together of concepts. What we are concerned with here is to see architecture in terms of thought, not theory or practice, but an actual thought, raw thought. This is what we can start looking at. What sort of thought do we see in the architectural work? Perhaps then we can make some strides forward.

PURINI I think that many architects would agree with me that the concept of construction is not enough for architecture. If you look at architecture simply as construction, there is always something missing, something more that architecture can reach for. But we can never pinpoint or define exactly what that missing part is.

DAMISCH An interesting coda to this relates to paper architecture – does paper architecture have to comply with different constraints? Does it have to be constructed? Does it have to be buildable, constructable? Imagine the sort of architecture that's never been built, never been constructed. Could we conceive of architecture without reference to construction?

AUDIENCE Paper architecture is still construction, but not functional – the triumph of constructivism over functionalism.

AUDIENCE The name missing here is that of Barthes – and the notion that our work is not to discover but to cover with a consistency the histories we have to tell. Now, concerning the notion of complexity, not as used by Venturi but rather when we say that our world has become more complex, we seem to be using the synonym *globalization*. I understand what globalization means at the level of the stock exchange, but I don't know what it means as far as architecture is concerned today. I think that we are faced with a structural difficulty here. We keep on working with notions of a universality dating back to the 18th century, to a time whose values have been lost. Secondly, there is a confusion over globalization and internationalism. The two terms are not substitutes for one another.

FORTIER Our problem is that a western is going to be shown in this auditorium in 15 minutes time, so since Patrick Berger was practically the only one to put his finger on questions of landscape in both concrete and transcendent terms, that is, not just architecture but space as a whole, I leave it to him to conclude.

BERGER Very simply, regarding this question of complexity, I'd like to say that architecture is some sort of a representation, and history is the history of concepts of representation, but it is also a construction and a programmatic shaping. It is its own complexity as far as representation is concerned. I don't know what categories there are here, but one can represent the world as either simple or complex. I would be in favor of the second type of representation.

3. Anymore Context?
The scale of cities today – their density, their breadth, their economies – and decades of unplanned growth have wreaked havoc with architecture's traditional notions of context, and the virtual community of the Internet suggests that regard for place is no longer necessary. What constitutes context in the image-saturated age of the sound bite? If the generic has become a new vernacular, how can architecture find its audience?

Arata Isozaki, study model, Shenzhen Cultural Center, 1998.

Arata Isozaki, model, Shenzhen Cultural Center, 1998.

An Extra-Context
Akira Asada
and Arata Isozaki

The problematic of "anymore" is suspended between the optimism of "much more (to come)" and the pessimism of "no more (to go)." However, today, as the tension between the two dissipates, a cynicism based upon the lethargic resignation of "no more" unilaterally prevails. Postmodernism sought to dissolve modernist norms: it aimed at deconstructing the monolithic theory of modernism from within, concurrently trying to recover the multilayered contexts that modernism had often ignored. But now even this postmodernism has faded away. What is dominant instead is the theory – or more correctly, the ideology – called "post-theory," which insists that theory, having been superseded by capitalism's de facto deconstruction of everything, is no longer effective. It observes that the specificity of contexts has been lost because of capitalism's global reshuffling. After delirious New York, more delirious Tokyo, and even more delirious Shenzhen – and other Asian cities amidst the bubble economy – it attracts attention as a specimen of such postcontextual chaos. Is not this tendency nothing more than a cynicism that ratifies the reality of that capitalism being globalized? Is not the ironical appreciation of Asian chaos – especially from the Euro-American stance – nothing more than postcolonial Orientalism?

Thus it is imperative for us to observe Asian cities from within. For instance, what has our postmodernist discovered in this very city of Shenzhen?

Could there be another alternative context? Now that the beliefs in the one and only universal context (modern architecture) and in everything being a context (the de-modernization of architecture) have both become obsolete, how might another new context appear?

With this question in mind, I present the following three cases. What they have in common is that they all appear as a consequence of choices and decisions that are determined neither a priori nor a posteriori; they are unpredictable and oscillating; they have the possibility of multifarious readings and are undecidable; however, what they engender, or what is engendered from them, becomes the context that grounds the architecture.

1. "One gold, one silver." Although it is invisible from the outset, a particular cultural cliché comes to function as the context of making the topos.

2. Shakkei (borrowing scenery). The external context intrudes, or the autonomy of the internal context is renounced.

3. The Archipelago. Heterogeneous subjects that appear in interstitial space automatically produce another, alternative context.

The city of Shenzhen, in the Pearl River Delta, is considered a tabula rasa city with no historical urban context. This almost deserted, barely inhabited village has grown, over the last twenty years, into a metropolis of four million, spurred by

China's "one country-two systems" policy. The design of the city's new cultural center, now under construction, had to be something different from the existing urban contexts of Beijing (traditional Chinese), Shanghai (modern Western classicist), and Hong Kong (contemporary internationalist). My proposal, selected in an international competition, takes the absence of context into consideration and creates a space that only responds to volume and movement.

In this new China, the process of determining a design is also new. When the basic design was submitted, many specialists were gathered from all over the country to review the proposal. And, in an unusual move, the results of their intensive discussions were reported to us – a new experience for me. The most important issue for the committee was how to technically realize the original competition design, which reflects the condition of a noncontextual topos. One particular problematic was raised. We had designed two buildings, a concert hall and a library, with symmetrical atria based upon a tree-trunk structure – what we called the "golden tree." The committee thought that the similarity of the two atria was confusing, and that there should be some distinguishing feature. I somehow thought of the gold and silver medals of the Olympics, and suggested that we use them to make the distinction. The committee immediately agreed, reasoning that this suited the old Chinese saying, "one gold, one silver." But another of my suggestions – to use copper for the tree-trunk support of another, minor part – was denied, because there was no saying that included gold, silver, and copper together.

In a place where no context was believed to exist there still lurked an invisible cultural context – as cliché. That is, an unexpected measure appeared. It seems to me that this idiosyncratic national custom concerning number, color, and order can be a motive for creating "another alternative" context.

In China today, there are three officially acknowledged ideologies: Marxist-Leninism, Mao's thought, and Deng's theory: Marxist-Leninism projects the communist society into the far future; for this to be done, Maoism continues the destruction of any established order by eternal revolution; and Deng Xiaopingism aims at the construction of a wealthy China by introducing a pragmatic market economy. There is no guarantee as to how they will coordinate in the future, except that the Chinese keep these poles because the number three is euphonious. By the opportunistic employment of the three poles, the infamous situation occurred: the government encouraged economic development, but when the demand for democratization intensified as a consequence, it was quick to crackdown – thus the massacre of Tiennamen Square. To state it clearly, we are critical today of the Chinese government, audacious in its violation of human

Above: Kenzo Tange, Tange House, Tokyo, 1953; below: Kiyonori Kikutake, Sky House, Tokyo, 1958

rights. On the other hand, will everything be fine if Western liberal capitalism with its Droit-de-l'Hommisme and market economy – as the only remaining universal norm – is forced upon the reality of China today? It does not seem so. Think of what is happening in postcommunist Russia. The idea of communism was immediately abandoned before being revised, and cynicism permeated the whole society, whereupon mature capitalism was suddenly and directly introduced without any consideration of the context of Russian society. Klepto-capitalism has diverted an extreme concentration of wealth into the vaults of the nouveau riches, while the rest of society has been impoverished and retroverted into a primitive system of barter exchange. It is from this apparent chaos that fundamentalism has begun to emerge, and this is less a rebirth than a new birth. The problem is not limited to Russia. From this standpoint, China's three-pole ideology structure seems interesting. What is primarily at work is certainly Deng Xiaopingism, while Marxist-Leninism and Maoism appear to be just pretexts or historical decor. Nonetheless, they are kept, with a strange persistence, as if poised for use according to different time spans. The relationship between them is neither like Kant's distinction between the constitutive use of Idea and the regulative use of Idea (in which the last is kept intact as purely ideatic and noninterventional), nor like the Hegelian-Marxist dialectic (nor, for that matter, like Adorno's negative dialectic, in which the synthesis is deferred to the indeterminate future). They are combined simply as the magic number three, like a euphony. Will they continue to result only in infamous opportunistic uses like those we criticize? Or is it a unique wisdom to sustain certain isms and thoughts for future use?

Shakkei (borrowing scenery) is a technique of Japanese garden design – the introduction of an external or distant landscape into an enclosed, artificially designed garden, like a stage backdrop. It might seem to be an economical, labor-saving way to make a spectacular garden, but in fact, it is an inversion of major and minor elements: the real subject of the whole garden is the back-drop of the landscape, while the artificial garden in front is just a device for capturing it. It is both a quotation from the external context and a device to dissolve the internal context into externality. This, I believe, is a method of looking for another alternative context.

For architects who began their careers by designing urban residences in big cities (like Tokyo), the model was Le Corbusier's Villa Savoye (1929). Both Kenzo Tange's own house (1954) and Kazuo Shinohara's house in Kugayama (1954) have a small garden in front with an open plan to capture the view. Kiyonori Kikutake's house (1957) also opens on to an external space; the main room is raised high above the ground and overlooks the whole city in the distance. At that time, though, Tokyo was not a spectacle of glittering lights, like,

for instance, the view of Los Angeles from the Hollywood Hills. Rather, the view looked out over a Tokyo filled with rows of temporary shacks built over bombed-out fields. Nevertheless, the gaze from the interior of these houses took in the external space, following the traditional form of Shakkei. As the metropolis grew denser, replacing natural landscapes and gardens and small houses, the gaze became one no longer looking out from the interior, but one counteracted with external and near gazes. Now the multidirected and intercrossing gazes form an unstable rapport.

Beginning in the 1960s, metropolitan residences began to be the objects of the gaze not only from the sides but also from above. The thought of being peered at and looked down upon shaped my first work. The N House (1964) gave up on the outward gaze and directed it totally inward. This was a 180-degree turn against the tradition of Japanese residential architecture. Both Tadao Ando's row house in Sumiyoshi (1976) and Toyo Ito's house in Nakano Honmachi (1976) also thwarted the outward gaze. Japanese urban residential space became totally enclosed within its frame, while the outward gaze was abandoned entirely. As a result, architecture in the city has to take either an offensive or defensive posture toward external urban space, mainly because high density has made borrowing scenery impossible by any means. Shakkei, which had defined the Japanese living custom as an alternative context, was no longer sustainable; living space became confined within the internal context of the self-enclosed box.

Today, the size of this container has been condensed to a microcosm and filled with the gadgets of modern life; the space has assimilated itself to the scale of the radio transistor; young people appear on city streets wearing these gadgets on their bodies. They walk around wearing the residential space itself, as it were. The outward and inward gazes that used to distinguish contexts are now constantly transposing, without any fixed standpoint. This state, in which innumerable gazes are randomly intercrossing, reminds us of the molecular movement of liquid. It is a total contextual meltdown.

If a prototype of Japanese architecture is the Ise Shrine, which is entirely rebuilt every twenty years, a prototype of a Japanese house might be found in Hojoki (Writings from a Three Square-Meter Hut), written by the hermit Kamono Chomei (1156–1216) in 1212. The essay expresses his sorrow about the impermanence of worldly things and advocates deliverance from it. It begins like this: "The flowing river never stops and yet the water never stays the same. Foam floats upon the pools, scattering, re-forming, never lingering long. So it is with man and all his dwelling places here on earth." The author eloquently describes the destruction of the capital and architecture by warring lords and natural disasters, and continues: "Then, well into my sixth decade, when the dew of life disappears, I built a little hut, a leaf from which the last drops might fall. I was a wayfarer raising a rude shelter, an old silkworm spinning one last cocoon. . . . As a house it is unique, three meters by three, the height no more than two. With no commitment to any one place, I laid no claim to land. I laid planks upon the ground and covered it simply. The joints are held with metal hasps. This is so I can quickly move if something should displease me. No trouble to build, for it would fill just two carts, the only cost the carter's fee." The author then begins to rhetorically depict the scenery of the four directions around Hino mountain, on the foot of which the hut is built, by referring to the famous sceneries in Buddhist scripture and Chinese literature. Here again, the context – the scenery – is fabricated rather than discovered. This might be another example of a borrowed scenery (Shakkei). After all, this 13th-century hermit built a hut – which is virtually mobile though less functional than Buckminster Fuller's – likening it to foam flowing down the river. Furthermore, in a sense, it might be a prototype for contemporary housing proposals: as puffs of foam flowing down the river of information.

Nevertheless, we cannot simply leave it with the pessimistic view of the impermanence of things in medieval Japan. Instead, let us turn our attention to another tradition – both hermitic and hermetic – the lineage of what Frances Yates called "Rosicrucian Enlightenment." One of its key terms was "Invisible College." In Theophilus Schweighardt's book, Speculum, from the early 17th century, there is an illustration, which, according to Yates, depicts the "Invisible College." The depiction is of an architecture that is made of stone, certainly larger than the three-square-meter hut, but rather small, and mobile, with wheels and wings. To Yates, this was a symbol of the intellectual network – that exists both everywhere and nowhere – imagined in the turmoil of religious conflict.

In what form can we conceptualize the "Invisible College" today? Can this be organized by a networking of an archipelago consisting of innumerable puffs of foam flowing down the river of information?[1]

I – 3

The metaphor of the archipelago – a collection of many islands – is poised to replace the model of the panopticon, the fixed-point surveillance system over homogeneous space. The center that radiates its gaze over all concerns disappears, and what appears is a mesh of points that are randomly placed. Certainly, the archipelago can be a model for the World Wide Web. The salient characteristic is that the difference (distance) in communication time, which used to stabilize the center, is maximally condensed. Linear time, which once supported the concept of design, is also absent. Conventional spatial (urban) and temporal (historical) models cannot be constituted in this network model. Rather, during the process of design, another alternative context

appears in the interstices between islands. New, unpredictable contexts are constantly built up during operations, neither a priori nor a posteriori.

Luigi Nono persistently employs the model of the archipelago in his 1984 opera, Prometeo. Each movement is called "Isola." Furthermore, the orchestra and chorus are dispersed, like the islands of an archipelago, and the sounds respond in harmony, whirling around the space and forming an acoustic vortex. The audience is placed in the interstices between the dispersed sources of sound. Because the sound itself streams within the space, no one hears the same "music." Rather, each audience member constructs their own music, according to their own position.

The concert hall of Akiyoshidai International Art Village (1998) was designed to host the premier of Prometeo. In contradistinction to a conventional hall with a center where orchestrated music is conducted by one conductor and equally distributed to each member of the audience, we designed a spatial mechanism in which the roles of performers and audience are interchangeable, where every point can be a stage for performance or an audience seat. This space was designed exclusively for the performance of Prometeo. Since then, the concert hall has been the site of various experimental performances and has been acknowledged as a model for a space for creating new music. What we discovered here is that another alternative context is autonomously generated in the interstices between islands, revealing the possibility that a network, that is, the Web itself, could be a context.

Gilles Deleuze presented his three types of power apparatus following and expanding upon Michel Foucault's analysis.

souveraineté – the rule of a transcendent sovereign from the outside.

discipline – the rule internalized within individual subjects by way of the internalization of the gaze through the panopticon.

contrôle – the direct surveillance and control by the omnipresent information network without mediation of the subject.

According to Deleuze, though all three categories coexist, the main tendency today is that of contrôle, which is becoming dominant as it replaces discipline.

If this is so, the task for today's architectural design or theory is to create a space that disturbs and escapes the omnipresent contrôle. Elsewhere we have mentioned Islands in the Net by Bruce Sterling. Now we might have to imagine an "archipelago in the net" as a model.

Another clue for us might be the concept of cryptic/cryptographic space. First, it suggests a crypt that escapes the omnipresent contrôle. (Here let us remember the importance Deleuze and Guattari give to the holely space [l'espace troué] – the dwelling of the first engineer, the smith – as categorically distinguished from both the striated space [l'espace strié] of sedentary people and the smooth space [l'espace

Above: Arata Isozaki, N House, 1964; below: Toyo Ito, U House, Tokyo, 1976.

Arata Isozaki, Akiyoshidai International Art Village.

lisse] of nomads.) And second, it indicates the disturbance of the information network by cryptography, the formation of minute enclaves by this disturbance, and then the networking of them. Here we run into a Derridean problematic. In the beginning, we mentioned the cynicism of "post-theory"; what is important, as opposed to this, is "postal theory" in the Derridean sense, whereby we may conceptualize an architecture not as a node of a transparent communication network but as a dead letter office (a storage place for undeliverable letters) – an allegory of a seemingly sterile yet nevertheless virtually creative discommunication. And here we can ask if Daniel Libeskind's great Jewish Museum in Berlin is a dead letter office and not only an ultimate incarnation of negative theology – the theology of void and silence. It is by contributing to the creation of cryptic/cryptographic space that architecture today can resist the movement of capitalism that seeks to level and arrange everything under the omnipresent contrôle.

Are these theoretical references assuming mere fantasy unrelated to architecture? We do not think so. These concepts continue to offer, though indirectly, important clues to architecture. If we stop learning from theoretical references, then there is no other choice for architects but to become skilled agents of capitalist production. We believe not in post-theoretic architecture, but in the possibilities of the postal exchange – including discommunication – between theory and architecture.

1 The English translation of **Hojoki** was borrowed from Yasuko Moriguchi and David Jenkins.

teaches at the Institute of Economic Research in Kyoto and is editor of the journal Critical Space.

is an architect in Tokyo. His realized projects include the Museum of Contemporary Art in Los Angeles, the Team Disney Building in Orlando, and the International Village of the Arts in Akiyoshidai.

François Roche

Between uncontrolled disorder and the excessive order of Euclid, there now exists a new region of fractal order, emerging out of the situation at hand and out of in situ analysis.
– Mandelbrot

In order to avoid taking a position and thus bypass a subject that, not without paradox, would open the debate opposing geographic particularity and American hegemony and end up in a major ideological conflict, I am going to confine myself naively to an exercise in decoding several videotapes, which I will present in the manner of the sequential images of a flipbook.

To begin, we have Charles and Ray Eames's celebrated journey, Powers of Ten, consisting of a continuous zoom from the intergalactic cosmos down to the cells of the human body, stopping at a picnic in a Chicago park along the way. The cartography breaks from the fragmentary visualizations in successive scales – from the orbit of astronauts to the descending outlook of an airplane pilot, an urban planner, an architect, a designer, a gardener, a dermatologist, and a molecular geneticist. In this representation of the world, locality is no longer synonymous with isolation; rather, locality is naturally connected to the global. Places and their surroundings can be reintroduced, such as they are, as elementary particles of a principle of reality in a continuum, a zoom that connects and ties together the ensemble of physical perceptions. The dualism that emerged out of the 18th century – on the one hand, nature, on the other, humanity – which allowed, among other things, for Western science to flourish, here loses its acuity.

But let us not kid ourselves – we are not talking about an instrumentality of representation alone but one partially of production, and one, more typically, of military domination (from Desert Storm to Kosovo) and the balance of power (see Wim Wenders' film Until the End of the World).

This geography in motion – which one could easily introduce today into the productive instrumentality of architecture – allows us in effect to seize and engage in real time, in the here and now, new hypotheses regarding the terrestrial crust, without reducing the complexity of the problem.

To illustrate this idea, one could cite a brief excerpt from Gilles Deleuze and Félix Guattari's A Thousand Plateaus: "[I]n the image of the rhizome, a map, not a tracing.

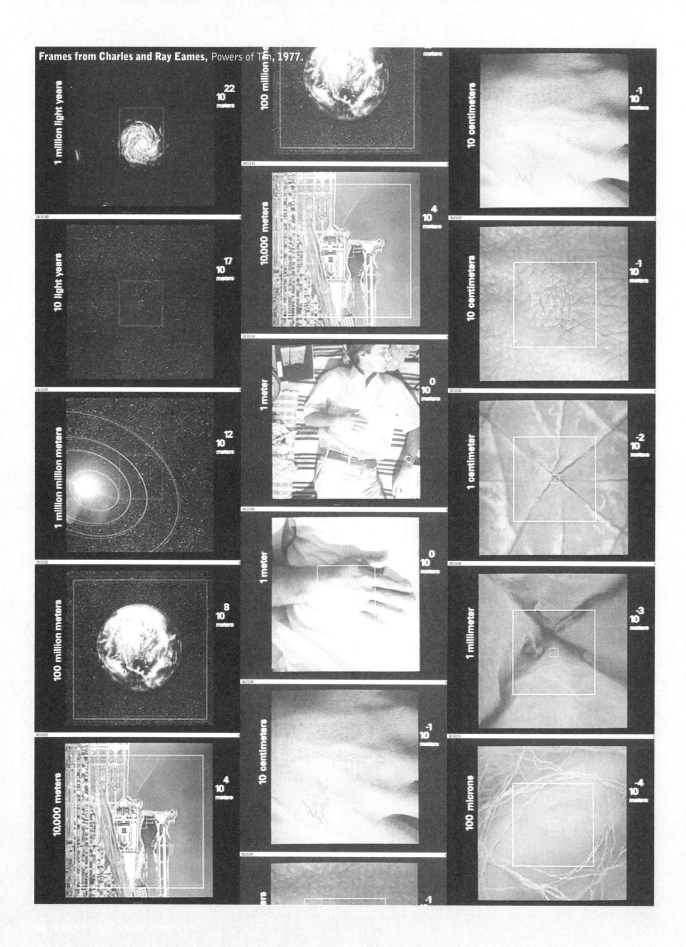

Frames from Charles and Ray Eames, Powers of Ten, 1977.

Make the map, not the tracing. . . . If the map fits the tracing, it will be because it is completely aligned with experimentation in touch with reality. The map does not reproduce an unconscious closed in on itself, the map constructs it." Decoding and space-measuring instruments – from the invention of tracing to the computer software used today – have favored the abstraction of the means of representation and projection. Architecture has thus modeled itself from the beginning on the blank page or the empty screen – decontextualized, deterritorialized – and the tracing has functioned as a substitute for reality, as an interpretative, projective system.

It is on these grounds that this tool, developing from geographic observation, radically confronts other techniques emerging from the reading of history – which in turn creates hierarchies, and in the process almost mummifies a conceptual quest for universality – as though it were the last avatar of fin de siècle romanticism.

By virtue of the implosion that has taken place in the political organization of territory, the Internet has accelerated the disintegration of these existing boundaries all the more rapidly – but it has done so by paradoxically favoring the exacerbation of a philosophy of localism. Through a phone jack, one can be in a farmhouse or on a tatami mat, yet still be part of the global village. No architecture is required to illustrate or symbolize access. The apparitions of Jacques Tati – those fantastic incarnations of technological modernity gone mad – no longer make sense.

The Eames's descent succeeds in fusing the perceptible reality of the world to its human conception. The context is no longer single-, but rather multiple-minded: rhizomatic and connected.

The second video sequence concerns a morphing among several stages of mutation, here tied to genetic errors in the DNA spiral. This miniscule provocation is designed to set off an inquiry into the very nature of the transformations that genetics never fail to produce in our bodies.

The ensemble of productive disciplines – medical, scientific, artistic, even sexual – today find themselves confronted with problems of transformation, of hybridization. All the while, architecture still continues to seek refuge in antediluvian, binary mechanisms of opposition – between patrimony and creation, mummification and destruction, rehabilitation and eradication. The conceptual and instrumental intellectual deficiencies that keep architecture from acting other than by these caricatural antimonies explain its incapacity to either apprehend or integrate the mutations in our society.

Paul White's video still of Björk (the Hunter) provides an example of an opposite condition. It develops through the animorphic transformation of a 3D animation on a

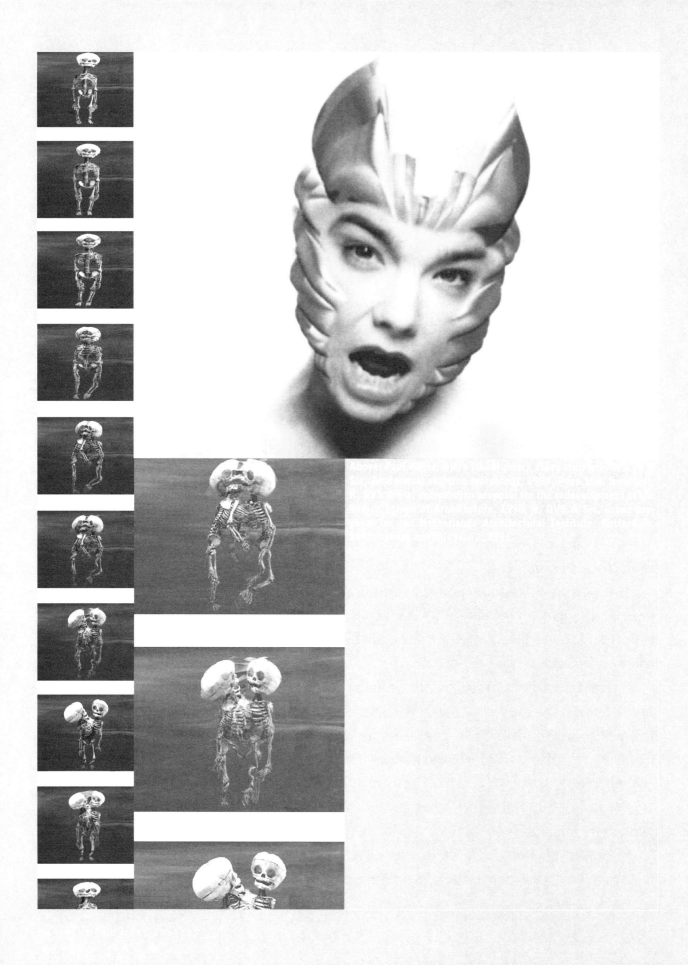

real face (reminiscent of those in the animated, humanoid film Tron), connecting and interweaving the virtual and the real, but also skin (digital and flesh), in a kind of ambiguous setting. This mutant – imperfect – dimension allows us to glimpse technology not as the fantasy of yet another "progressive" declaration but rather as a tool of contextualization, of hybridization.

But one can easily see in the virtual a rapidly disappointing, rapidly becoming metaphoric, fictional condition. Ghettoized within the intrinsic performances of the machine, it could appear to be – given its deterritorialization – the last avatar of deconstruction, in the service of the pixel. Are paths taken by the information revolution any longer of importance if the virtual is to abandon itself to the pure virtuosity of the object and its representation?

The deformation processes arising out of sequential morphing relate to these interrogations. Beyond the fascination with technological tools and the artificial metamorphosis it engenders, it is rather the operational function that should concern us.

The more the morphed transformation appears to "deceive," inert in its metamorphosis, the more the urban or architectural project appears to allow itself to be dominated by the preexisting situation. By contrast, the more the morphing allows itself to be read in all its artifice, the more the projection seems this time to be deterritorialized. Morphing thus reveals the degree of the decontextualization of hypotheses and – in a constant back and forth between deduction and induction as the successive stages are read and reread – operates to validate or weaken the pertinence of choices in a strategy of "making do with less."

It is no longer a matter of pitting the project and its context against each other, like two distinct hypotheses, but rather of connecting them by the very process of transformation. The project no longer emerges from an abstract projection; it emerges from a distortion of the real.

These two models of territorial intervention are radically different. One consists of the projection of reasoned, admissible Euclidean forms – arising directly from geometrical abstraction (deconstructed or not) – that apply themselves to the site like a conceptual mental grid. The other, of a totally different nature, acts to exacerbate a response in prolonging the complexity of the site itself. The first dominates the territory in order to demonstrate the preeminence of man in the situation. It is a pure projection of the spirit and, within the range of the consummation of concepts and images, prolongs modern ideals. The other draws back, humbled, in order to allow itself to be absorbed by the preexisting equilibrium. It is mutant, excerpted from the probable,

more difficult to obtain, and on the contrary, invites us to contemplate that "for want of better ideas, we had better observe."

The morphing video clips presented here are the expression of that position. Depending on what the projects are, the skin of the photographic or cartographic image molts and metamorphizes into the same envelope by aspiration and into the same matter by extrusion, and undergoes manipulations on the order of folding-in or puffing-up. The pixels – which are none other than fractal fragments of reality – rearrange themselves in a series of genetic mutations. The context is no longer idealized, conceptualized, or historicized, but rather becomes a substratum of its own transformation. Therein lies a political difference. The virtual instrument paradoxically becomes a principle of reality.

These mutations, visualized as so many subcutaneous piercings, function on several registers, several possible identifications. The loss of integrity seen on the sequenced tapes thus reveals the ambiguity of the probable identities, hesitating as it does between the processes of sickness and degeneracy, genetic transformation, substitution, and in vitro evolution.

The transformations of the body and of its sexuality – whether by silicone or collagen – into the antipodes of the Cyber-Robot of Metropolis are its preamble. The contemporary prosthesis is made from flesh; the functional excrescence is made from reconstituted artificial derma. The body is not denied, though it is exacerbated, hypertrophied.

François Roche practices with R, DVS & Sie. P/B:L Architects in Paris, whose work has been featured in many exhibitions, including Mutations @morphs in Orléans and Urbanismes at the École des Beaux-Arts in Nîmes.

Saskia Sassen

Each phase in the long history of the world economy raises specific questions about the particular conditions that make this economy possible. One of the key properties of the current phase is the ascendance of information technologies and the associated increase in the mobility and liquidity of capital. There have long been cross-border economic processes – flows of capital, labor, goods, raw materials, tourists – but to a large extent these took place within the inter-state system, where the key articulators were national states. The international economic system was ensconced largely in this inter-state system. This has changed rather dramatically over the last decade as a result of privatization, deregulation, the opening up of national economies to foreign firms, and the growing participation of national economic actors in global markets.

It is in this context that we see a rescaling of what are the strategic territories that articulate the new system. The partial unbundling, or at least weakening, of the national as a spatial unit due to privatization and deregulation and the associated strengthening of globalization have developed conditions for the ascendance of other spatial units or scales. Among these are the sub-national, notably cities and regions; cross-border regions encompassing two or more sub-national entities; and supra-national entities, i.e., global digitalized markets and free trade blocs. The dynamics and processes that get territorialized at these diverse scales can in principle be regional, national, or global.

I locate the emergence of global cities in this context and against this range of instantiations of strategic scales and spatial units. In the case of global cities, the dynamics and processes that get territorialized are global.

1. Elements in a New Conceptual Architecture

The globalization of economic activity entails a new type of organizational structure. To capture this theoretically and empirically requires, correspondingly, a new type of conceptual architecture.[1] Constructs such as the global city and the global-city region are, in my reading, important elements in this new conceptual architecture. The act of naming these elements is part of the conceptual work. There are other, closely linked terms which could conceivably have been used: **world cities**,[2] **supervilles**, **informational city**. Thus choosing how to name a configuration has its own substantive rationality.

When, in 1984, I first chose to use the term **global city**, I did so knowingly – it was an attempt to name a difference: the specificity of the global as it gets structured in the contemporary period. I did not choose the obvious alternative, **world city**, because it had precisely the opposite attribute: it referred to a type of city which we have seen over the centuries, and most probably also in much earlier periods in Asia than in the West. In this regard it could be said that most of today's major global cities are also world cities, but that there may well be some global cities today that are not world cities in the full, richest sense of the term. This is partly an empirical question for me; further, as the global economy expands and incorporates additional cities into the various networks, it is quite possible that the answer to that particular question will vary. Thus the fact that Miami developed global city functions beginning in the late 1980s does not make it a world city in that older sense of the term.

2. The Global City Model: Organizing Hypotheses

There are six hypotheses through which I organized the data and the theorization of the global city model. I will discuss each of these briefly as a way of producing a more precise representation.

First, the geographic dispersal of economic activities that marks globalization, along with the simultaneous integration of such geographically dispersed activities through telecommunications, is a key factor feeding the growth and importance of central corporate functions. The more dispersed a firm's operations across different countries, the more complex and strategic are its central functions – that is, the work of managing, coordinating, servicing, financing a firm's network of operations.

Second, these central functions become so complex that increasingly the headquarters of large global firms outsource them: they buy a share of their central functions from highly specialized service firms: accounting, legal, public relations, programming, telecommunications, and other such services. Thus, while even ten years ago the key site for the production of these central headquarters functions was the headquarters of a firm, today there is a second key site: the specialized service firms contracted by headquarters to produce some of these central functions or components of them. This is especially the case with firms involved in global markets and nonroutine operations. But increasingly the headquarters of all large firms are buying more of such inputs rather than producing them in-house.

Third, those specialized service firms engaged in the most complex and globalized markets are subject to agglomeration economies. The complexity of the services

they need to produce, the uncertainty of the markets they are involved with either directly or through the headquarters for which they are producing the services, and the growing importance of speed in all these transactions, is a mix of conditions that constitutes a new agglomeration dynamic. The confluence of firms, talents, and expertise from a broad range of specialized fields makes a certain type of urban environment function as an information center. Being in a city becomes synonymous with being in an extremely intense and dense information loop. This is a type of loop that as of now still cannot be replicated fully in electronic space, and has as one of its value-added features the fact of unforeseen and unplanned mixes of information, expertise, and talent, which can produce a higher order of information. This does not hold for routinized activities, which are not as subject to uncertainty and nonstandardized forms of complexity. Global cities are, in this regard, production sites for the leading information industries of our time and the strategic sites on key information loops.

A fourth hypothesis, derived from the preceding one, is that the more headquarters outsource their most complex, unstandardized functions, particularly those subject to uncertain and changing markets and to speed, the freer they are to opt for any location because the more the work actually done in the headquarters is not subject to agglomeration economies. This further underlines that the key sector specifying the distinctive production advantages of global cities is that of highly specialized networked services. In developing this hypothesis I was responding to a very common notion that the number of headquarters is what specifies a global city. Empirically it may still be the case in many countries that the leading business center is also the leading concentration of headquarters, but this may well be because there is an absence of alternative locational options. But in countries with a well-developed infrastructure outside the leading business center, there are likely to be multiple locational options for such headquarters.

Fifth, these specialized service firms need to provide a global service, which has meant a global network of affiliates or some other form of partnership, and as a result we have seen a strengthening of cross-border, city-to-city transactions and networks. At the limit, this may well be the beginning of the formation of transnational urban systems. The growth of global markets for finance and specialized services, the need for transnational servicing networks due to sharp increases in international investment, the reduced role of the government in the regulation of international economic activity, and the corresponding ascendance of other institutional arenas, notably global markets and corporate headquarters, all point to the existence of a series of transnational networks of cities. One implication of this, and a related hypothesis for research, is that the economic fortunes of these cities become increasingly disconnected from their broader hinterlands or even from their national economies. We can see here the formation, at least incipient, of transnational urban systems. To a large extent it seems to me that the major business centers in the world today draw their importance from these transnational networks. There is no such thing as a single global city: the global city is a function of a network. In this sense there is a sharp contrast with the erstwhile capitals of empires.

A sixth hypothesis is that the growing numbers of high-level professionals and high-profit-making specialized service firms have the effect of raising the degree of spatial and socio-economic inequality evident in these cities. The strategic role of these specialized services as inputs raises the value of top-level professionals and their numbers. Further, the fact that talent can matter enormously for the quality of these strategic outputs and, given the importance of speed, the fact that proven talent is an added value has brought high rewards to these firms and professionals. Types of activities and of workers lacking these attributes, such as manufacturing or industrial services, are likely to get caught in the opposite cycle.

A seventh hypothesis is that one result of the dynamics described in hypothesis six is the growing informalization of a range of economic activities which find their effective demand in these cities, yet have profit rates that do not allow them to compete for various resources with the high-profit-making firms at the top of the system. Informalizing part or all production and distribution activities, including services, is one way of surviving under these conditions.

In the first four hypotheses, my effort was to qualify what was emerging as a dominant discourse on globalization, technology, and cities that posited the end of cities as important economic units or scales. I saw a tendency in that account to take the existence of a global economic system as a given, a function of the power of transnational corporations and global communications. My counterargument was, and remains, that the capabilities for global operation, coordination,

and control contained in the new information technologies and in the power of transnational corporations, need to be produced. By focusing on the production of these capabilities we add a neglected dimension to the familiar issue of the power of large corporations and the capacity of the new technologies to neutralize distance and place. A focus on the production of these capabilities shifts the emphasis to the **practices** that constitute what we call economic globalization and global control.

A focus on practices draws the categories of place and work process into the analysis of economic globalization. These are two categories easily overlooked in accounts centered on the hypermobility of capital and the power of transnationals. Developing categories such as place and work process does not negate the centrality of hypermobility and power. Rather, it brings to the fore the fact that many of the resources necessary for global economic activities are not hypermobile and are, indeed, deeply embedded in place, notably places such as global cities, global-city regions, and export processing zones. It also brings to the fore the fact that it takes capital fixity to produce hypermobility.

This entails a whole infrastructure of activities, firms, and jobs that is necessary to run the advanced corporate economy. These industries are typically conceptualized in terms of the hypermobility of their outputs and the high levels of expertise of their professionals rather than in terms of the production or work process involved, and the requisite infrastructure of facilities and nonexpert jobs that are also part of these industries.[3] Emphasizing place, infrastructure and nonexpert jobs matters precisely because so much of the focus has been on the neutralization of geography and place made possible by the new technologies.

Dealing with place brings with it the problem of boundaries. These are at least of two sorts, the boundary of the territorial scale as such and the boundary of the spread of globalization in the organizational structure of industries, institutional orders, places, and so on. In the case of the global city I have opted for an analytic strategy that emphasizes core dynamics rather than the unit of the city as a container – the latter being one that requires territorial boundary specification. Emphasizing core dynamics and their spatialization (in both actual and digital space) does not completely solve the boundary problem, but it does allow for a fairly clear trade-off between emphasizing the core or center of these dynamics and their spread, both institutionally and spatially. In my work I have sought to deal with both sides of this trade-off: by emphasizing, on the one hand, the most advanced and globalized industries, such as finance, and, on the other, by looking at how low-budget and low-wage sectors, including the informal economy in major global cities, is articulated with some of the leading industries.

Finally, the detailed examination of three particular cities in my earlier work, **Cities in a World Economy**, brought to the fore the extent to which these cities collaborate through their very specific advantages rather than simply competing with each other. In focusing on global finance it became clear that the growth of the major centers was partly derived from the growing network of financial centers. In looking at the broader network it also became clear to what extent it was and remains characterized by a pronounced hierarchy among this growing number of centers that constitute it.

The growth of networked cross-border dynamics among global cities includes a broad range of domains — political, cultural, social, criminal. There are cross-border transactions among immigrant communities and communities of origin and a greater intensity in the use of these networks once they become established, including for economic activities that had been unlikely until now. We also see greater cross-border networks for cultural purposes, as in the growth of international markets for art and a transnational class of curators; and for nonformal political purposes, as in the growth of transnational networks of activists around environmental causes, human rights, and so on. These are largely city-to-city cross-border networks, or at least it appears at this time to be simpler to capture the existence and modalities of these networks at the city level. The same can also be said for the new cross-border criminal networks.

Recapturing the geography of places involved in globalization allows us to recapture people, workers, communities and, more specifically, the many different work cultures, besides the corporate culture, involved in the work of globalization. It also brings with it an enormous agenda for research, one that goes beyond the by now familiar focus on cross-border flows of goods, capital, and information.[4]

In the two final sections I develop two particular issues that illustrate some of these ideas concerning the dynamics between centrality and networks in a global economy, and city-to-city networks in realms other than the economic.

3. In the Digital Era: More Concentration than Dispersal?

Several of the organizing hypotheses in the global-city model concern the conditions for the continuity of centrality in advanced economic systems in the face of major new organizational forms and technologies that maximize the possibility for geographic dispersal. Historically centrality has largely been embedded in the central city. Have the new technologies and organizational forms altered the spatial correlates of centrality? Yes, they have.

There is no longer a simple, straightforward relation between centrality and such geographic entities as the downtown, or the central business district (CBD). In the past, and until quite recently, the center was synonymous with the downtown or the CBD. The spatial correlate of the center can assume several geographic forms. It can be the CBD, as it still largely is in New York City, or it can extend into a metropolitan area in the form of a grid of nodes of intense business activity, as in Frankfurt or Zurich. But perhaps the most starkly novel space of centrality is that constituted through the growing intensity of networks connecting cities across borders. This is a space that is partly deterritorialized and partly deeply embedded in vast concentrations of various types of materiality.

The world of global finance illustrates these various conditions well. This is the most globalized, digitalized, and dematerialized industry, with some of the most hypermobile firms and talents. It operates to a very large extent in digital space, yet also has produced the highest levels of spatial concentration in major cities and has, in all major financial centers, raised their level of functional specialization. Further, even as it becomes increasingly globalized and incorporates a growing number of financial centers worldwide, what really stands out in the evidence is the extent to which there is a sharp concentration of the shares of many financial markets in a few financial centers.[5] We are seeing both consolidation in fewer major centers across **and** within countries and a sharp growth in the numbers of centers that become part of the global network as countries deregulate their economies. São Paulo and Bombay, for example, joined the global financial network after Brazil and India deregulated, at least partly, their financial systems. This mode of incorporation into the global network is often at the cost of losing functions which they had when they were largely national centers. Now the leading, typically foreign, financial, accounting, and legal service firms enter their markets to handle the new cross-border operations that local firms are thought to be unable to do. The incorporation typically happens without a gain in the share of the global market that they can command, even though they add to the total volume in the global market and even though capitalization in their national market can rise sharply.

Why is it that at a time of rapid growth in the network of financial centers, in overall volumes, and in electronic networks we have such a high concentration of market shares in the leading centers? Both globalization and electronic trading are about expansion and dispersal beyond what had been the confined realm of national economies and floor trading, so to speak. Indeed, given globalization and electronic trading one might well ask why financial centers matter at all.

The continuing weight of major centers is, in a way, countersensical. The rapid development of electronic exchanges, the growing digitalization of much financial activity, the fact that finance has become one of the leading sectors in a growing number of countries, and that it is a sector that produces a dematerialized, hypermobile product, all suggest that location should not matter. In fact, geographic dispersal would seem to be a good option given the high cost of operating in major financial centers. Further, the last ten years have seen an increased geographic mobility of financial experts and financial services firms.

The next section briefly illustrates some of these patterns, in order to move on to an attempt at interpreting and explaining this apparent contradiction.

3.1 Expansion and Hierarchy

There is powerful evidence indicating the enormous levels of concentration in a limited number of top-ranked financial centers even as the overall volumes of the industry have grown sharply and the number of financial centers in the global network have increased rapidly. London, New York, Tokyo (notwithstanding a national economic recession), Frankfurt, and Paris regularly appear at the top **and** represent a large share of global transactions. They are increasingly seen as the five leading command centers in the global economy. Hong Kong is a close sixth, but it is not clear that it will retain that position much longer as it is slipping in many of the markets.

By early 1999, 25 cities accounted for 83 percent of the world's assets under institutional management. These 25 cities also account for roughly 48 percent of the total market capitalization of the world, which stood at 20.9 trillion dollars (U.S.) in early 1999. Yet, within this group, five or six cities command the largest share of the worldwide market. London, New York, and Tokyo account for over one-third of global institutional equity holdings, as of the end of 1998, after a 32 percent decline in Tokyo's value over 1996. London, then Tokyo, New York, Hong Kong, and Frankfurt represent the major share in all international banking. London, Frankfurt, and New York account for an enormous world share in the export of financial services. London, New York, and Tokyo account for 58 percent of the foreign exchange market, one of the few truly global markets; together with Singapore, Hong Kong, Zurich, Geneva, Frankfurt, and Paris, they account for 85 percent in this, the most global of markets.

This trend toward consolidation in a few centers is also evident within countries. In the U.S., for example, New York concentrates all the leading investment banks with only one other major international financial center in the rest of the country, Chicago. Sydney and Toronto have equally gained power in continental-sized countries and have taken over functions and market share from what were once the major commercial centers, respectively, Melbourne and Montreal. So have São Paulo and Bombay, which have gained share and functions from, respectively, Rio de Janeiro in Brazil and New Delhi and Calcutta in India. These are all enormous countries, and one might have thought that they could sustain multiple major financial centers.

But these same trends are also evident in smaller countries. In France, Paris today concentrates larger shares of most financial sectors than it did 10 years ago, and once important stock markets like Lyon have become "provincial," even though Lyon is today the hub of a thriving economic region. Milan privatized its exchange in September 1997 and electronically merged Italy's 10 regional markets. Frankfurt now concentrates a larger share of the financial market in Germany than it did in the early 1980s, as does Zurich, which once had Basel and Geneva as significant rivals. The stock market capitalization of Frankfurt is today five times as high as the total for the other six regional stock markets in Germany, when in 1990 it was merely twice as large – this in a country characterized by considerable multipolarity in its space economy. This story is the same for many countries. What stands out is that this pattern toward the consolidation of one leading financial center is a function of rapid growth in the sector, not of decay in the losing cities.

There has been geographic decentralization in types of financial activities aimed at securing business in the growing number of countries becoming integrated into the global economy. Many of the leading investment banks have operations in more countries than they had 20 years ago. The same can be said for the leading accounting and legal services and other specialized corporate services. And it can be said for some markets: for example, in the 1980s all basic wholesale foreign exchange operations were in London. Today these are also distributed among several other cities (even though their number is far smaller than the number of countries whose currency is being traded). But these trends do not undermine the patterns of ongoing concentration described above.

4. Why the Need for Financial Centers?

There are, in my view, at least three reasons that explain the trend toward consolidation in a limited number of centers rather than massive dispersal, even as the global network of centers expands.

4.1 The Importance of Social Connectivity and Central Functions

First, while the new telecommunications technologies do indeed facilitate geographic dispersal of economic activities without losing system integration, they have also had the effect of strengthening the importance of central coordination and control functions for firms and for markets.[6] Major centers have massive concentrations of state of the art resources that allow them to maximize the benefits of telecommunications and to govern the new conditions for operating globally. Even electronic markets such as NASDAQ and E∗TRADE rely on traders and banks that are located somewhere, typically in a major financial center.

One fact that has become increasingly evident is that to maximize the benefits of the new information technologies you need not only the infrastructure but a complex mix of other resources. Much of the added value that these technologies can produce for advanced service firms depends on the externalities – the material and human resources; state-of-the-art office buildings, top talent, and the social networking infrastructure that maximizes connectivity.

A second aspect that is emerging with greater clarity concerns the meaning of "information." There are two types of information relevant to these operations. One is the datum, which may be complex but comes in the form of standardized information easily available to these firms: e.g., the details of a privatization in a particular country. The second type of information is far more difficult to access because it is not standardized. It requires interpretation/evaluation/judgment. It entails negotiating a series of datums and a series of interpretations of a mix of datums in the hope of producing a higher order type of information. Access to the first kind of information is now global and immediate thanks to the digital revolution. But it is the second type of information that requires a complicated mixture of elements, not only technical but also social – what we could think of as the social infrastructure for global connectivity. It is this type of social infrastructure that gives major financial centers a strategic role.

In principle, the technical infrastructure for connectivity can be reproduced anywhere. Singapore, for example, has technical connectivity matching that of Hong Kong. But does it have Hong Kong's social connectivity? We could probably say the same for Frankfurt and London. When the more complex forms of information needed to execute major international deals cannot be gotten from existing data bases, no matter what one can pay, then one needs the social information loop and the associated de facto interpretations and inferences that come with bouncing off information among talented, informed people.[7] The process of making inferences/interpretations into "information" takes quite a mix of talents and resources.[8]

In brief, financial centers provide the expertise and the social connectivity that allow a firm or market to maximize the benefits of its technological connectivity.

4.2 Cross-border Networks

The global financial system has reached levels of complexity that require the existence of a cross-border network of financial centers to service the operations of global capital. But this network of financial centers will increasingly differ from earlier versions of the "international financial system." In a world of largely closed, national financial systems, each country duplicated most of the necessary functions for its economy; collaborations among different national financial markets were often no more than the execution of a given set of operations in each of the countries involved, as in clearing and settlement. With few exceptions, such as the offshore markets and some of the large banks, the international system consisted of a string of closed domestic systems. The global integration of markets pushes toward the elimination of various redundant systems and makes collaboration a far more complex matter, one which has the perhaps ironic effect of raising the importance of leading financial centers.

This has brought with it a new kind of "merger," connecting financial markets across borders. The two most important forms are the consolidation of electronic networks that link a very select number of markets and the formation of strategic alliances among financial markets. The Chicago Board of Trade was until recently loosely linked to Frankfurt's futures exchange, DTB, and the Chicago Mercantile Exchange, to the Paris MATIF. The New York Stock Exchange is considering linking up with exchanges in Canada and Latin America and has opened talks with the Paris Bourse. The National Association of Securities Dealers acquired the American Stock Exchange in June 1998. This has set off other combinations, notably the merger of the Chicago Board Options Exchange and the Pacific Exchange. NASDAQ's parent company is having similar talks with Frankfurt and London. Perhaps most spectacular is the link-up between the London Stock Exchange and Frankfurt's Deutsche Borse in the summer of 1998, with the goal of attracting the top 300 shares from all over Europe – a blue-chip European exchange. Paris reacted by proposing that some of the other major European exchanges should create an alternative alliance, a proposal which, as of March 2000, will be a reality.

These developments make clear a second important trend that in many ways defines the current global era. These various centers do not just compete with each other: there is collaboration and division of labor. In the international system of the postwar decades, each country's financial center, in principle, covered the universe of necessary functions to service its national companies and markets. The world of finance was, of course, much simpler than it is today. In the initial stages of deregulation in the 1980s, there was a strong tendency to see the relation among the major centers as one of straight competition among New York, London, and Tokyo, the heavyweights in the system. But in my research on these three centers I found clear evidence of a division of labor. What we are seeing now is yet a third pattern, where this cooperation or division of functions is somewhat institutionalized: strategic alliances not only between firms across borders but also between markets. There is competition, strategic collaboration, and hierarchy.

4.3 De-Nationalized Elites and Agendas

National attachments and identities are becoming weaker for these global players and their customers. Thus the major U.S. and European investment banks have set up specialized offices in London to handle various aspects of their global business. Even French banks have set up some of their global specialized operations in London, inconceivable even a few years ago and still not avowed in national rhetoric.

Deregulation and privatization have further weakened the need for **national** financial centers. The nationality question simply plays differently in these domains than it did even a decade ago. Global financial products are accessible in national markets and national investors can operate in global markets. It is interesting to see that investment banks used to split up their analyst teams by country to cover a national market; now they are more likely to do it by industrial sector.

In **Losing Control?**, I have described this process as the incipient de-nationalization of certain institutional arenas. I think such de-nationalization is a necessary condition for economic globalization as we know it today. The sophistication of this system lies in the fact that it only needs to involve strategic institutional areas – most national systems can be left basically unaltered. Japanese firms operating overseas adopted international accounting standards long before Japan's government considered requiring them. In this regard the wholesale side of globalization is quite different from the global consumer markets, in which success necessitates altering national tastes at a mass level.

Major international business centers produce what we could think of as a new subculture. The long-standing resistance in Europe to M&As, especially hostile takeovers, or to foreign ownership and control in East Asia, signals national business cultures that are somewhat incompatible with the new global economic ethos. I would argue that major cities contribute to de-nationalizing corporate elites. Whether this is good or bad is a separate issue; but it is, I believe, one of the conditions for setting in place the systems and subcultures necessary for a global economic system.

5. The Global City as a Nexus for New Politico-Cultural Alignments

The incorporation of cities into a new cross-border geography of centrality also signals the emergence of a parallel political geography. Major cities have emerged as a strategic site not only for global capital but also for the transnationalization of labor and the formation of translocal communities and identities. In this regard cities are a site for new types of political operations and for a whole range of new "cultural" and subjective operations. The centrality of place in a context of global processes makes possible a transnational economic and political opening for the formation of new claims and hence for the constitution of entitlements, notably rights to place. At its limit, this could open the way for new forms of "citizenship."

The emphasis on the transnational and hypermobile character of capital has contributed to a sense of powerlessness among local actors, a sense of the futility of resistance. But an analysis that emphasizes place suggests that the new global grid of strategic sites is a terrain for politics and engagement. The loss of power at the national level produces the possibility for new forms of power and politics at the subnational level. The political space of the city is concrete and allows for a variety of projects outside formal political systems. Further, insofar as the national as container of social process and power is cracked, it opens up possibilities for a geography of politics that links subnational spaces across borders. Cities are foremost in this new geography. One question this engenders is how and whether we are seeing the formation of a new type of transnational politics that localizes in these cities.

Immigration, for instance, is one major process through which a new transnational political economy and translocal household strategies are being constituted. It is one largely embedded in major cities insofar as most immigrants, certainly in the developed world, whether in the U.S., Japan, or Western Europe, are concentrated in major cities. It is arguably one of the constitutive processes of globalization today, though one not recognized or represented as such in mainstream accounts of the global economy.

This configuration contains unifying capacities across national boundaries and sharpening conflicts within cities. Global capital and the new immigrant workforce are two major instances of transnationalized actors that each have unifying properties internally and across borders, but they find themselves in contestation with each other inside cities. Researching and theorizing these issues will require approaches that diverge from the more traditional studies of political elites, local party politics, neighborhood associations, immigrant communities, and so on through which the political

landscape of cities and metropolitan regions has been conceptualized in urban studies.

One way of thinking about the political implications of this strategic transnational space anchored in global cities is in terms of the formation of new claims on that space. The city has indeed emerged as a site for new claims: by global capital, which uses the city as an "organizational commodity," but also by disadvantaged sectors of the urban population, frequently as internationalized a presence in large cities as capital. The "denationalizing" of urban space and the formation of new claims by transnational actors raise the question, Whose city is it?

This is a space that is both place-centered, in that it is embedded in particular and strategic locations, and transterritorial, because it connects sites that are not geographically proximate yet are intensely connected to each other. If we consider that large cities concentrate both the leading sectors of global capital and a growing share of disadvantaged populations – immigrants, many of the disadvantaged women, people of color generally, and, in the megacities of developing countries, masses of shanty dwellers – then we can see that cities have become a strategic terrain for a whole series of conflicts and contradictions. We can then think of cities also as one of the sites for the contradictions of the globalization of capital, even though the city cannot be reduced to this dynamic.[9]

*   *   *   *

Economic globalization and telecommunications have contributed to produce a spatiality for the urban that pivots on cross-border networks and territorial locations with massive concentrations of resources. This is not a completely new feature. Over the centuries cities have been at the crossroads of major, often worldwide, processes. What is different today is the intensity, complexity and global span of these networks, the extent to which significant portions of economies are now dematerialized and digitalized, and hence the extent to which they can travel at great speeds through some of these networks, and the numbers of cities that are part of cross-border networks operating at vast geographic scales.

The new urban spatiality thus produced is partial in a double sense: it accounts for only part of what happens in cities and what cities are about, and it inhabits only part of what we might think of as the space of the city, whether this is understood in terms as diverse as those of a city's administrative boundaries or in the sense of a city's public imaginary. Some forms of this new urban spatiality operate today at a whole variety of scales, not just that of the city narrowly defined in geographic-administrative terms.

Global cities around the world are the terrain where a multiplicity of globalization processes assume concrete, localized forms. These localized forms are, in good part, what globalization is about. Recovering place means recovering the multiplicity of presences in this landscape. The large city of today has emerged as a strategic site for a whole range of new types of operations – political, economic, "cultural," subjective. It is one of the nexi where the formation of new claims, by both the powerful and the disadvantaged, materializes and assumes concrete forms.

1. Here Giovanni Arrighi's analysis in **The Long Twentieth Century: Money, Power, and the Origins of Our Times** (London: Verso, 1994) is of interest, in that it posits the recurrence of certain organizational patterns in different phases of the capitalist world economy but at higher orders of complexity and expanded scope, and timed to follow or precede particular configurations of the world economy.

2. Originally attributed to Goethe, the term **world cities** was relaunched in the work of Peter Hall, **The World Cities** (New York: McGraw Hill, 1966), and more recently respecified by John Friedmann in "Where we stand: A decade of world city research," in Paul L. Knox and Peter J. Taylor, eds., **World Cities in a World-System** (Cambridge: Cambridge University Press, 1995), 21–47, and in Richard Stren, "The Studies of Cities: Popular Perceptions, Academic Disciplines, and Emerging Agendas," in Michael A. Cohen et al., eds., **Preparing for the Urban Future: Global Pressures and Local Forces** (Washington D.C.: Woodrow Wilson Center Press, 1996), 392–420.

3. This brings with it an emphasis on economic and spatial polarization because of the disproportionate concentration of very high and very low income jobs in the city compared with what would be the case at a larger scale, such as the region or the country. A focus on regions, in contrast, will lead to an emphasis on broad urbanization patterns, a more encompassing economic base, more middle sectors of both households and firms.

4. Further, by emphasizing the fact that global processes are at least partly embedded in national territories, such a focus introduces new variables in current conceptions about economic globalization and the shrinking regulatory role of the state. (See generally Kris Olds et al., eds., **Globalization and the Asian Pacific: Contested Territories**, (London: Routledge, 1999). That is to say, the space economy for major new transnational economic processes diverges in significant ways from the duality global/national presupposed in much analysis of the global economy. The duality national versus global suggests two mutually exclusive spaces – where one begins the other ends. One of the outcomes of a global city analysis is that it makes evident that the global materializes by necessity in specific places and institutional arrangements, a good number of which, if not most, are located in national territories.

5. See Saskia Sassen, **Cities in a World Economy**, updated edition (Thousand Oaks, California: Pine Forge/Sage Press, 2000), chapter 3, for a more detailed presentation of data and sources on the subject covered in this section. See also Janet L. Abu-Lughod, **New York, Los Angeles, Chicago: America's Global Cities** (Minnesota: University of Minnesota Press, 1999), and Liane Mozère, Michel Péraldi, and Henri Rey, eds., **Intelligence Des Banlieues** (La Tour d'Aigues: Editiones de l'Aube, 1999).

6. A growing number of financial markets have "owners" now and are run by something akin to firms, and hence also involve central management functions.

7. It is the importance of this input that has given a whole new importance to credit-rating agencies and consultants of all sorts. Part of the rating, or consultancy, has to do with interpreting and inferring. When this interpreting becomes "authoritative" it becomes "information" available to all.

8. Risk management, for example, which has become increasingly important with globalization due to the growing complexity and uncertainty that comes with operating in multiple countries and markets, requires enormous fine tuning of central operations. We now know that many, if not most, major trading losses over the last decade have involved human error or fraud. The quality of risk management will depend heavily on the top people in a firm rather than simply on technical conditions, such as electronic surveillance. Consolidating risk management operations in one site, usually a central one for the firm, is now seen generally as more effective. We have seen this in the case of several major banks: Chase and Morgan Stanley Dean Witter in the US, Deutsche Bank and Credit Suisse in Europe.

9 See John Eade, ed., **Living the Global City: Globalization as a local process** (London: Routledge, 1996).

Saskia Sassen is professor of sociology, The University of Chicago, and Centennial Visiting Professor, London School of Economics. Her most recent books are **Guests and Aliens** and **Globalization and its Discontents. The Global City** is coming out in a new updated edition in 2000.

Police Box, Chofu.

The Context of the Self
Kazuyo Sejima

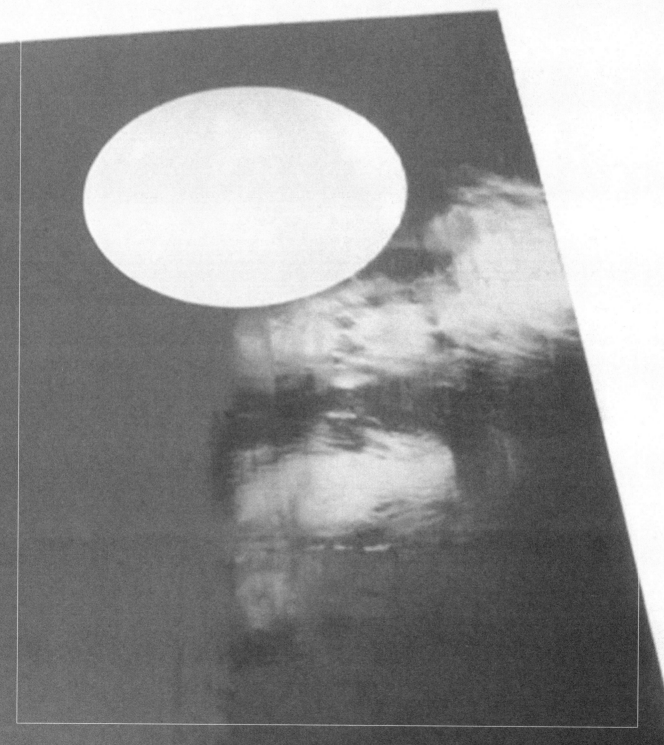

Saishunkan Seiyaku dormitory for women.

Multimedia workshop.

Gifu Kitagata Apartment.

Kazuyo Sejima is principal of SANAA Ltd./Kazuyo Sejima+Ryue Nishizawa Associates, Tokyo. Her projects include the Police Box in Chofu and the Saishunkan Seiyaku dormitory for women.

Rem Koolhaas

In a way, I am one of the least successful members of the Any conferences in the sense that I have been talking for the past three years about issues that don't seem to be interesting to anybody else. I have spoken about architecture in China without any noticeable effect, and I have spoken about the impact of shopping on current architecture, also without noticeable effect, even though it was a very suggestive theory. So I feel rather lonely, although this is to some extent the summary of my experience.

I will begin by introducing two things: first, a recent journey to Nigeria as part of the Harvard Project on the City and as part of an investigation of the urban condition in West Africa, and then its apparent opposite, though in many ways it is actually similar, the replacement of Schiphol Airport in Amsterdam. We must all remain conscious of context; I sometimes have the feeling that I am one of the few people who is interested in theorizing and assuming the consequences of globalization. In that sense, the combination of these two subjects – Nigeria being a country of abject poverty, pervasive corruption, and a complete absence of infrastructure – seems farfetched. Nevertheless, I believe it is a relevant issue. Take, for example, Lagos, the capital and most important city in Nigeria. Nobody knows how big it is. It might be 15 million people or 20 million people. At first sight it doesn't look like a city. I was expecting an internally chaotic, desperate, and even depressing condition. Second, it became very clear that partly through its incorporation in the system of globalization, even a city like Lagos is completely consumed with organization of a kind, and consumed with a generation of economic activity on a scale which perhaps at first sight is imperceptible to us but is nevertheless pervasive in its totality. I have never had the sense of an entire city being so involved in a single pursuit. It makes for a very modern condition, a very contemporary condition, and maybe in its looseness and in its absence of strictly architectural or urbanistic manifestations of the urban condition, it contains, perhaps, a prognosis of things that could exist here in the future.

For example, in one area of Nigeria, every stone in the river has a daily schedule. If you look at the immediate environment, you see this seemingly disorganized plan, but because each part of the immediate environment is rented out for specific hours to specific people, there is a plan underlying the entire territory. This very small segment of the river is disciplined and maintained with incredible rigor in a seemingly self-organizing, but in fact deeply organized and recorded, system of division. The same underlying pattern is visible, for instance, in what at first sight seems a typical African hill: the earth is red and the car wrecks are pervasive. But in fact it is not merely a junkyard. If you look carefully, you discover that it is actually part of a pattern in which the entire hillside functions according to simple and minimal means. For instance, pits are dug so that cars can drive there and be maintained, covers can be unfolded, and little huts turned into garages. The place is also a system, a so-called mechanical village. With unbelievable ingenuity, fake spare parts from Mexico and Taiwan are organized to maintain the largest fleet of Mercedes cars from the 1980s and 1990s anywhere in the world. This seamless organization seems, at first sight, villagelike or ancient, but is in fact a very smooth, contemporary form of organization, making Nigeria the country where, for instance, the motor block of a Mercedes can be married to the motor block of a Peugeot for additional power and effect. These villages have a kind of pervasive totality, and are not to be underestimated in terms of ingenuity and systematicness and connection to our own world. There are more Mercedes in Nigeria than in the whole of Germany.

Another thing that at first sight looks like a desperate situation or a junkyard is in fact inhabited by a crew or shift of people who are not scavenging but are organizing all the debris into its smallest component parts. They create, disassemble, and dismantle a superficially random heap into the most organized and systematic process of disassembling I have ever seen. Through tiny, minute economic interventions, this apparent mound of garbage is disassembled into parts that can then take their place in the Nigerian economy. Of course this is a miniature economy, but it is a system that works with incredible energy and creativity, so that there is a kind of planning in Nigeria where suddenly entire sections of the city, like in a Mondrian painting, seem to turn a single color: black, for instance, for old car engines, or systematically white for one color of plastic, or yellow for foam rubber. This may be the best analogy for a city like Lagos.

Lagos is perhaps very similar to the City Of Exacerbated Difference (COED) that I identified in the Pearl River Delta in China. It is perhaps the only sustainable model of the city – a city that consists of radically different parts that define themselves in relation to all the others, and that coexist through the interactions between all components. It is a city where organization is more overwhelming than in any other urban system I have seen before. In the center, for instance, one can observe the area of an apparent rubbish heap. In its lower-middle portion, one can make out the gridlike remnants of a

Sorting in Lagos, Nigeria.

Western urban condition and recognize triple-bypass bridges that go from the island to the mainland. Here, the organization is so extreme that at different points on the bridges it becomes too dangerous to pass at certain hours of the day. More than any other, this system requires an incredible amount of information from every inhabitant in order either to avoid a mishap or to be part of a mishap, and those two roles are both obviously played. The bridges enter the European city through a labyrinthine infrastructure; it is misleading to call it a cloverleaf because they are incredible receptacles where money arrives and, in the clutches of unbelievably chaotic conditions, where, in an almost mythological way, one is supposed to get lost in some system of catacombs where, again, the entire design of the system promotes small economic transactions in the name of progress and justice.

One can also perceive the moment at which infrastructure arrives in the city. There is an unbelievable crust, teeming with activity, mostly economic activity, that is ready to receive or deal with any arriving car. The intensity of life, the sorting, the auto repair, and also agriculture, cows, and other animals, is all part of this single, vast, and unbelievable organization. What is fascinating is how this organization, through some basis of communications, is also part of our own world. In Nigeria, financial transactions function as a fetish. Money, in spite of endless devaluations, is never printed in larger denominations, rendering every financial transaction grotesquely visible – enormous bags of money have to change hands. The money is very rarely crisp but rather is archaeological and almost too ephemerally imprinted. But here again, what remains fascinating is how similar the transactions are to the mechanisms by which we now dictate or describe architectural space. Very importantly, it is part of a specific context or a single space in which architecture can and must unfold. We discovered recently that the acronym YES is formed by the names of the three major currencies. This is a manifesto, and this virtual space is more pertinent than the space of the computer per se.

Now we go back to Europe, back to the Netherlands. A system of major arteries crosses Europe, and by apparent coincidence, most arteries converge in the Netherlands. A diagram of the most intense traffic flow – the flow of goods in Europe and the other goods between East and West – shows again that those enormous vectors converge in the Netherlands. The Netherlands carries the brunt of this enormous traffic, which has nothing to do with people but simply with the flow of goods and economies. There is a small paradox that nobody realizes in my country, namely, its relative density. We are not far from being the densest country in the world. But if you look at the density of the urban condition, you see a cluster of cities – Amsterdam, The Hague,

Rotterdam. The density is half that of even London, so there is an undeclared paradox and an undeclared latency in Dutch culture that we are the densest country, but we live in the least dense environment. This has been for a very long time a quality and a form of attraction that reaches through the enormous intensity and almost exaggerates an increase in all the flows, becoming an almost untenable model. Since we are so incredibly democratic and have such an occurrence of centrality, the area that we call Randstad is the most urbanized condition of the Netherlands, with Amsterdam to the north, Rotterdam in the south, and The Hague. This is an area where six million people live. There are something like three hundred different municipalities, and each considers itself important. Each village in Holland has declared its own periphery and its own center, and therefore a system which, in terms of the focus of the world, is an incredibly important point, yet has an administrative disarray and disorganization that makes it unable to handle or exploit that condition. One result is that basically every city has to expand, and there are many expansion projects planned before the year 2020. Essentially, a culture that has a self-image of urbanity is in fact indulging in an incredible process of suburbanization at a very rapid pace, and therefore exacerbating its absence of centrality and its absence of management. What we analyzed is the effect, or the strangeness, of this if you add one key, red element – Schiphol, Holland's principal airport. This strange form is actually the area that is hindered or impacted by the noise pollution, etc., of the airport. The densest country in the world has one of the busiest airports, and this busy airport is almost superimposed in a straight way on this system. Most of the country, then, lies in this affected zone. It is not surprising that there is a plan to shift the airport to an island in the sea, making us the first European country with an Asian strategy. This move will liberate in one stroke a huge area in the center, a huge area of new land in the densest country of the world, therefore allowing us for the first time to exploit and experiment with centrality, with real density, and a contemporary version of metropolitan conditions. It enables all these extensions to be located in a single place and liberates the country.

By some fluke we have become the architects, or the planners, involved in considering what could be done with two tabula rasa situations: one in Nigeria and one in the Netherlands. What I think is becoming increasingly important, and what I think is the main effect on architecture of the current economic globalization, is that the significance of the traditional meanings and vehicles of architecture are no longer relevant. There are other languages and other forms of mediation that are becoming crucial. Because the airport is a project with a large political charge and also a large economic

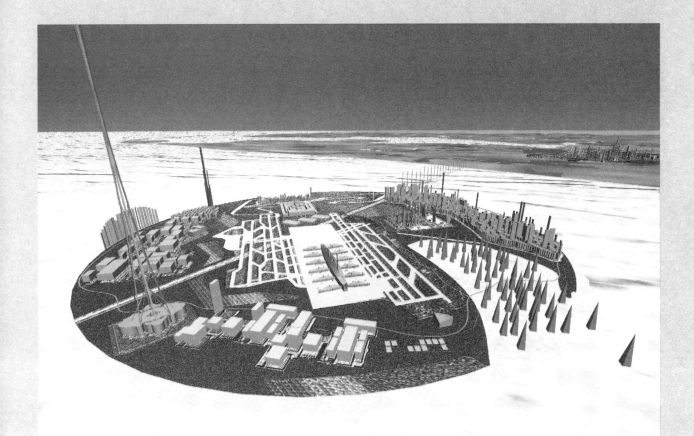

Above: airport island proposal, North Sea; below: currency study.

Logo for the Netherlands. © Office for Metropolitan Architecture.

dimension, we are forced, in a way – but we have also gleefully experimented – to come up with other ways of recording ideas. For instance, we have invented a new logo for the Netherlands. Our first gesture was to suggest that the new logo could be improved, so that the entire country could be a circle with a free zone, and the area of the airport could be the heart of that circle. We then copyrighted that logo, so the Netherlands is the only country that has been copyrighted in terms of its future. We will build a real urban condition there, but we are also thinking and looking at how – and this is where the money is equally important, or as emphatic, as in Nigeria – we will work on the island. We can work on the island because the Dutch economy has started to behave suddenly in a very eccentric way. It doesn't follow the German economy anymore; it now follows the American economy. As the first country in Europe to do this, we have become a tiger economy according almost to an Asian model.

The whole of Western Europe is dominated by four airports, each saturated and each suffering acute political problems in terms of expansion – DeGaulle, Frankfurt, Heathrow, and Schiphol. On this island there could be a receptacle in Western Europe for the busiest port of the world, of unlimited capacity and unlimited access because it is an island. This could then give the Netherlands a disproportionate presence in this part of the world. It has been incredibly sobering for us is to realize how the development of this language has given us access to debates and architectural discourses that were previously totally inaccessible to us.

Rem Koolhaas is the principal officer of the Office for Metropolitan Architecture (OMA) and teaches at Harvard's Graduate School of Design. He is the author of Delirious New York and, with Bruce Mau, S,M,L,XL.

As Saskia Sassen said, is context a term or is it a fiction? I don't know, but I wonder if anybody here wants to try to ask a question that will pull it together.

The postmodern condition was characterized by the end of master narratives, yet it seems that globalization is becoming a new master narrative. To what extent can we take terms like *global*, *local*, and *globalization* as attempts to normalize a gaze from the Occident toward the Orient? Or are these terms themselves too embedded in ideas of the 1960s and '70s, and therefore not important in our era?

I would say there is an ongoing reconfiguration of the master narrative, but it's happening through the structuring of very specialized orders that cross borders. There is definitely a master narrative involved in the economics of globalization today, but it concerns only part of what we've always considered economics. It's transnational; it crosses borders, so it destabilizes existing meanings. Though the notion of a master narrative is prevalent, its representation is partial, highly specialized, and it involves a different geography, one that disembeds itself from the national, so there's a novelty to it. There is something to explore, to detect, to decode, etc. At the same time, there are multiples, new "master narratives" that are configured differently. They're not contained; the containers have changed.

There is another sort of master narrative about the other, the hybrid, the subaltern. Is the multiplicity of these cross-border specialized master narratives a master narrative in itself? Or does that set a landscape where these multiples can actually engage and destabilize the whole notion of a master narrative? I have the impression right now that this is where we stand — with the possibility of destabilization. When I was talking about this frontier zone, I described a new politics of the right to place that is being engendered, and which comes out of multiple presences in one site. So from where I look at things, and I do think that the question of position is crucial, I see that we can now deal with a multiplicity of narratives, thereby destabilizing the modernist version of the master narrative. Language is our cage; not English, but the language of a master narrative. What I am intrigued by, and why I like Any conferences, is the possibility of experimenting in other domains. What does that mean architecturally? It has to be a problematic that lies beyond the hyperspace of international business — beyond those very familiar tropes.

Given that there are emerging master narratives for globalization, and that they serve to normalize Western culture's view, or gaze, toward the Orient, are these concepts outdated or are they still useful?

This is a very hot subject in certain milieus. In terms of economic globalization this is a big issue. Is it Americanization? That's the language being deployed. To answer this, I would say no. I think calling it Americanization doesn't get us much farther. There is an operation of power that is enacted through an American project. It's not just the state; it's the international standards for legal and financial reporting. I want to dehistoricize the process — we shouldn't be stuck with this term *Americanization* simply because of the contemporary power of the United States. American hegemony, in itself, is a blinding presence. Globalization is predicated on the partial denationalizing of elites — corporate elites, government elites, etc. The global project inhabits certain structures of national states, including the French state. These are partial inhabitings; they are strategic presences. They are not predicated on majorities. Consequently, the question of the master narrative has to be reconfigured. The ultimate question is whether or not we are dealing with a master narrative in terms of these very strategic instantiations. This is a far more sophisticated mode of empire than the British, the French, etc. It doesn't need the majorities. It doesn't need to change your hearts and minds — only the consumer market firms, etc. I do think that Americanization and similar types of gazes obscure certain things. In China, for instance, the local financial firms operate in a global strategic zone that is increasingly institutionalized via adopted international standards. Yet when they go back home they can still operate with a national economic system that has its own national accounting and legal systems. These Chinese operations have already reconfigured themselves to work partially in international standards and partially in local standards. Calling that Americanization misses something. It's possible that using the language of Americanization becomes the enactment of a Western gaze. But there is something else happening, and it's coming from the inside. For instance, China's globalization is coming to fruition through some of its very specialized elites — media elites, cultural elites, government elites, and economic elites. The process is better thought of as denationalization, not Americanization.

Yes, globalization might be a new master narrative, but it's not the dominant one. Posthistory itself is a master narrative today. They say that history is over and we are well into a posthistorical inertia. But that very story is nothing more than a master narrative in itself, and it is dominant today.

The pessimistic version of this inertia is a pessimism of "no more," and an optimistic version of this story is a certain enthusiasm about multiplicity, complexity, etc.: there is still more to come and greater complexities to come. I think it is important for us to somehow grow out of this closure, this new dominant master narrative, to find a new complex combination of what is global and what is seemingly local, just as Saskia explained.

In this context I would like to ask a few questions to my Japanese colleagues. Arata Isozaki explained the context of so-called Japanese minimalism quite explicitly. People say that Tadao Ando's minimalism is wonderful. And yes, it is wonderful, but precisely because it is against the background of urban chaos. Outside, there is a chaos where more is more, but inside the impeccable minimalist space, less is regarded as more. I would like to know what the younger architects, like Kazuyo Sejima, feel in this context. She's so versatile in playing with complex urban situations. And I have one question to ask Isozaki. In Japan, in our information society, you are confronted with the impossibility of deciding the profile and contour of the building. But in China you seem to make use of archaic mythology, symbolism, and even numerology. Do you really believe in Chinese mythology or do you just pretend?

ARATA ISOZAKI The question is, how, as architects, do we take in the real cultural context dominating a given area? For example, Tokyo appears as a chaos, and the architect has difficulties making a proposal or precipitating change in the city, or making something stimulating within the existing infrastructures. A few years ago I criticized a very large-scale project in the city. I think that each project in Tokyo is maybe three times, five times bigger than the *grands projets* in Paris. In Tokyo there are a huge convention hall, a kind of city hall, and an opera house. I called these projects simply "big piles of trash." There doesn't seem to be any meaning to the architectural fabric around Tokyo Station, only a kind of junk that people worry about using and maintaining. After I voiced this criticism, I subsequently suffered problems with people in the government not giving me any more projects. But I stand by my criticism. Architects have no idea how to create big gestures. So, given this situation, the only possible way to work within the context of Tokyo is to go inside, to work on the interior. This is one kind of context – understanding the surrounding context of a specific city like Tokyo. Now, when I'm working in China, I use a lot of traditional Chinese cultural symbolism, but these appear not from the outset but by chance, along the way. In China, the simpler the architectural object the better, so I proposed simple numbers with colors and simple forms. The interesting thing about the Chinese context is that there is no single client. Every decision-making process is very bureaucratic, very complicated. The easiest way to reach accord with the many people involved was to propose simple, culturally symbolic works. So in this way, I have been very much influenced by the processes of making and working in China through the local traditions or local cultural contexts. Wherever I work, I like to start without any preconceptions, without any preconceived ideas, and to learn from and embrace local cultural contexts.

KAZUYO SEJIMA I think that young people, especially in Tokyo, don't have any expectations about architects, only of more general activities or events. They only see architecture as a slick smooth box. I think the Pompidou here showed some flexibility twenty or thirty years ago, but now the urban condition is very different, so architects must think about this flexibility. The context has completely changed. Physical context is still very important, but everyday we receive information via mobile phones or e-mail, so the context surrounding us now is really a virtual one.

PETER EISENMAN I am quite struck by the different analyses of context. One was presented by our Eastern colleagues, who seem to think that Tokyo is chaos and that the reaction to chaos is to turn inward and become minimal. Then I look at Rem Koolhaas's presentation of Lagos, and he sees in what we would normally describe as contextual chaos a fantastic series of orders, and I think that's incredible. This is what one is always looking for – order within chaos. Then Rem gives the coup de grace to his own position when he comes to the Netherlands. Probably he's too close to the Netherlands, because he sees a chaotic situation and then does what they did in Tokyo – he takes away the condition that promotes the chaos and puts it into a minimal abstraction on an island, and then reorganizes the chaos into a gridded box of stuff – again a minimalism. I'm curious if Rem sees any difference in his analysis, which is incredible, and his solution, which seems very much like Ando, Ito, Sejima, etc. Could he comment on that?

REM KOOLHAAS Yeah, I'd love to.

EISENMAN I've hit you a tennis ball that you can really swing at.

KOOLHAAS I think that you must have misunderstood me because I've always been completely allergic to the word *solution*, and I've never recognized any single one of my operations as in any way addressing a program. I was showing a kind of manipulation and a rhetorical device that has enabled us to enter a particular discourse outside architecture. You should not persist in reading it as an architectural emblem. It is a kind of formalist logo . . .

Logo?

A logo, right. It has a kind of formalist power in domains beyond architecture and therefore creates a particular space, or maybe an economic architecture, in which we can do certain completely different things. So it has nothing to do with how we organize in the Netherlands but is somehow a singular emblem worth a million words and worth a million hours of discussion, because it somehow crystallized something that became completely self-evident. So it's just a device.

Rem, I wondered if you could speak in a more expert way about the types of logos, or diagrams, you are referring to. If we just say that this is a logo and it's detached from architectural or urban techniques, in some circles that's a kind of heroism of the logo, and in others it's a vindication, it's an attack on it. So instead of taking a side that's good or bad, could you talk a little bit about different urban diagrams? The colonial Netherlands might have used a grid both as a logo and as an organizational technique – the same way graphic designers would have used a grid fifty years ago. Now graphic designers are using a lot of logos, like you are – asymmetrical elements or primitives like circles placed out of balance. There's a very precise character to your logo that's different from other colonial logos, so I wonder if that's important or whether it's just something you throw away.

It is a pity is that my presentation was slightly aborted because it was actually continuing with this whole domain of logos and graphic design and design with words, because I think that this project – and I think it is unique to this project – really severed almost all connections with urban form, or with the diagram as we use it professionally, to enter a completely other virtual domain where clusters of words, or clusters of concepts, could be represented in ways that were completely abstract and that resonated with language and political discourse more than with anything even remotely related to form. I think in that sense it was a kind of radical break.

Will there be some kind of formal byproduct the way there was with the grid? Because I'm sure the grid started that way, and the grid you showed doesn't organize any better than the serif spirals, but still there's a byproduct. Are you interested in that byproduct?

You mean will there be as a result a byproduct?

In terms of a physical organization.

Or will there be physical evidence?

Yes.

I don't think on the mainland, but I think that because the mainland is the mainland and it's already too completely taken care of and too dense, in fact, to even remotely begin to make that kind of operation. But what is interesting, of course, is that this project represents two absolutely opposite conditions that have to be approached partly in the same way. One is already a highly charged historical context, and the other is an absolute, overt tabula rasa that almost never occurs. And I think that has been fascinating for us. The tabula rasa is, of course, the one area where you could make a logo literal.

I had the chance a few months ago to attend a conference on globalization. After that meeting, in Vancouver, and the meeting now, where we are discussing the global, I have the feeling that we are speaking about abstractions. Global is abstract; local is factual. Local involves people; the global is some kind of computer project. It can break down at any moment. I think it would be all right to give at least an equal role to the local, and local communication systems, word-of-mouth systems that we in French call *téléphone arabe*, which is far more efficient than all the computer systems. It never breaks down.

I would add one other thing. It was very clear at this Vancouver meeting that there is absolutely no economist who has any idea as to what's going on in the economy, because they don't allow for the unpredictability of individual acts. The existing economic system of power deals only with abstractions. I am not against abstraction, but it has to be balanced with the nonabstract, the factual part.

Let me quickly say that part of the global is inhabiting very specific localized communities of individuals. I don't think the global versus the local can be fruitfully subsumed today under this duality, abstract/nonabstract. I think that part of the issue that is coming out of the discussions yesterday and today is that some of the local is inhabiting a digital space, which you might think of as abstract, but some place or locality within the digital is not abstract either. A lot of what's going on is still about inhabiting old forms – I don't mean old versus new but longstanding forms, where some of these dualities capture more than they do with some of these particular issues that we're addressing. The materiality of Nigerian money, for example, or lots of paper, is a false materiality, because what is operational in that materiality, what seems so terribly local and anachronistic, is that it comes to life insofar as it enters a cross-border circuit that is a financial operation. It may serve local transactions in the Nigerian economy, but it also wants to jump circuits, so its materiality is very ambivalent. In the local situation it's one thing. Once it enters a financial circuit and becomes part of a cross-border operation, it suddenly assumes a different meaning. So one way of responding to what you are saying is that the global and local today cannot fruitfully be subsumed under the vocabularies that we have used to understand them. A lot of what I think of as excavating needs to be done to understand what we mean by the local and what we mean by the global. Throw in the digital, throw in dematerialization, and you get a totally different landscape. I have long tried to argue that the only way that this global financial system that we have today — which is global, digitized, and dematerialized in its outputs and in a lot of its operations — can exist is because we have a strong subculture within a financial, cross-border subculture. The way individuals communicate with each other goes way beyond the actual operations necessary for that financial transaction to happen. It's embedded in certain trust systems, in certain conceptions of what can sell as an instrument. All I'm trying to say is that there is a lot of ambiguity to these global/local dualities.

All of us know that there is an incredible link between the economy and architecture, so in one sense we could say that architects are the slaves of the economy. For me, this is a secondary issue. The primary issue is that the economy has its own goals, which are not the same goals as for architecture or thinking in architecture. In its fullest dimension, the economy and architecture have to be split. Only in a secondary field do we know that architecture depends on the economy. So I would like to argue that architecture should overcome both the notion of the global and also the notion of the local, because otherwise we will always exist under the shadow of economics.

If there is a specificity as to what the architectural might represent as opposed to building, the built environment, construction, infrastructure — all the necessary instrumentalities — it is that even when at its most instrumental (i.e., you are building a building within which financial transactions are going to happen, within which people are going to live), something else still has to be happening. I think of this in my field in terms of theory. Theory cannot just stick with describing and explaining what's happening on some operational level. Something else has got to be happening, a signaling of something else. In the context of the material that we might think architecture is embedded in, something else has to happen besides the instrumental, and perhaps that is what you are alluding to. Now, speculating on what that something else might be, is, I think, dangerous. What I object to is the representation that something else is added to the instrumentality that is being enacted through this architectural event. When it serves to misrepresent the instrumentality, I get uncomfortable, because then you enter a realm of communication that challenges legibility, but a legibility that doesn't have to use the language of the instrumental. Of course there are follies, and there are things that are meant not to be instrumental, but a lot of architecture has an instrumentality attached to it. The question is, how do you go beyond that instrumentality? What else can the architect do besides build the building that does whatever it does?

I want to go back to the point of departure of all this — the idea that context may still have some usefulness. What seems to emerge here is not an alternative category but rather some sort of convention, the notion of a condition in architecture or of a word that is made instrumental by architecture, even if it is not defined within this framework. And what I got from the territorial observations in Rem's and Saskia's presentations is that a global/local opposition is not relevant. We can see this in current political events, and in the European strategies which led Paul Virilio to say that while the bombs are falling on Serbia it is not a good idea to speak of architecture — which is why he isn't here this morning. This would seem to indicate that this national question exists not only in terms of reality but also in very concrete geopolitical/practical terms. So it would not be prudent, since we are here to simulate an evaluation of the ending century, to forget about nationality while it is thrown in our face in a very violent way. What I saw in a number of the presentations this morning was a duty to observe, practically a moral duty to open up to the world, especially the worlds which are not legible, to record, to bear testimony, to codify, and also to animate and move these conditions. In this discussion, what seems to be emerging is this idea of overcoming the limit of the architectural field. In particular, I'm struck by the importance of geography, of cartography, and the idea of representation, which is not only the simple fact of putting architectural things in a computer but a way to operate spatially and to architecturally strategize economic reality.

FRANCO PURINI I followed very carefully this morning's presentations and I want to stress something concerning Rem's presentation. His logo would propose a synthetic ideogram to represent Holland as a single city. But all cities have had some sort of ideogram imposed on them that dominates their lives. It is interesting to contrast the destruction of identity through the proposal of an archetypal pattern that will stretch the existence of a possible process of recognition. The mental image of the globalized world is also one that leads you to think of diptychs – that is, the dialectic between global and local is not drawn in a very big shape, but rather is just distributed all over the world, and there are cracks in the representation. Rather than thinking of a project of architecture as interpreting whole cities or countries, I interpret these conflicting proposals at a very small scale. Globalization leads you to think of something that is at a global scale, but the realization of space is actually at a very small scale.

I don't understand the breakdown between global and local, what form that takes in terms of a project. It does seem that things are going well beyond the local context – for example, what was done for refugees in Zaire by very quickly putting up emergency buildings using technologies that are not local at all. Often they have to use technologies that couldn't be used locally, but local techniques are called upon in terms of the materials used. It might sound naive to say that this condition could be applied to architecture, but it could be used in a very meaningful way in situations that are perhaps extreme – after natural disasters or wars between different ethnic groups, for example.

SASKIA SASSEN There is a certain kind of imbrication of the local and the global. That is why I came up with the global city – a site that is complex, thick, big, and where the global materializes with its function of a network. I do think that the global has thickness and complexity attached to it, and that it is producing a particular kind of spatiality, that it has specific modes of the temporal that are operational. The project that Frédéric described in Zaire, in which a technology from elsewhere is embedded within an existing condition, explodes its relationship with that local, but it's not outside of that local. At the moment, I am working on a project that involves recovering the specificity of the global without thinking of it just in terms of the nonlocal. It's another way of specifying.

The other point that I want to make is about scaling – the local, the regional, the national, the global. One of the ways in which the imbrication of the global and the local is transformed is that it destabilizes inherited, or partly inherited, hierarchies of scale. The local is no longer simply in a hierarchy of scales beneath the regional, beneath the national, beneath the international. In fact, the local can reconfigure itself in a scaling where it is part of the global. This destabilizing of existing hierarchies of scale is a crucial issue in specifying this relationship between the local and the global.

AUDIENCE This question of globalness is something very interesting. It's true that economic forces are bringing these new relations to bear, breaking up preexisting concepts and structures. We hear it in our discussions today, but we also see it happening In the protection of a local scale, a national scale. Look at the issue of war. Without a very strong national or ethnic identity, we would not have some of these conflicts. It's not a question of Americanization, or American imperialism. No, it's the economic force, the might of all of the Western countries, in fact. They are the driving force behind this globalization, and these are war economies – economies based on an enormous investment in weapons. The source of conflict nonetheless remains the question of nationality, belonging, things that can be identified, perhaps, in terms of language and architecture and other areas. Saskia, do you still believe that it makes sense, that it's meaningful, to look at this difference between global and local?

SASSEN In my reading there is a lot of renationalizing. It's the national with which we have lived and which has constructed much of what we are, so there is no way that it can simply be wiped away. It is always there, and it often forms the frame through which a lot of conflict takes place. In my new research project, I deal with the national state. The national state produces some of the necessary instrumentalities for the global economic system, so the national is deeply imbricated. But the more important and abstract point that might connect with broader interests in this audience is the fact that we have lived with national states that have deployed enormously powerful and effective wills to nationalize most of our institutional orders, including the question of identity – always partial, never complete, never successful in its totality. I disagree with those who think that the ascendance of the global represents simply the disappearance of the national state. I think this is not correct. But I do think that it comes back to my previous point: if we are going to understand the meaning of the global, then we've got to excavate the field. There is an archaeology to be had here, and I don't just mean in the Foucauldian sense, but literally.

LAMBERT Personally, I find it absolutely fascinating that in a conference on architecture most of the questions relate to economic issues.

CYNTHIA DAVIDSON I want to make a link that I haven't heard the panel make. This discussion about the global and the local is for me an old dialectic. The most radical thing that's been proposed here about the local is the logo of Rem's. The idea that there could be a logo for Holland – I picture Dutch people wearing it on their T-shirts the way athletes have Nike symbols on their uniforms – enters the local into a sort of global, capitalist branding operation that represents the local in a completely new way. In terms of the local Parisian context, or the chaos of Tokyo, the local may be evolving into something else entirely. But the logo that Rem introduced today seems to be a movement toward keeping the local up with the speed of global transaction.

4. Anymore Architecture?
In today's system of global capital, is everything destined to become generic systems of infrastructure or can new forms of specificity emerge? Can architecture sustain any autonomy in its forms and content or will it be subsumed within social, economic, and political practices?

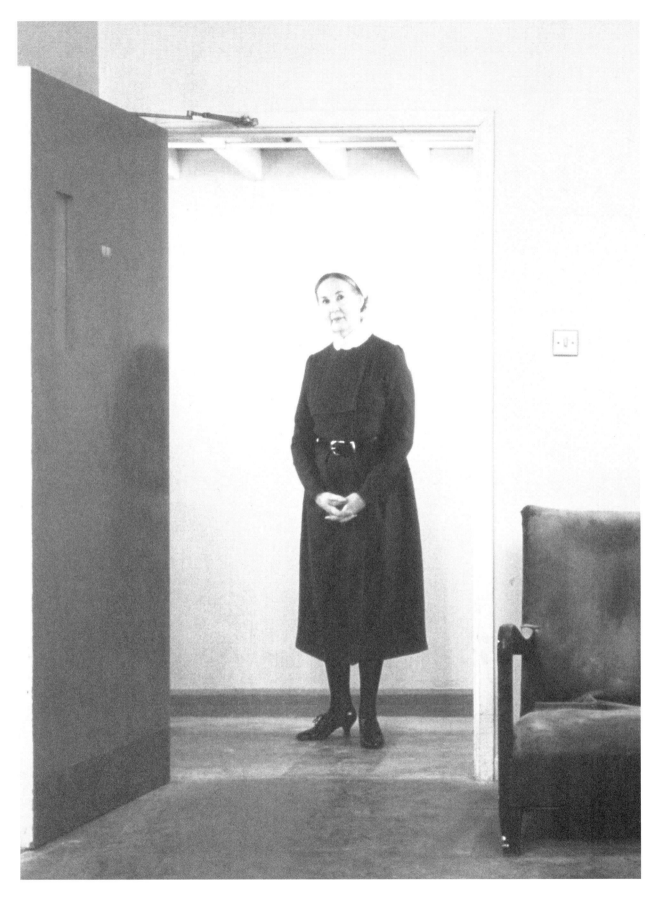

Anymore
Specificity?
Rosalind E. Krauss

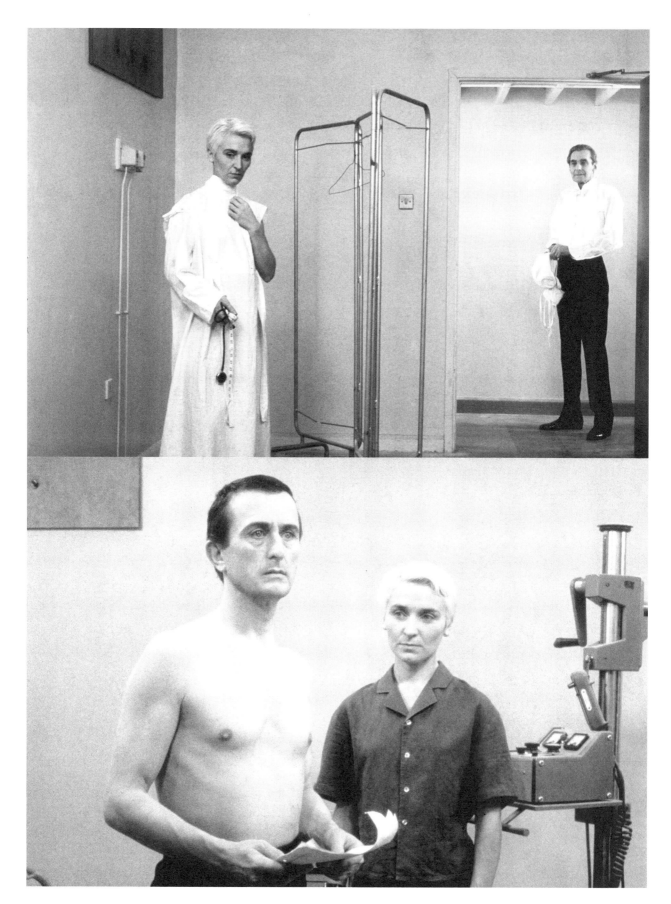

Previous pages, left, and above: James Coleman, INITIALS, from his Projected Images Series, 1994.

The ebullient character of the "anys," with their theme of proliferation and promiscuity – anyone, anywhere, anytime, anyhow – announced a kind of deconstructionist hedonism, the joy of self-deferral, the pleasure of self-duplication, the thrill of self-abandonment. "Anymore," however, sounds a different note, which may in itself contain some kind of lesson about the specificity of the signifier. Redolent of Edgar Allen Poe and mournful in tone, it rings with a ravenlike sound, chiming, now, with "Nevermore": an "any" with regret somehow souring its breath as we approach the endlessly touted millennium.

It is in this spirit not exactly of regret but of skepticism about the triumphalist claims of the nonspecific, which is to say about the expected gains for art contained within the deconstructionist promise, that interests me in this context. Although I find myself on a panel devoted to architecture, my comments will have to focus on the domain I know something about, namely, the visual arts, with the hope that it will be possible to extrapolate from one field to the other. After all, the question "Anymore Architecture?" is framed as a problem in specificity; and it is indeed medium specificity that I want to address.

For the last 30 years the avant-garde has congratulated itself on having buried the very idea of specific mediums along with any grounds for their claim to autonomy. Whether this was done in the name of conceptual art and its shift from the specific to the general (as in Joseph Kosuth's declaration: "Being an artist now means to question the nature of art. If one is questioning the nature of painting, one cannot be questioning the nature of art. . . . That's because the word **art** is general and the word **painting** is specific. Painting is a kind of art"); or was effected in order to take up the critique of the aesthetic institution as such, as sketched by Peter Berger in his **Theory of the Avant-Garde**; or was formed in alignment with Michel Foucault's attack on disciplinary authority, and thus involved propping its various examples on the proliferation of new, transdisciplinary discourses that developed as a result, avantgarde practice is now almost universally carried out in the name of hybridity, parergonality, the indeterminacy of networks, all of them recodings of the same message: that the specific medium – in fact any notion of a medium – is "history."

But history has a funny way of biting the hand that feeds it. By now a tiny segment of those identified with the avant-garde are beginning to experience their own co-optation by what Fredric Jameson has termed the "cultural revolution," which is to say the ultimate cunning with which advanced capitalism exploits radical artistic practice by allowing it to prospect within the cultural imaginary and thereby to open up new spaces within a subject now programmed to participate in – and be colonized by – the next stage of capital.

In no matter how minor a way, the two services that the avant-garde has rendered the cultural revolution involve spectacle, on the one hand, and globalization on the other. Accordingly, the installation practices that are by now the universal language of multidisciplinarity have been incapable of resisting absorption into the transformative system of spectacle in which everything, now distanced as imaginary display, is repackaged as entertainment. Similarly, the very reconfiguration of all material objects into the condition of the image has turned the physical into the virtual, thereby making the experience of the work of art more and more porous to cybernetic transcoding. The result of this leveling is not only to drain the work of art of anything that could be called its own specificity but also to empty out the specificity of the aesthetic as such by dumping it into the swamp of experience in general, so that everything from shopping to watching wars on television takes on a kind of aestheticized glow.

There are, however, certain artists, who, while they still identify themselves as avant-garde and continue to believe in the verdict that declared the traditional mediums, like painting and sculpture, dysfunctional, are nonetheless finding themselves committed to the idea of specificity, and thus to some kind of renewed notion of a medium. In the cases I am thinking of, namely that of the Irish artist James Coleman and that of the South African William Kentridge, the medium with which each has become engaged has to be understood as a kind of new invention, a medium built on a particular technical support, different in each case, but from each of which is derived a set of specific conventions used to speak the language of the medium.

That each artist is conscious of the sui generis nature of his medium is marked by the fact that each has produced a particular name for his practice. For Coleman, whose support is the decidedly low-tech contraption of the slide-tape, which is to say, a timed projection of slides accompanied by a sound track, the name he has used since the late 1970s is "projected images." For Kentridge, whose support is something like animated film – although he has managed to strip animation not only of its technical prowess but almost of its very capacity for movement – the rubric he has insisted on is "drawings for projection."

In gravitating to supports of a decidedly commercial, or mass-cultural, nature, both artists are clearly stating their distance from the high art assumptions of the traditional media, assumptions that have long since been compromised by the utter acquiescence of postwar painting and sculpture to commodification. But at the same time, in embracing the lowest possible end of the technical spectrum, they have also refused to participate in the heady futurism of the technological celebration that has increasingly swept video, photography, and film into the embrace of cyberart. Indeed, part of the point each one is making about technology itself is the rapidity with which it renders each of its stages obsolete. The photographic slide – indeed, photography in general – is now on the way to being replaced by the digital camera; the hand-drawn animated film has not only been supplanted by computer graphics but the photographic basis of the cinematic medium itself is now deeply compromised and outmoded by the digital image. But the other part of this point – and this goes directly counter to the technophilic euphoria that has engulfed the latest round of art practice – is that it is only at its moment of fading into obsolescence that a technical support actually becomes available as an aesthetic medium.

This was a lesson long ago pronounced by Walter Benjamin, who saw that it was precisely at the moment at which a given technology is eclipsed by another that it is able to produce an outside to the totality of technologized space. In this regard, he looked to outmoded optical devices from the 19th century, particularly the stereopticon slide, which he used as the model for his concept of the dialectical image, seeing all of these as opening up the possibility of brushing the phantasmagorical against its own grain.

Exactly what the processes of inventing a medium might be would take too long to present here, as would an explication of how each of these artists has conceived his own project as the constitution of a recursive structure through which to generate the conventions necessary to the unfolding of a medium and to acknowledge the embeddedness of these conventions in the technical support itself. Telegraphically, I would simply point to a few features in each case.

For Coleman the slide-tape is structured between movement and stasis, between, that is, the narrative progression that thrusts one image beyond the other as the slides change in the carousel and what Roland Barthes has signaled as the particular genius of the production in its total indifference to storytelling, and thus in its opening onto what he called a third, or obtuse, meaning. To continually retrieve the atemporality of the single slide from within the flow of a temporal sequence is at the heart of Coleman's understanding of the medium he is forging, and to do this he has had recourse to various strategies.

One of these is to line his actors up as if for a final curtain call so that the images repetitively thematize the outside of the narrative space. Another involves adapting a convention peculiar to the kinds of anecdotalized images – to use Barthes' collective term for comic books, photo-novels, and stained glass windows – with which Coleman associates his project. This convention, which I have elsewhere called the **double face-out**, derives from the inefficiency of a static medium to choreograph emotional exchanges between the protagonists of a given drama, since to cut back and forth between the faces of two characters would waste far too much narrative space.[1] Thus at great pitches of intensity, instead of confronting each other, the two are inevitably shown one behind the other and both facing outward toward the viewer. Pressed against the realities of a planar dimension it cannot overcome, the double face-out's own flatness thereby takes on a compensatory gravity as it becomes the emblem of a reflexive acknowledgment of the impossibility of the visual field to deliver its promise of either lifelikeness or authenticity, even while it liberates that field into an ever-intensified visuality.

If Coleman locates his medium within the ebb tide of photographic technology, Kentridge situates his at the moment of the absolute eclipse of drawing. His "Drawings for Projection" are charcoal drawings whose progression and – since he is constantly erasing and remaking them – whose retrogression are cinematically tracked by making a single-frame record of every slight extension or deletion of the line. The result of this, when projected, is something like an animated film, although, in contradistinction to cel animation or even to the primitive flip book, his process does not involve the proliferation of images but rather an extreme parsimony. An eight-minute film, for example, might be composed of no more than thirty separate drawings.

But the result of the erasures and the build-up of their residue is to make one feel the density of the graphic substance itself, which, along with the systolic

pulse of the unfolding line, invests the visual field with a particular corporeality and gravity. This phenomenon is at direct odds with the kind of liberation from both gravity and mortality that characterizes animated film in general, a freedom that led certain theorists and critics of cinema – I am thinking of Stanley Cavell and André Bazin – to disqualify cartoons from the medium of film in the first place. Cavell, for example, says: "The world inhabited by animated creatures . . . is essentially a child's world. [The difference between it] and the world we inhabit is not that the world of animation is governed by physical laws or satisfies metaphysical limits which are just different from those which condition us; its laws are often quite similar. The difference is that we are uncertain when or to what extent our laws and limits do and do not apply (which suggests that [within the world of animation] there are no real laws at all)."[2] It is in this abrogation of law that Cavell locates the rupture between animation and the medium of film, which both he and Bazin qualify as geared to the world of reality and therefore necessarily photographically based. This notion of law is not just physical but also moral, since the release from both gravity and stable identity also constitutes an escape from responsibility.

Bazin was writing in the '50s and Cavell in the '60s, addressing a situation that preceded not only the outmoding of cel animation, but the outmoding of the photographic basis of film, as more and more footage is generated by computer graphics. What this means is that not only has the proliferation of the image exponentially increased but the possibility of its automation and the total control this makes possible has rendered the "real" itself obsolete, supplanted by the gravity-free field of a **Star Wars** euphoria.

It is at just this juncture that we find the invention of a medium that restores gravity to a kind of drawing that exists nowhere but in the field of projection, at the interstice between its appearance and disappearance in a movement it also resists; it is at this juncture that this invention takes on a particular importance. The relevance of this kind of moment for the specificity of the architectural medium resides in the yielding of certain design practices to computerization. I am not referring to the use of the computer as a graphic tool but rather as a design alternative, one that, imitating its use in aeronautics, rocketry, and shipmaking, encourages architecture to slip off the shackles of gravity and thus out of a certain notion of tectonics and of embodiedness. I have in mind Frank Gehry's Guggenheim Museum Bilbao which, as a kind of **Star Wars** architecture, constitutes, for me at least, just another version of Mickey Mouse.[3]

1 See my ". . . And Then Turn Away?': An Essay on James Coleman," October 81 (Summer 1997); and "Reinventing the Medium," Critical Inquiry 25 (Winter 1999).
2 Stanley Cavell, The World Viewed (Cambridge, Massachusetts: Harvard University Press, 1971), 169–71.
3 For a discussion of Walter Benjamin and Mickey Mouse see Miriam Hansen, "Of Mice and Ducks," South Atlantic Quarterly 92 (January 1993); and "Benjamin and Cinema," Critical Inquiry 25 (Winter 1999).

Rosalind Krauss is a professor of modern art at Columbia University and a cofounder of **October**. Her books include **The Optical Unconscious** and **Bachelors**.

Archery Range, Barcelona, Spain, 1985–96.

Enric Miralles

There is a kind of nostalgia when we ask ourselves, Anymore?
There is the assumption of a past and a future.
But architecture has a different approach to time.
It lives in a kind of continuous present.
Anyway, we are talking about time,
And I will try to offer an answer in two ways.

First is to see one's own work as a kind of continuous field of research,
where curiosity about architecture has produced a series of elements.
where Igualada, Huesca, and Archery Ranges have been transformed into
Bremerhaven, Mollet, etc., and ultimately into the Edinburgh Parliament.

In this sense, time does not exist. It is a kind of parallel situation.
A kind of technical approach.
The construction of genealogies.

Second, time is embedded in places, in things.
It has a kind of material quality.
Every case, every specific situation, guides the project in a completely new way.

It is at this moment that fear makes the architect choose,
within a very limited number of options, that which we call "architecture."

This is where nostalgia appears.
The fear of not finding the best possible performance
Anymore.

On the contrary, accepting the complexity and richness
of every new situation seems to be the way to keep
enlarging the possibilities of our profession.

I feel that enlarging the capacity to be identified with reality,
accepting radically different notions of time in different situations,
is what we need to work toward.

Let us take the previous list of projects,
connected with a specific treatment of geometry
in relation to the earth construction of buildings,
and make a new list.

Unfinished (Igualada)
Double (Huesca)
Dichotomy (Archery Ranges)
Social landscape, imagination (Mollet)
Time as layers (Bremerhaven)
Not being specific (Edinburgh)

It seems that **ANY** parallel thinking,
any kind of **Dr. Jekyll and Mr. Hyde** situation,
allows the work . . . to continue.

Enric Miralles is principal of Enric Miralles and Benedetta Tagliabue Associated Architects, Barcelona, and a professor at Harvard's Graduate School of Design. His projects include the Meditation Pavilion in Unazaki and the New Scottish Parliament in Edinburgh.

Best Wishes,
Mike

Import and Export
Bernard Tschumi

Jean-Luc Godard, Week End, **1967.**

Most of the Any conferences have been about imports and exports — about importing from other disciplines into architecture, and exporting from architecture into other areas of knowledge. Anymore in Paris is also about importing: from France to America, or from America to France. This implies mixing, compressing, expanding, informing, deforming. It is about heterogeneity and hybrid bodies rather than homogeneous purity, about the singular rather than the generic.

An "event" or occurrence happened to me ten days ago – a violent car crash. Indeed, some pieces of me are still in the car. While in the hospital, I thought about importing and exporting, about the exchange of forces between dynamic and inanimate objects, and between France and America.

Remember the centrality of the car to French movies and novels of the 1950s. These "mythic, fabulous objects," as Kristin Ross calls them in her excellent book **Fast Cars, Clean Bodies**, in which she analyzes American influences on France, characterize the French fascination for speed at the wheel. After all, Albert Camus, Roger Nimier, and Françoise Sagan all made headlines as they encountered large plane trees in fast sports cars, and either died in the meeting of the two or were seriously hurt. French intellectuals discovered American culture violently. Sartre read American hard-boiled detective novels brought to France by G.I.s and developed a unique writing style – philosophy hammered out in short, pugnacious sentences, à la Dashiell Hammett or Peter Cheney. Car crashes became part of the myth. From James Dean's ultimate movie ending to Jean-Luc Godard's multiple and repetitious car wrecks in the film **Week End**, the worlds of driving and movies were woven into the lifestyle of the era. As Godard said at the time: "Il n'y a de cinéma que le cinéma américain." "There is nothing but American cinema."

Of course the fascination with car culture was part of a larger phenomenon, namely, postwar industrialization and the complete change this meant for French culture. This affected every aspect of living: cars, Frigidaires, and other "modern" appliances were all part of everyday life. All were different forms of domesticity that shared one common aspect: quick living, clean living, "quick" and "clean" thinking. The American curtain wall – epitomized by Park Avenue towers – took over the world. Architecture was proving it all: architecture now coincided with lifestyle; form and function were finally synonymous.

Import-export: thirty years later, French theory (as it was called in America) crossed the Atlantic. The lesson of the car crash had finally returned home: no more heroic purity but rather dislocations, deconstructions, dissociations, ruptures, collisions.

Of interest were both the fascination and the rejection generated within American architectural culture by the concepts proposed by French writers and philosophers. On the one hand, we witnessed an extraordinary attraction, as almost all universities or institutions of learning became fertile ground for research and invention, impregnated as they were by concepts that clearly broke away from popular local conventions such as the vernacular, neoclassicism, high modernism, Las Vegas, and so on. But, simultaneously, we witnessed a rejection, because these concepts argued for hybridizations, for grafts and contaminations of all sorts, and these contravened received ideas about what architecture was.

Indeed, it is as if the purity of high modernism always returns as the inescapable "truth" of architecture. Born in the 1930s, refined in the 1950s, it permeates everyone's unconscious. Import and export allow temporary contaminations, disjunctions, and transgressions into other fields and territories, but they are soon, and inevitably, absorbed and synthesized into a larger whole. They are "recupéré," as the French say, namely, reintegrated. Today's "recuperation" is performed by the software we all use in our projects — Form Z, Alias, Maya, and others. All of our projects share the same common denominator: rectilinear or curvilinear, they are all smooth, coherent, and visually comfortable.

Hence the question: Is there an architecture that cannot be "recupéré," an architecture that constantly pleases but also disturbs at the same time, an architecture that is celebrated and attacked simultaneously? This would be an "architecture of events," where what happens in it, and through it, is more important than what is reported. Car crashes or . . . Architecture . . .

I even became interested in those hybridizations that are the ultimate "effects" of the "crash": bones and titanium, carbon steel, skin grafts, and stitches. Nothing is pure anymore.

Bernard Tschumi is dean of The Graduate School of Architecture, Planning, and Preservation at Columbia University, and practices architecture in both New York and Paris.

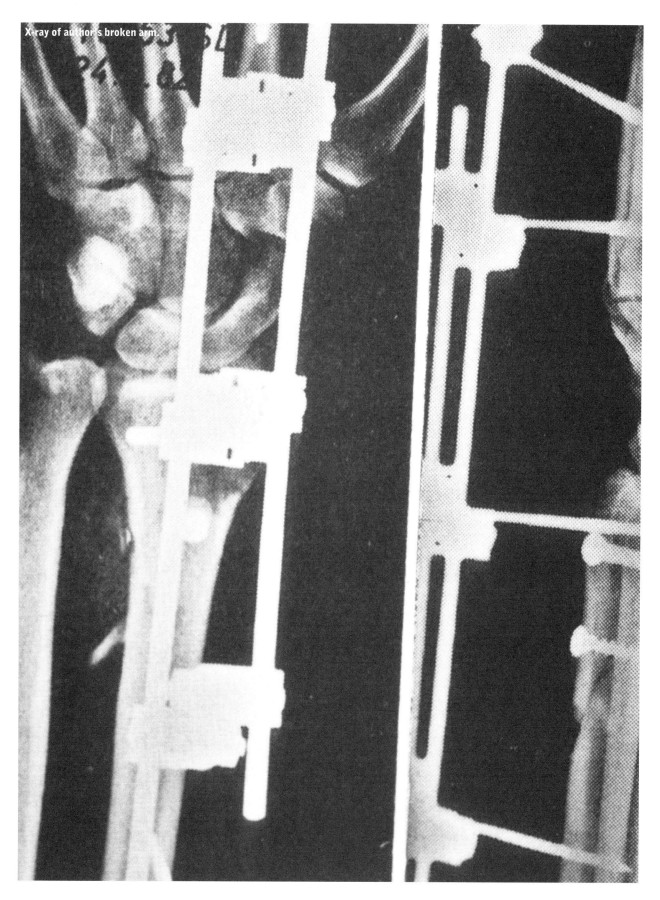

X-ray of author's broken arm.

French advertisement for an American refrigerator.

The Structure of Experience

Lars Spuybroek

"We designers are the inventors of images of freedom."[1] Sanford Kwinter's crucial sentence in his fillip on post-Koolhaasian Dutch architecture first struck me as completely ridiculous ("Go read Foucault! – an architecture of freedom can never be anything other than an architecture of power."), exactly because Dutch architecture today is nothing but a gridding of images: an ongoing attempt to save the Dom-ino model, where image (wall), action (floor), and structure (columns) seem to be forever separated. But then the thought occurred to me that it could mean the images themselves could be structural and therefore must be blurred, part of the background. Obviously freedom lies in the potential of seeing, the potential of action – not as in a freedom of choice but in an experimental tension within the choice-making machine named body.

Suppose it were possible to paint a picture of freedom. Would it have to be a very bad painting, very academic, perhaps something with a prisoner looking out of a barred window, the rays of the sun falling in, the eyes in a gaze? Even if the painting were more intelligent, something monochromatic and sublime, once we had painted an image of freedom and hung it on a wall, most of us would start laughing – it would be like a Monty Python scene; we would all realize that the image is there where the freedom is not. All freedom would be occupied by the image, the image would obliterate the freedom. Were we inventors of images of freedom and were we actually to invent such a thing, would it be best, then, to hide it, to have the absence of the image of freedom? Then again, how would we let everyone know that we hid the image, that we can now finally enjoy our freedom because its image is safely locked away? Realizing, or materializing, this void is indeed our main task, but only with the knowledge that it cannot be an image on the wall or a hole in the floor. How can we be connected to the unseen; how can the unforeseen happen?

Let us stay with this image of freedom as the void. It has often been stated that it would suffice to replace the determined with the undetermined, to replace the defined with the undefined, the fixed plan with the open or free plan. This has been reasoned as follows: when life produces images, moving things, furniture, the only way for architecture to provide for this so-called "lived" freedom is to retreat out of the experience, to take a few steps back in scale into pure tectonics, support, and service. In order to create the greatest common denominator of all possible movements, architecture must retreat into the empty envelope, the empty hall, into providing pure infrastructure and structure; in short, architecture must move toward urbanism. Instead of the old crystalline architecture that disciplines behaviors into pure habituation, we are, then, left with an open field, the open field of sheer indifference. In this view, the body is like the Master of the Universe, god of all things: it produces effortless program; it throws its actions into an outside world like light into darkness.

Alas, this tireless Cartesian machine is a fictional character (mainly Dutch in origin); no act simply takes place in an open space, no movement is unrelated to another. Already in the late 1940s, Maurice Merleau-Ponty had stated that, on the one hand, action is nothing but the world passing through the subject and, on the other, that as organisms we are only structurally opened to the world; that is, only our bodies define what constitutes the outside world. Here he is already departing from the classic distinction of idealism and realism, even of knowledge and world. There is no either/or: the world is neither pure interior (solipsism) nor the body pure exterior (representationalism). I am in the world and the world is in me. This is a topological condition that cannot be described by something volumetric, something with an outside and an inside. Its geometry is not descriptive but looks at the dimension of the relationship rather than the volume; it is a matter of electrical and genetic flesh only, purely structurally related – what Francisco Varela and Humberto Maturana call "structural coupling."[2] Cognition is lived experience, not located anywhere, not located in the subject or in the world. Subject and world coevolve, they coemerge, they structurally lock into each others' trajectories because of their transformability, their plasticity. If there is any intentionality involved, one cannot speak of it without the millions of movements in the world that are structurally coupled to the millions of movements that condense into a structured body of experience. We then must conclude that there cannot be any pure intention. No act is grounded, no act is to be grounded, every act is in its essence ungrounded or groundless; thus an act is only free when it is a jump, when it leaps over this internal and existential void of freedom. It must surely be a jump because the body is tense; a tense, elastic structure charged with all these other movements, "old," abstract movements that are absorbed within the proprioceptive substrate of the body – old movements that have been sublimated into higher structures that have a tendency to act in the present. Merleau-Ponty refers to this as "abstract movement,"[3] a movement in the body that not only coordinates all actual actions but also structurally and topologically connects all possible movements. It is a movement as an abstract capacity, the movement available in the body, a "background tension," he calls it, following the Gestaltists of the 1920s. In fact, this movement only becomes available to the body through the many actions performed in everyday life; it is not given, and one can also lose it.

Movement is made up of movement. The abstract and the real feed back and forth continuously, but only through the plasticity and elasticity of the structure. This concept of tension is particularly critical to the notion of intentionality, where the body is seen solely as purposeful, as a mechanistic machine that has to start itself up every time a goal comes into view. Every act springs from this background tension, a

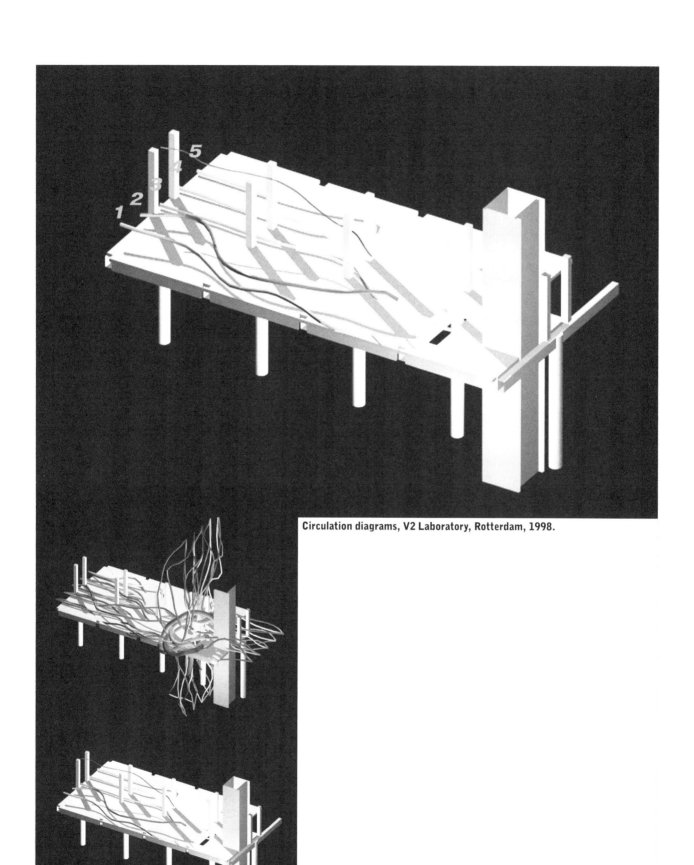

Circulation diagrams, V2 Laboratory, Rotterdam, 1998.

real, actual movement that "releases itself from neurological anonymity"[4] within a body where millions of processes go on simultaneously. In this view, subject and object must be deeply intertwined, hardly distinguishable, as are action and perception, the motor and the sensory. This is a fundamental critique of the architectural program: the mechanistic layout of all human behavior within a built system viewed purely as tasks, routines, and habits.

Suppose this habituation, this crystallization of behavior, were more of a bottom-up emergence of repetition, an order emerging from different patterns of collective and individual processes. In this instance, an act is never completely certain, it always differs from itself and is always ready to shift into another act or even to slide into a "free" act. When every act, however intentional, is also oriented sideways, a significant amount of in-between program could unfold, both undetermined and unprogrammed "program." Every path would then be part of a field, because every trace is first written within this soft field, the deep surface of the body, as in the classic concept of chreodes. The body is a beach, and architecture can only appeal to this bandwidth of action when it also becomes a beach – at least partly. I would like to try to take the topological view of the body and connect it to a topological view of program, connect it to a topology of architecture, and even of structure.

An architecture of the free is then one where the void is absorbed by matter, where it is not the other side of matter but saturates it, makes matter responsive, a soft matter, not weak, where the softness has become part of the geometry. It is not matter in space but space in matter. Instead of opposing media and architecture, image and movement, perception and action, elevation and plan, or tectonics and textiles, I merge them. I opt for a geometry of the mobile, where the geometry becomes part of the furniture and the movable: a geometry of waves and media. Here we must go from a geometry of fixed points to one of springs,[5] where a point opens up and becomes part of a line, a sensitive zone in the line, a point that can both contract or expand and build relations with other lines into a coherent flexible system – because the soft is much stronger than the rigid: a tectonics of the responsive, of the springy and the flexible. In such a system, movement never really dissipates and leaves the structure, and the structure never solidifies. The building may be static, but the architecture is never at rest.

The architectures of both the fixed and the open plan – the crystallization of both the habituated and the wild – focus on the end of an act, its objective or goal. They both say: no matter how an act emerges from the neurological jelly, it always comes out as a vector in space, an intention directed toward a goal. The only difference is that the intention of the first is singular, and the other, plural. In this case, we would always be on the other side of freedom: behavior fixed in either mono- or multifunctionality. Viewed in time, this architecture always reacts to an act in the same way, either through discipline or indifference. This other architecture is an architecture of the responsive, it is interactive, where action occurs between body and world and causes them to merge into one experiential system. This alternative architecture, a "liquid architecture,"[6] locates itself at the start of an act, in the affect, at the possibility of action, in the haptic field of potentials. The direction of this vector is a coevolving of world and body, it is a direction without an outside or ground. In this sense, surely space is a by-product of movement, and movement does not take place in space. The void is the other side of the eyes; space is in the body. We should not forget that an act is always directed toward situations that have not yet become actual. This architecture does not wait for the real, does not passively wait for things to come, for life to happen; it is itself part of life, active, charging the present, electrifying the now, multiplying the contemporary with motor geometry, energizing the real with rubbery, plastic, responsive interactions. We inhabit time more than space; we have to build houses in time more than in space. (Do not believe architects who say that we occupy space, and that our intentions are directed in space.)

The rest is a question of methodology. Instead of moving toward the urbanist and the empty shell, leaving the movement to furniture, this architecture moves itself into furniture, where architecture nestles itself in twirls, displacements, and shifts. It maps all movement as movement in tectonics itself, it absorbs the minutia, the tiniest things, a voice, a muscle tone, a cup falling, a pile of papers. The need to connect all of the things we do, all of the concentrations, to live either fluently or in tension, to make chains of actions without seams or hesitations, is interpreted in architecture, where it becomes structural. This architecture materializes the undetermined, it determines the undecided, not by deciding on a name but by articulating the nameless. It shapes the formless and the informal – it finds a structure of experience without prescribing any specific experience. It maps potentials within a medium that is highly structured but soft; it restructures by coordinating these potentials, and here it opens up to the real. Within this soft coordination, the real emerges and never comes back the same way; now experience and geometry are merged in matter. In this conceptual continuum it becomes possible to synthesize action, perception, and construction.

The V2 Lab is part of the V2 Organization, an arts and technology collective based in Rotterdam. The lab is meant to be a space where artists and programmers cooperate on a crossroads of private and public money. We developed two diagrams, one conceptual, the other mechanistic; one of architecture, one of the building. We merged both by interference onto a higher level, where the abstract movement of both architecture and body share one continuum, resulting in real, actual actions.

Interior views, V2 Laboratory, Rotterdam, 1998.

First, we mapped the (desired) movement in the building. This is the classic method of dealing with behavior and the organization of behavior in an office such as this. We analyzed quantifiable schema of all actions as they are seen through the purely mechanistic filter of running lines, bubble-diagrams, flow charts – habits, tasks, work, all actions viewed as repeatable. We know that we strive for this, we long for repetition. All actions are described by vectors within an additive system of architectural elements: walls, stairs, an elevated floor, a table, more tables. Actions can only safely repeat themselves if they do not interfere with others. Clients generally have the tendency to draw these kinds of diagrams – which is essentially okay – but architects generally have the tendency to materialize these diagrams – which is not.

Second, we mapped all that is in tension, all possible movement; rather than keeping events apart, we connected them through a medium in a topological relational system of potentials. This model is made up of soft matter ("rubber"), the so-called "springs and strings" model: when forces go into it, it not only deforms but also responds. This is done by making a structure of springs to control the geometry of strings. The springs are determined by five parameters: elasticity, damping, incompressibility, density, and friction. One can make them very stiff or very wobbly; the character of the material is related to the dimension and form of the machine. "Data" and "scape" are not separate entities; the "scape" is already a structure with a certain capacity to absorb certain information. In this structure there are no points, only zones of contraction and expansion. In this structure there are no lines, only coordination of the various zones by waves.

We do not freeze the form and start thinking about how to materialize it. We start thinking how we should read the (second) conceptual model of springs and strings through the (first) mechanistic model. The system is made up of four groups of five strings connected to a large central spring. The V2 Lab was designed with one of these groups, i.e., five strings running parallel to each other and connected by more (invisible) springs. We started reading the vibrating five strings through the organizational model. So, for instance, line number five moves up, ergo: "a table." But at the same time, line number four moves down, ergo: "an entry to an elevated corridor." Three moves up high: "the elevated floor." Two: the same. One: too expensive and cut out. So, instead of materializing the mechanistic diagram in a system of separate entities, they are all read as modulations within a system of variability. Then all of the five, now four, lines are connected by ruled surfaces; what results is a dented surface that does not neutralize the longitudinal orientation but rather only partly absorbs the lines. That is, lines are pure orientation, and when connected within a single surface they generally tend to lose that orientation. Here this is partly saved because the ruled surfaces (which connect curves with straight lines) create a variety of folds with a different sharp-

ness. When the fold between two ruled surfaces is sharp it orientates more in the longitudinal direction of the lines, and when it is less sharp the difference between both surfaces is smoothed out, and the orientation becomes multidirectional. The surface introduces extra, lateral movements. There is an increase in order, exactly the way lines emerge in dune formation; they emerge out of the surface, the field of sand, but do not separate themselves from it. They orient the surface with the wind; the surface stays more flexible and multidirectional. Generally we read either one or the other, field (open) or line (direction), but the ordering principle is actually in between.

Let us focus on a single spot: the table-contour derived from line number five, and the corridor derived from line number four. What is this surface in between? According to Bart Lootsma, it comes very close to Xenakis's ruled surfaces for Metastasis, geometry as a score, this time not for playing music but for dancing, for introducing dance into the program. The actual connecting of the one contour (table) to the other (corridor) is in fact a morphing, a transformation of a table into a corridor, and this materialized in-between is actually larger than the objects/edges themselves. Habituation, tasks, and performance are still there: you can sit at one side with three people and work, for on this edge it is 100 percent table. The other line indicates 100 percent corridor: people simply walk from the flat, existing floor onto the new, elevated floor via this curved surface. It exactly follows the mechanistic diagram where corridor and table were separate entities. But then this is all swallowed up by the materialization of the undecided: the potential of the program (which of course is not programmed) is in the field, the ruled surface. Because the edges have a name (table, corridor) but the in-between has not, there is no way one can say where the floor stops and the table begins. Generally architects spend their energy on what has a name, not on what hasn't.

When we concentrate on actual movements, the actual motion-capture diagrams of actual behavior, we see how they both merge. Of course, if we trace behavior a thousand times around this area, more than half of the lines coincide with the running lines of the mechanistic scheme. But here one can see what actually happens. Action regains its bandwidth, its elasticity, its potential, purely related to feeling. The vibrations of the (rubber) lines of the strings reemerge in the traces of behavior; it is the same tension, in different materials (cyberrubber and neuroflesh meet through wood). Suppose one morning one feels exceptionally happy or excited; one could, after entering the space, suddenly accelerate, run over the surface alongside the table and then walk on into the corridor (this actually occurs quite often). Or, one could just walk straight on, bored – either way, you always have to choose whether to go left or right of the column. Sometimes people lie down on the large surface between table and corridor, drink their tea there in the afternoon when they are in need of a pause, or walk up the surface to speak with the manager who is three feet below, sitting at the table. This beach between objects, this beach moving through the standard additive elements, was not in the program, it is an intensification of program, or more precisely, a tensification of program. And it is exactly because the undetermined (the morph) is materialized that it creates tension and freedom. It did not say in the program, "We want a space were we can lie down in the afternoon to drink our tea." The standard option of leaving-things-open-in-between, as a "space of accidents," the Farnsworth model, is exactly not doing that. The animation does not stop, there is no final equilibrium, the machine does not leave the architecture when it is realized as form. The diagram does not stop being a machine when materialized, and, more importantly, the diagram was never immaterial in the first place; it was constructed in the (hyper)rubber of the strings and springs model. This is exactly where the movement goes or, even, where the "rubber" goes. The material of the rubber is shared over time, through concept and percept, by the conceptual machine, the materials in the built structure (plywood and rubber and plastic), but also of the flesh, the neuro-electrical flesh. It is shared and thus not located, not anchored. It is the nonlocated affect that is distributed over diagram and matter simultaneously.

In essence, the "movement in the building" is charged with "movement in the architecture"; that is, the abstract movement of morphing from a table into a corridor. This topology is linked directly to the abstract movement in the body, the proprioceptive bandwidth of action, the potential of action. Every general intention is charged with a lateral sideways orientation, and therefore every straight line comes out as a wave. One movement interferes with the other; it multiplies it, and therefore both merge; actual and memorized movement interact; movement of body and geometry act within one continuum. This is why habits should not be set against free movement, play, or experiment. Habituation is an increase of order. It makes our rhythms stronger than ourselves; but even when repetition is at a high level, it should never be simply crystallized in a top-down order of building. It should be different each time it returns, it should emerge time and time again, negotiating with the background time and time again. The plasticity of the structure and the body interact continuously, sometimes to form crystals of behavior, and sometimes to slip and become new.

1 Sanford Kwinter, "FFE: Le Trahison des Clercs," **Any** 24 (1999), 61–62.
2 Humberto Maturana and Francisco Varela, **The Tree of Knowledge: The Biological Roots of Human Understanding** (Boston: Shambala, 1987). Later Varela widened the crucial concept of **autopoiesis** and **structural coupling** to the level of perception, looping it into action with the notion of "enac-

tion." See: Francisco J. Varela, Evan Thompson and Eleanor Rosch, **The Embodied Mind** (Cambridge, Massachusetts: MIT Press, 1993), especially chapter eight.
3 Maurice Merleau-Ponty, **The Phenomenology of Perception** (New York: Humanities Press, 1993), especially chapters three through five.
4 Ibid.
5 The term **springs** refers to the machines we use to generate structure. These "strings and springs" models should be opposed to "lines and points" as they exist in drawings. As the drawing moves from sketch to ink, from complex to simple, the machine is basically simple in its layout but becomes a complexity when informing it with action. Springs first came up in the Hypermatter plug-in for 3DStudioMAX, and later in Maya's SoftBody Dynamics.
6 Liquid Architecture, the title of Marcus Novak's influential text in **Cyberspace: The First Steps**, ed. Michael Benedict (Cambridge, Massachusetts: MIT Press, 1991). He then related the inherent liquidity of the digital to architecture, but basically to an architecture of satisfying needs, a topological variation on plug-and-play. We shift this to the architecture of the liquid itself, where architecture doesn't satisfy but rather charges desires. Therefore, it should always be read between organization and structure, information and form, diagram and matter, because it remains partly unformed, articulated but informal.

Lars Spuybroek is with **NOX Architects in Rotterdam. Among their many projects are Foamhouse, bBeachness, V2-Engine, Flying Attic, and Two-D-Tower.**

The Specter of the Spectacle: Ghosts of the Real

Peter Eisenman

Proposed Staten Island Institute for Arts and Sciences, St. George Ferry Terminal, New York, 1999.

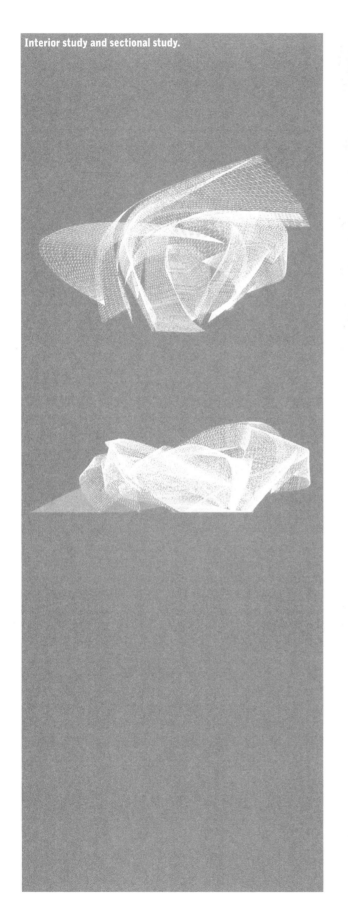

Interior study and sectional study.

Palace on the outskirts of London, made possible structures such as the Eiffel Tower, which were almost pure spectacle, no longer erected to accommodate events and their participants but rather designed for pure viewing. The Eiffel Tower existed in real space and time, even though its relationship to the viewing subject had changed. The viewer had become passive, no longer a participant, and "distracted."

With the rise of the middle class came the concept of leisure, placing even more importance on spectacles both as events and as buildings. This change in how people used time also involved a change in how they used space. These changes were paralleled by a shift from public spectacle to one of private display. Correspondingly, the space of the public realm of the spectacle was diminished as private venues for similar functions flourished. A further transference from the outside to the inside occurred with the advent of film and the still camera. It was now possible to exchange the space of the spectacle from occasional and uncontrolled occurrences to the controlled space of an everyday performance in a movie theater. But the movie houses themselves were far from everyday. They were the new pleasure palaces of the 1920s, where the now private, commercial, internalized spectacles were enacted. With interiors suffused with a dreamlike opulence and exotic themes from faraway places, the audiences were no longer limited by the real dimension of space and time. The cinema as spectacle, while allowing for the erasure of real time and space, also turned the burgeoning middle class into a crowd of passive spectators. As the observer became increasingly passive and introverted, the housing of these spectacles became increasingly extroverted, producing the Centre Pompidou in Paris and now the Guggenheim Museum in Bilbao.

Another moment of the spectacle that must be noted as critical to this discussion, both as event and structure, is the Nazi party rally staged by Leni Riefenstahl and Albert Speer at the Marschfeld at Nuremberg in 1934. Here the actual event became a simulation, a stage set for a propaganda film. This was a situation much like the medieval pageants, where the subject of the event became the participants in that event, but with a critical difference. The participants in this monumental rally would become both the observers and the observed, creating a condition of spectator/voyeur, both outside of and within the more sinister propagandistic program. In a desire to turn a collective mass into the spectacle of the will, of the **Volk**, the rally used one

medium, the live event, as the vehicle for another medium, the film. This provoked a double simulation: the live spectacle not only questioned the nature of what was real but was also the beginning of the substitution of the reality of the physical container, i.e., architecture with the appearance of a container – floodlights as arcade. This double simulation erased the former dialectical difference between model and copy, and hence began to question the traditional qualities of reality: the unexpected, the unprogrammed, and the contingent. The idea of the unexpected architectural experience was lost to the certainty of the programmed time of the framed image. Accident, chance, and coincidence were lost to the certainty of the film. Historically, within a dialectical consciousness, the spectacle had represented reality; now the spectacle had become the simulacrum. Further, as the condition of the subject had been problematized, so too had the dialectical conditions of reality and simulation.

In contemporary historical consciousness, two distinctions have been made: one between the spectacle and the event, the other between architecture and the theme park. While both relate to the eye-catching nature of the object/spectacle in relationship to the subject, they define these distinctions differently. Critical to the difference between the spectacle and the event is the different role played by the subject, or observer. The event is in the time of the present and the observer/subject is part of that action. In this context, the viewer is both object and subject. In the spectacle the observer/subject has become removed from the present and occupies a different, perhaps even critical, role. Thus any discussion of the spectacle contains the question of where the subject is in relation to the object, precisely because the spectacle, as opposed to the event, no longer occurs in the real time of the present. The art historian Norman Bryson, for example, has questioned the position of the subject by contrasting the French term **regard** (translated as "the gaze" in English) with the French term **coup d'oeil**, or "the glance." In this sense, the spectacle today would seem to involve the subject in the removed position of the glance as opposed to the involved position of the gaze.

Debord argues in another context that the spectacle proclaims itself as the dominance of appearance over reality, that the spectacle is largely a question of image, not an image of structure. In this context, social life becomes a set of appearances. For Debord, the spectacle is a visible negation of a life that has invented a visual

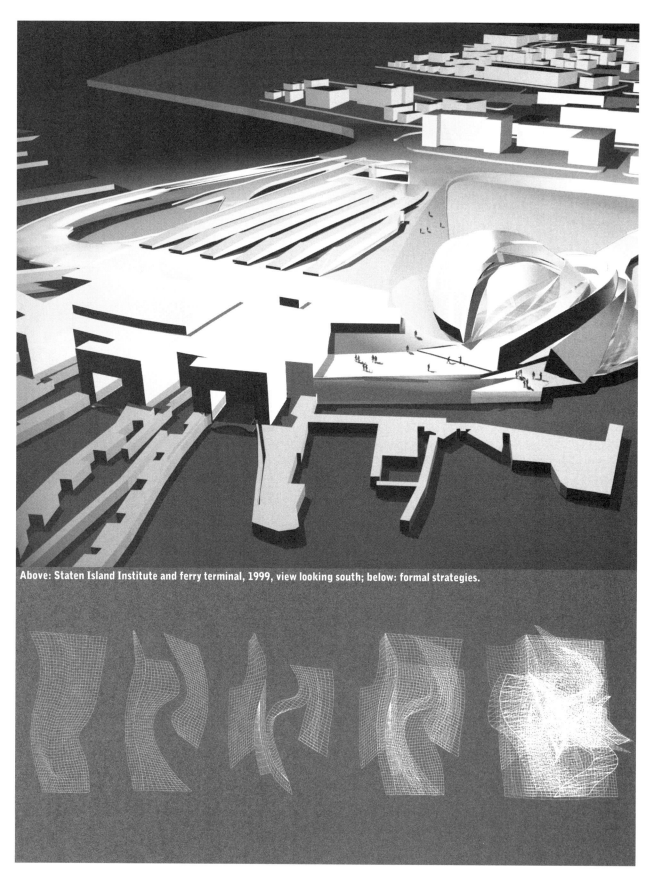

Above: Staten Island Institute and ferry terminal, 1999, view looking south; below: formal strategies.

form for itself. Precisely because of its problematic attributes, the spectacle questions the former distinctions between spectacle and nonspectacle, between the real original and the simulated copy. An issue for architecture now becomes how to conceptualize the former difference between the virtual and the real, how to see these no longer as different but rather as a condition where both exist simultaneously. Thus, in a new definition of the critical project, the spectator, whether real or virtual, whether involved through the eye or the body, could become, in a sense, an active presence as both subject and object in a spectacle that was no longer clearly different from the event.

The second distinction that needs to be questioned is one between the theme park and architecture. In the theme park, the experience of place is made to be the same for everyone, much like Coca-Cola is made to taste the same in the United States as it does in Argentina. It necessarily has to be that way in order to guarantee the same experience each time. However, architecture, to maintain its criticality, had to allow for the unexpected, the inadvertent, the contingent, and the coincidental, enfolding and blurring the different readings made by different subjects. The critical architectural project was not directed at the same experience for every observer. It was not a repetition of sameness but rather a repetition of difference. The critical project of dialectics posited architecture in opposition to the theme park; the critical project after dialectics would blur this opposition, and thus suggest the possibility of both. This could be seen by the possible repetition of the dimension of time in architecture, not only as narrative time but as a time disjuncted from the bodily experience of the subject. Traditional architecture proposed a disjunction in time that was internal to the object, not to the time of the event. Architecture, in this sense, proposed a clear distinction between real time and virtual time. The theme park, on the other hand, is instructive because it attempts to erase this distinction, producing a more homogeneous, one-to-one time experience for its subjects. The idea of the virtual produces a condition of oscillation, a blurring of the distinction between reality and its simulacra, at the same time that both exist in real space.

The issue of blurring was crucial in our project for the Staten Island Institute of Arts and Sciences. In the 19th century, the museum as an icon of the privileged class was set apart from the daily life of commerce. Museums in New York, Boston, and Philadelphia were located in parklike surroundings and situated as palaces of culture. Today these palaces have been replaced by two new settings that represent the ebb and flow of commercial culture – the computer terminal and the travel terminal (airports, bus and train stations, car parks). With this dynamic condition of human movement, new hybrid facilities are appearing: shopping malls, airport hotels, cineplexes. These shifts seemed to lead naturally to another hybrid, the museum and the terminal; that is, to moving the museum out of the garden and into the daily flow of people – 18 million passengers a year at the Staten Island Ferry Terminal. The terminal then would become the entrance and **aula magna** of a new museum. We were asked to dissimulate the function, that is, to produce an object that was also a dissimulation of its function. It was not to look like a building or a museum. Thus the blurring of ground, function, and container was played out in the project.

The forms of the Staten Island museum are an attempt to obscure the relationship between figure and ground. The project combines Gilles Deleuze's idea of smooth and striated space and then blurs their difference with the sense of an invertebrate piling up of the ground. This approach produced a figuration from a heaving ground surface without articulating either a spatial or functional center. Rather, while it looked like a centrally organized space, it was conceived as a series of spatial striations, an integration of smooth, feltlike spatial strips that appear not as whole cloth but as a series of linear elements. The disjunction between the inside and the outside becomes critical to this condition of irresolution.

The Staten Island project began with a finely gridded Cartesian matte, which was eventually turned into smooth topological strands that retain in their striations a memory of their original gridding. In the twelve diagrams of the process of transformation, the movement from a Cartesian mesh (ground) to a figured set of striations is achieved by passing a flow through the matte, analogous to the pedestrian flow through the ferry terminal. The resultant interior space is not formed by function, nor is it centralized, but appears to be a random overlay of layers revealing spaces which appear and disappear at a glance, not allowing the observer to have a directed route or a fixed gaze. It is the space of a voyeur who can see without being seen, and who at the same time is also seen by unseen eyes.

*   *   *   *   *

In this context, the specter of the spectacle becomes the possibility for a new criticality that is no longer

Staten Island Institute, interior view.

Discussion 4

FRÉDÉRIC MIGAYROU My first question, for Peter Eisenman, concerns the unity of the outside world of architecture that he defines as spectacle. How is it possible to create a new interrelation between architecture and the people who are living in it?

PETER EISENMAN I'm interested in the possibility that a critical consciousness about the body – as opposed to cartoons and Mickey Mouse – proposes a way of dealing with another kind of affect. Of course, I get nervous listening to Lars Spuybroek speak about affect because, as Rosalind Krauss said to me, Lars makes Frank Gehry's work look like the Parthenon. This is probably all I can say. In listening to the presentations today, I think we have real problems communicating and understanding what each of us means by affect and the body and reality and space and time. I think we have a lot of things to define before we talk about a general notion of how some new interrelation might happen.

MIGAYROU Bernard Tschumi, along these lines, what is your definition of *event*? In terms of the notion of the body, you reference it in a quite different way than Lars Spuybroek. Is there a constituent experience of architecture different from the disposition of architectural culture?

BERNARD TSCHUMI Let me try to be specific by using an example that does not come from architecture but from filmmaking, and then try to help Peter answer the question he was asked.

EISENMAN Thanks.

TSCHUMI It's so good to be in this room. You know, there is a history of film in this place. In the 1920s, a Russian filmmaker and theorist named Kuleshov devised an experiment involving a figure, the absolutely static face of an actor, in front of a succession of different backgrounds. The first background to this passive face was a series of trees in the wind. Then you saw another shot of the same face – exactly the same, no different – with a railway station with people leaving. A third one showed a war scene. The last one was a domestic scene. Kuleshov would ask the audience what they saw. What expression was on the face of the actor? And it was, of course, quite fascinating to hear that every one of these shots had been perceived as a different expression, a different emotion, on the face of the actor, even though the actor was always the same. Through this, Kuleshov devised a theory of how montage

makes two things work together. Maybe this can help us find a definition for *affect*. It certainly can help us find a definition for event. Event does not exist without the space in which it takes place. Events in architecture are intensely related; they cannot be separated – architecture becomes different. When Peter showed his slides, very consciously I'm sure, he showed a picture of the Staten Island museum, once with a background of New York City, of lower Manhattan, and then with the background of the River Seine on the Right Bank. I felt as if I was witnessing the Kuleshov effect. My reaction was one of horror – I was horrified with the New York thing – wow, what a shocking vision. But I felt very comfortable with Peter's building here in Paris. Now, Peter, tell me about what you were trying to do.

EISENMAN What interests me about history and events is that they are pure fiction. If you saw in my slides a picture of Paris, then someone slid it into my slide tray without my knowledge, which could be the case, since the people who prepare my slides often test me to see if I am aware of what I'm talking about. I guess I missed it.

MARK TAYLOR My question concerns the relationship of Peter's remarks to Rosalind's. If I understood you correctly, Peter, you're worried about a loss of a certain kind of criticality that's in the notion of spectacle as it has emerged. And yet, again if I understood what you were saying correctly, criticality is not a necessary element of spectacle. There is a certain potential for a certain criticality in a certain inscription of spectacle. Rosalind, if I understood you correctly, especially your closing remarks on Bilbao, you have a similar concern about the role of spectacle in architecture. But it wasn't clear to me whether you agree with the potential, or possibility, for a kind of critical role for spectacle or not. In other words, is the reading of spectacle that you're both working with similar on this point of its critical potential or lack thereof?

ROSALIND KRAUSS I am very interested in Peter's development of what I heard him suggesting, which is that within spectacle itself it is possible to wrest a kind of logic, and in doing so you could get some kind of a critical relationship to spectacle. I would be really interested to see how that would work. The idea that there are all these phenomena that I understand to be maligned phenomena, like spectacle, but that we might be able to convert from within – to engage with them in a way in which we are both inside them and able to be critical of them – seems to me to be a gambit that we saw operating within cultural studies as it developed in the 1980s; the idea that there is a liberating aspect of consumption. It was sort of shopping as a form of resistance. A whole, rather obvious discourse developed about how you could read Harlequin romances, not intellectually, not as a form of anomie, but as a liberating event for the women who consumed that sort of trashy literature. This seems to have been interesting for about a minute and a half, but it's become very obvious that there is no resistance, that this sort of theory is inside the worst forms, the most debilitating forms of capital exploitation. I really think we have to question it and be very, very suspicious of it. I don't mean to say that I would have to reject it from the outset. If Peter thinks he can wrest some form of criticality from within spectacle itself, I would be incredibly interested to see that happen.

EISENMAN Where architecture, I think, differs from the other visual arts is that no client I know is going to hire an architect to produce a critical project, that is, to produce a project of negativity about either their being or their corporation. Therefore, how is it possible to build a critical project in architecture when this is precisely what clients are not interested in? And not only are they not interested in critical projects, they're not interested in any form of ideology other than the one they subscribe to. That self-subscribed ideology is supposed to be hidden in certain aesthetic manipulations. I was trying to suggest that to dismiss outright a corporate client or the sudden collapse of media into the spectacle without examining the history of this relationship, how it has been used and how it operated at certain times, would be to throw away an interesting possibility. That's really all I was saying. At the end of my talk I said that Staten Island was a very dangerous project for us because it bordered on the spectacular. It bordered on being consumed by the very constituency that, if they knew what it was, would be against it – by the way, a very conservative constituency, the most conservative constituency in New York. The real issue is, how is it possible to maintain a critical project? Because, you see, no one realizes that there isn't a Grand Central type space with glorious light coming in, etc. We have never showed the model of the project to anybody because they would run like crazy if they thought that's what we were building. Now, I know that Giuseppe Terragni showed a model of the Casa del Fascio to the people, who voted it in, and then he built something completely different. They were absolutely horrified when this thing started coming out of the ground. They said, "Well this isn't what we thought we had approved." I don't know how architects can operate other than in some kind of subterfuge in attempting to make their preferred buildings appear. This is what I was saying about a disjunction between appearances and the facts of a situation; we may be forced to

work with appearances that seem at first glance to be critical or consumable, when in fact the actual reality is not the case. I am interested in projects that can't be photographed. That is, they can't be consumed by media, or they're not designed to be media. It's interesting that many of the architects I know design only the postcard view of a project and that's it. To try and overcome this tendency is one of the things we are talking about today.

GREG LYNN Maybe I could provoke the panel, because there's a calmness that I was deeply disturbed by when Rosalind said that only as media is replaced with its latest incarnation can a true aesthetic emerge from the media that's being outdated. I personally find that deeply troubling. I came up with two ways out of this issue. First, isn't that more of a historical position about aesthetics than a theoretical position about aesthetics? Because one could see in any number of instances a theory of a media before the emergence of the media itself. The second way out would be to argue that in some ways media and commerce are not so much threatening art practice as becoming more artistic than ever before. Instead of saying that art is turning into media and needs to be replaced by some new moment in order to be aesthetic, the fact is that media is becoming more and more aesthetic all the time. I'm wondering if at some point in the future corporate media might be more artistic than art practices.

KRAUSS Well, that, of course, is the argument that Fredric Jameson makes – that there is no aesthetic domain anymore because everything is aesthetic. There's been such an explosion that no simple distinction exists anymore. So, in response to the question whether there can be any autonomy, Jameson's answer would be no, autonomy is finished. He would agree with you there. I feel that as beings with the capacity to make choices, and not simply submit to our masters, we have to somehow wrest autonomy back. I do certainly appreciate that architects have to build for clients and that those clients are corporate clients. Somebody this morning asked how much freedom you have as an architect; whether you are really serving a group of masters that you're utterly beholden to. Obviously this is a very, very sensitive issue. It's one that you all have to talk about. Not being an architect, I can't talk about it, but I think there are artists now who really feel that to play into the hands of the sort of inevitability of the technological and the cybernetic is incredibly dangerous, and they wish to pull back in various, specific ways.

TSCHUMI I'd like to return a question to Greg. You used the word *media*, but media has at least two meanings, a little bit like the word *opera* – the opera is both the building and the performance, right? Media is also both the means of communication, let's say the technology, and the mode of communication – in other words, the ideology. We use the word *media* without making a distinction between the two. There is a risk, then, of misunderstanding that the means of communication, in other words, the technology, is something that can be diverted, turned toward goals for which it was not designed, and therefore be a place of freedom. The mode itself, how it is used by the prevalent society, by the establishment, the people in power, is something else altogether. My concern these days is that the status of the media is not a technological issue but a cultural issue – for example, the Gulf War aestheticized on our TV screens. In the same way, the general media, especially in America, will only talk in aesthetic terms when it examines architectural issues. It will only talk about what a building looks like in terms of the spectacle, because everybody understands a spectacle.

ENRIC MIRALLES Media, in relation to communication, in a way goes too far out of our hands. One becomes almost like a spectator, not at a spectacle but of the thing that is happening, which detaches us from our work. Currently my office is in the middle of designing the Scottish parliament. We are completely confused because we are subject to brutal attacks in the press about every act, every comment we make, everything we do.

IGNASI DE SOLÀ-MORALES I would like to say to Peter that it's very dangerous to use the Guy Debord idea of spectacularization, because spectacularization for Debord is basically related to commodities, and then you relate that commodity to the Guggenheim in Bilbao. It's true that through the media the building appears as a spectacle, but it's no less true that the Guggenheim is an important tool for political action – political action in a Basque territory that basically identifies itself with terrorism. This is to suggest that there is an important effect that is not architectonic but political. Architecture is as polysemous as other cultural productions. Today there is something very ambiguous called "city marketing," which has to do with the development of cities and which plays a very important game. We are now in a city, Paris, that recently played a key role in this regard. The main investments, the so-called *Grands Projets* of Mitterrand, were basically a city marketing strategy.

EISENMAN In my presentation, I was trying to make a distinction between Albert Speer's involvement at Nuremburg and Frank Gehry's involvement at Bilbao. First of all, when I was at Bilbao, a group of Basque separatists came to make a

protest, a mediated protest. They had a huge banner; they stood in front of the building and waited for the TV cameras to come; the TV cameras came and filmed for a minute; then the protesters all high-fived and off they went. There was no intentionality on Frank Gehry's part to participate in this kind of thing. Speer's participation was very different. I was trying to suggest that we have to be careful not to involve ourselves a la prima in the situation that Speer found himself in. I was not suggesting that Gehry had anything to do with that kind of involvement. It so happens that the building lends itself to being photographed for just such media experiences.

LARS SPUYBROEK You can never control the way people photograph your building. I mean, there's no way that you can paint crosses on the pavement to show where the photographer should stand.

EISENMAN I never said you could.

SPUYBROEK No, but if you build a building, it will automatically be absorbed into the media. It will always find its way in.

EISENMAN The difference, Lars, is that Speer's Nuremburg project was set up as media. It was set up to be mediated.

SPUYBROEK But there's no way that one can build a building that is not already mediated. We think media; we live media. We are surrounded by media. I spend half of my day connected to some kind of wire or another: in my car, at my computer, the television, whatever. We constantly occupy this – I wouldn't even call it mediated space – media. You can either use it or misuse it. The technology itself is enormous, but it is no longer a medium between one thing and another, like a hammer or a car used to be. Media is much more vague and blurred than any architectural concept of space ever was, and if you build an architectural object, it will immediately plunge into that space, into this blurry atmosphere. You can't control that.

EISENMAN Are you suggesting that it doesn't matter what we do as architects because media will do with it what it wants?

SPUYBROEK No, I would ground a building in two ways, to the earth and the sky; that is, toward something physical and concrete and toward something transient and ephemeral. Both of these conditions are part of media. Throughout this discussion, media has been presented as something bad, controlled and run by people like Bill Gates. But media is so interesting. I mean, we can make architecture out of it. The whole concept of space is already tilted in such a way that media is taking over. The old concept of the polis was constructed by architectural means, but with media you can never talk in terms of space or perspective again. So why use space or perspective again in a building?

MIRALLES I think it's difficult to talk about these issues because we all just talk about what we really feel is necessary for explaining our thoughts or our working methodologies. For instance, I really admire the slides you showed, Lars, and the ideas you discussed, but I felt that the computer images that generated those ideas were completely unnecessary. This is where we should be able to criticize ourselves – the tools we employ, and whether we really need them or not. For example, how much do we really rely on media, in terms of communication, to produce our buildings? How much do we really need media and the specific techniques of representation to deal with our thoughts? The building that you showed was completely formed in your mind. It has nothing to do with the computer images that you showed. It was very beautiful, a fantastic image, but I think that you have a thought in your head and then you use the computer as a kind of mirror. Like the mirror in the bathroom – you look at yourself in the morning and say, "Aha, I have an idea." It happens sometimes. In the case of Albert Speer, media was absolutely necessary. Without media, we could say that the project wouldn't exist. But in the case of Gehry, I have the feeling that the project could exist without media.

TSCHUMI I think the discussions taking place today are fascinating, touching upon issues of the event, issues of the spectacle, and, of course, issues of the media. But when media is discussed I get worried about the inevitable confusions – that media is all around us, yet we cannot control it, and so on. I understand that Paul Virilio is not going to come to the conference today, so I'm going to quote him on something which was in a slightly different context, but which I think is very useful: "The difference between the technology of construction and the construction of technology." In other words, one could say that architects are not necessarily involved in the technology of construction but, inversely, should be involved with the construction of technology. Substitute media for construction, and I would be more inclined to say that architects should not be involved with the media of construction but with the construction of the media. I'm absolutely convinced that we have a certain amount of power in directing interpretation, and that we should not see ourselves as the victims of an overall ideology that surrounds us. Architects have been extremely good at literally building up history – preparing the ground on which our work has been

interpreted. Many people around this table have had that accusation leveled at them. I think we have the power that the media always denies us. The general media always says, "You should not talk about your work; you should build. We will talk about it." But architecture now is beginning to follow the art scene of the 1960s, when artists started to say what they were trying to do rather than waiting for the critic's interpretation. So in this sense I find it absolutely fundamental that we be involved with the construction of the media as well, and not only with the media of construction.

AUDIENCE I have a question about systems theory for Peter Eisenman and Lars Spuybroek. Peter said that it was important for him in his architecture to question reality at the same time that it is reality – a questioning of reality in reality. Now, a German sociologist once defined the function of the system of art in modern society as the function of questioning reality within reality. So to me it seems that what Peter is presenting is the question of how architecture could be part of the system of arts in modern society. Only art has this function – questioning and, at the same time, making reality from within reality. This is why we have art in our modern society. So, on the one hand, we have good modern artists doing architecture, perhaps even with a specific means of architecture, as Rosalind Krauss was asking for. And on the other hand, we have Lars Spuybroek talking about structural couplings. These couplings are precisely about linking the undifferentiated, what you get between systems. Either we go for undifferentiation or we go for de-differentiation in architecture. Each one obviously produces different results.

EISENMAN Yesterday Frédéric mentioned Corbu's Maison Dom-ino and that when it was put forward, in 1914, it was a critical gesture. It was not an explanation of a new means of construction. It was an attempted critical gesture, just as Corbu's five points and four compositions were each critical gestures. Now, those same gestures put forward today wouldn't have any criticality because all of the systems and discourses that we're operating in have changed. I would argue that there remains, in every discourse, an autonomous condition that remains autonomous until it is brought into a state of criticality. In other words, it's already there, perhaps repressed by normalcy or traditional typologies or traditional ways of looking at things. The minute it becomes operative it could become critical material, but then that critical material is absorbed into a normal condition and we have to look again within that autonomous material to find a new criticality. That's the situation I find myself in, and I think it's a repetitive cycle. I believe, for example, that Bramante created autonomous material out of the work of Brunelleschi and Alberti so that Palladio could make critical material, which then was absorbed into the English country house and became normalized. I believe that throughout history we're involved in finding these kinds of autonomous materials to become critical, which then get absorbed into a normal condition.

FRANCO PURINI Bernard Tschumi spoke earlier of a dialectic between homogeneity and heterogeneity, and about the introduction of certain forms of incompatibility. Now, looking at his project under construction, we can see that it is built on the model of gradation. It's an old model of composition that has been known from the earliest stages of the history of architecture, and I'd like to have some clarification on this point because I think it's important. Similarly, I think that Miralles' project is one that has lost shape – the innovative load and the provocative plastic load have been put at the service of a program of representation. Both Tschumi's and Miralles' projects, therefore, seem to raise the question of representation. After a century that has been endeavoring to negate representation, why are we returning to it? In the 1930s in Italy we used to say that there was a problem in returning to order, the problem of standardizing avant-garde research in order to bring it back to a practical, communicative level. I think that the spectacular that we talked about this afternoon is indeed the distance between a thing and its constitution. The real architect, it seems, does not want to represent this. He wants to hide his building. The problem for me is, how can we hide the spectacular quality as a contradiction between a visual reality and its raison d'être?

TSCHUMI Franco, I'm very happy that you are making a specific criticism, because the mode of analysis that you suggest is exactly the one that I am questioning. I would argue that this mode is based on typologies, on morphologies, and on composition. You said that the school was a model of composition known since the beginning of the history of architecture. So what? Why not? In other words, there are certain typologies, certain organizations of space, that are used to define an interior space and that have been there for a long time. In the same way, I have been attacked for a building [Lerner Center] that I'm doing in New York where I use certain elements based on 19th-century neoclassical typologies. But this is not what the project is about. In many ways these things are used as found objects, as things that preexist. It's simply in their rearrangement, in order to provoke a number of situations, that the architecture lies. It's not about conditioning a design but about designing conditions. In this particular case, the conditions are what I'm interested in.

Whether the building is going to use poured concrete, whether it will have ramps or not – this is not the issue. A lot of the work that I've been involved with, including that building, is about a certain type of programmatic invention. At no moment did you discuss this issue of program. I'm not interested in composition; I'm interested in the form of montage, however old-fashioned that may be.

MIRALLES *La vie c'est difficile*. I don't know what to say, because you establish through your work a direction with existing bodies of knowledge. Composition is a series of rules that repeat. I think that through composition one can find the opposites, the differences between architects. I feel, for instance, that between your work, Bernard, and my work, there are a lot of differences. But then we could establish a kind of dialogue. We could share mutual interests. In the end we could discuss basic things, like transparency. Peter says, "I'm interested in not showing the inside on the outside." I really don't care if he shows the inside or the outside. The only thing I care about is a certain ambiguity, a certain kind of doubt posed by the building – for example, the way Peter talks about the building both as an organization of bits and then as a whole, unique space.

AUDIENCE What are the new means for transgressing feelings of space in architecture? I'm not talking about models or drawings or computer programs that make promises of a real, physical, architectural future, but about more straightforward expression; the casting of wood in concrete, for example. And from there, maybe the panel can talk about the critical project – what is the critical project in architecture?

SPUYBROEK I like to avoid any criticism or any criticality in my projects. I think that if you start a project with a criticism of typology, with a criticism of structure, or a criticism of media, then suddenly you become caught up in a dialectic that won't lead you anywhere. So when I start with the idea of media, I don't criticize the medium but rather I misuse it, experiment with it, not trying to read anything into media but trying, like artists do nowadays, to invent something within media, or within technology, that brings me into another architecture. This is a sort of mutant way of working with technology – trying to invent through media something that you can generate as an operative means in architecture to create architecture. Using media as a pure diagrammatic tool to create matter.

MIGAYROU But according to this view, Peter Eisenman also uses media in this way.

EISENMAN Frédéric, you always say these things to me, and I always have to say yes, it's true!

YONA FRIEDMAN I think that any built building is media, and it is media for a very long time – far longer than its imagined life span. I also think that when we speak about a communication process, this process should include a public. You only spoke about communication in terms of the tools of architecture, in construction. But there is another residue of meaning at the other end, when a building is completed and is absorbed, as a built message, into a public arena.

RENATO RIZZI I think that architecture has to be critical so as to engage critics in thinking about architecture. Critics, though, tend to be drawn to technique – technique in the most general sense – as the fundamental body of knowledge for Western civilization. Technique, as I see it, is not the tools of the discipline, but it has a theological, metaphysical significance. Mark Taylor could explain this far better than I, but technique is what makes every object isolated, autonomous. So I agree with Peter when he says that architecture has to be critical, but critical of what?

EISENMAN I would like to say one thing that I think is very amusing about this problem of architecture and the critical. None of us architects, art critics, theorists, and historians would be here today if we were not engaged in what we thought was a critical project. Bernard, like many of the teachers and architects here, trains his students in Alias and Silicon Graphics computer techniques. People who want to get involved in the "real world" go into animation and begin to work for Disney and Microsoft and other corporations at enormous salaries. They come out of architecture school and immediately make four or five times what architects typically make. I think that anybody who goes into architecture is already taking on, for some dumb reason, a critical project, because it is no way to make money today, given the kinds of skills and techniques that architects are trained with. For instance, I asked somebody the other day to do a Web site for me, and he said, "It'll cost you $20,000." That's what lawyers charge. I can't afford to tell a client, "Yes, we would like to do a project, but before we look at it you have to give us $20,000." That wouldn't be possible. So, given the commodification of society and where we are as architects, we are nowhere in terms of real commodification. We don't have to worry about being critical projects. We are critical projects.

5. Anymore Technology?

Architectural imagination is stimulated by new technology, be it condensed in objects such as airplanes and spacecraft or diffused in digital systems. The most remarkable input here is not related to building technology in the narrow sense but is due to the broader realm of models, processes, and visual schemes produced by science and industry. Can architecture's inventiveness inform technological culture? Or is architecture the passive receptacle of technical strategies that constantly redefine its space of action?

Digital Semper
Bernard Cache

"Digital Semper." To put these two words together seems like a contradiction in terms. Starting with an analysis of the first word, however, I will try and dismantle the apparent contradiction.

L'atelier Objectile, which I created with Patrick Beaucé, experiments with technologies in architecture by focusing primarily on software development in order to digitally design and manufacture building components. Beginning with a period dedicated to building research, furniture design, and sculpture, we worked for more than ten years with the French company TOPCAD in designing complex surfaces in order to debug our developing software. Three years ago we created Objectile and started to focus our work on flat and supposedly simpler components like panels or doors in order to tackle the problems generated by the industrial production of varying elements.

Industrial production forces us to confront many basic problems like zero-error procedures and stress-free MDF panels. A key element in digital manufacturing is to avoid bending a panel when machining one of its faces. Our experience now enables us to think of a fully digital architecture like our museum project and the pavilion we recently built on the occasion of the Archilab conference in Orléans. The four elements of this pavilion are the result of previous experiments with screens, panels, and tabletops. In that process, we noticed that our approach had a clear affinity to Gottfried Semper's theory as he articulated it in Der Stil (1863) not only because we come to architecture through the technical arts, or because we came to invent new materials in order to create new designs, but because our interest in decorative wooden panels is consistent with Semper's Bekleidung Prinzip (cladding principle). Even our investigations into the generation of software to map key elements of modern topology, like knots and interlacing, consist of a contemporary transposition of Semper's Urmotive or primitive pattern.

What does it mean today to refer to Gottfried Semper? Why, in 1999, should we look back to the 19th century just as everybody claims the 21st will be digital? And why focus on Semper, whose architecture seems to reveal nothing but the Renaissance historicism rejected by the Moderns?[1] Are we not in a very different period? We live in an age not of iron but silicon. Why would we need to reconnect the end of our iron, concrete, and glass century to the history of wood, stone, clay, and textiles? Do we not run the risk of a new technological determinism, by which the information age, the so-called "third wave," would create a second break with the past, definitively negating any historical experience, leaving us with no alternative other than a choice between the dinosaurs and the space shuttle? Or should we not instead be reminded that information technologies themselves are deeply rooted in the past? The computer is not an Unidentified Flying Object that landed one day in a California garage.

Let us recall a few examples of current computing issues that lead us back to the 19th century, if not earlier. We could begin with the Fast Fourier Transform Integrated Circuits, which you can find in any digital television set. Joseph Fourier, who discovered the mathematical method for coding the picture of the future, had worked alongside Champolion, his companion on Napoleon's expedition to Egypt, and who had found a way to decode hieroglyphs (1822) with the help of Quatremère de Quincy's cousin. We could also cite Sadi Carnot, inventor of the Second Law of Thermodynamics (1824) that Richard Feynman, the great physicist hired by IBM, paired with Maxwell's Demon (1867) in his 1996 lectures about "Reversible computation and the thermodynamics of computing"[2] – lectures whose topic is the long-term future of the computer. We could also discuss the all too familiar, yet often misinterpreted, chaos theory, the mathematics of which were worked out by Henry Poincaré. Recently, Michel Serres has brilliantly demonstrated how these mathematics share a common structure with Claude Debussy's musical composition, as well as with Charles Péguy's book on history, Clio, ou dialogue de l'histoire et de l'âme paienne.[3] And, last but not least, we could mention the integration of Desargues's geometry into modern CAD software.

Even if computer science cannot contemplate its future without returning to old debates, we should certainly expect architecture to benefit from reacquainting itself with its past in order to take advantage of information technology. We believe that cyberspace need not lead to cultural amnesia. We believe that innovation can be linked to history, without the return of a prehistory or the advent of a science fiction.

Our interest in Semper stems from his concise articulation of technology and history in architecture. But today we will leave aside the anthropological aspect of Semper's conception of history in order to focus instead on the structure of his theory, which I will summarize in the following four propositions:

1. Architecture, as with the other fine arts, finds its fundamental motivation in the technical arts.
2. The four major technical arts are: textiles, ceramics, tectonics, and stereotomy.
3. Among these four technical arts, textiles lend many aspects to the other three techniques.
4. The knot is the fundamental mode of textiles, and therefore of architecture, inasmuch as this monumental art is subordinated to the cladding principle (Das Bekleidung Prinzip).

This, of course, is too straightforward a summary, for when we get into the matter and read Semper's text carefully, we quickly realize that these summations are complicated further. Immediately following his introduction, Semper enunciates the four categories of materials according to physical criteria. Materials can be pliable, like fabrics; soft, like clay; elastic, sticklike elements, like wood; or dense, like stone. Semper then immediately switches to the second enunciation of four categories, no longer distinguishing materials but activities, or what we will call procedures. These are the famous technical arts: textiles; ceramics; tectonics (i.e., carpentry); and stereotomy (i.e., masonry).

At first sight, the second list seems to be redundant, given the first one. But then Semper makes a series of puzzling remarks. He tells us that "Not only have the four categories to be understood in a wider sense, but one should be aware of the numerous and reciprocal relations that link them together." To be sure, each of the four techniques applies to a privileged material from which originated the primeval motives. Nevertheless, procedures were also developed for each of the other materials. Thus, ceramics should not be restricted to earthenware but should also include objects made out of all kinds of materials, like metal, glass, and stone. Equally, brickwork, tiles, and mosaics, although made out of clay, should not be directly related to ceramics but rather to stereotomy and textiles, considering the fact that they are used both to compose masonry works and as cladding materials for the walls themselves. Semper follows with various other examples, creating a rather disconcerting impression. Textiles can no longer be considered to be made out of fabrics, and clay does not suffice to explain ceramics. All four technical arts remain abstract categories elaborated throughout the pioneering Der Stil.

However, things become clearer if we switch from a linear reading to a tabular one. The two lists of materials and procedures, far from paralleling one another, should rather be articulated as a table (table 1), since we can find occurrences of each type of material for every type of procedure. Semper himself briefly explains his methodology in the second chapter of the introduction. Each technical art must be analyzed from two perspectives. One should first look at what he calls "the general-formal aspect" (Allgemein Formelles), which accounts for the intention or the purpose (Zwecklichkeit) of the works. Only afterward should one consider "the technical-historical aspects" (Technisch-Historisches) and analyze how these intentions or purposes have been realized throughout history, according to various local factors. Semper illustrates these two approaches by taking the example of the strip which holds an object in the shape of a ring. Semper points out that in the general-formal analysis, "One should only consider certain characteristics, so to speak, abstract, which relates to the strip as something that links, while the question of its various forms, according to the expression of the concept within linen, silk, wool, and in wood, baked clay, stone or metal, should be relegated to the historical-technical analysis."[4] We have then, on one side, the general procedure of linking, and on the other, the various materials through which this procedure is applied. But then Semper warns us that one cannot expect too much rigor in the distinction of the two approaches, since the function of a product also requires the use of appropriate materials. Hence the abstract procedure cannot be thought of in isolation from the historical material.

Table 1 Historical and traditional materials

Abstract Procedures	Textile	Ceramics	Tectonics or Carpentry	Stereotomy or Masonry
Fabric				
Clay				
Wood				
Stone				

The table prevents an oversimplified reading of Semper's system; a reductiveness that I was lucky enough to avoid in two, opposing ways. While Alois Riegl complained about the materialist reading of the so-called Semperians, according to which art forms would be strictly determined by materials, Otto Wagner, in his Modern Architecture (1896), criticized Semper's symbolist approach (although he could not help placing wreath-bearing angels on the top of his 1903 modern Post Office in Vienna). Riegl focused on the material, while Wagner isolated the abstract procedure from the material, each considering only one single part of Semper's system. More generally, this tabular structure explains why the style of Der Stil makes reading Semper so complex and consequently so prone to oversimplification. Semper approaches and returns from his major themes like the weaver's shuttle passes over and under weft threads (table 2). His thinking on the surface is hard to account for in the linearity of his writing, which would explain why two of Semper's key arguments, that of the knot and that of the mask, find their ultimate development only in footnotes.

Table 2 Historical and traditional materials

Abstract Procedures	Textile	Ceramics	Tectonics	Stereotomy
Fabric	Carpets, rugs, flags, curtains	Animal skin flask, ex: Egyptian situla		Patchwork?
Clay	Mosaic, tiles, brickwork cladding	Vase-shape earthenware, ex: Greek hydria		Brickwork masonry
Wood	Decorative wooden panels	Barrels	Furniture, carpentry	Marquetry
Stone	Marble and other stone cladding	Cupola	Trabeated system	Massive stonework, Goldsmith's

In a way, we could argue that the structure of this table has been worked out by Semper himself, inasmuch as we could consider that writing is only one of many modes of thinking – a type of intellectual activity among which we could also posit architecture (Ut scriptura architectura [table 3]). Indeed, in the proposal given to the approval committee, Semper explained how the two museums built in Vienna, the Art History Museum and the Natural History Museum, illustrate the

Top: Objectile, door, 1998; bottom: Objectile, panel, 1999.

dualities of his practice and his theory, between his writings and his buildings. Harry Francis Mallgrave has brilliantly commented on the structure of the facades of these monumental pieces of architecture.[5] In the Art History Museum, each of the three stories was assigned a specific iconography related to one of the three factors affecting the development of primitive patterns according to Semper's definition of style. The ground story is dedicated to the materials of the various technical arts (what Semper called the external factors). Moving upward, the main floor is dedicated to the social and religious conditions of art, and the statues on the roof reify the individuals who opened significant new paths in art (the two types of internal factors). Hence, we have a vertical organization of the facade progressing from the material conditions of art toward its spiritual achievements; in other words, a progression from the material to the immaterial. This vertical progression is articulated with a horizontal opposition between classical and romantic tendencies in each of the arts, Doric being opposed to Ionic, Raphael to Michelangelo, Mozart to Beethoven; oppositions that anticipate later writings like Renaissance und Barok by Heinrich Wölfflin, or Abstraktion und Einfuhlung by Wilhelm Worringer, not to mention The Birth of Tragedy, in which Nietzsche opposed Apollo to Dionysus. So, each facade is organized as a table, and this tabular structure is applied to the four historical epochs allocated to each side of the building: Antiquity, the Middle Ages, the Renaissance, and Semper's present.

Table 3

The built book: The Art History Museum (1869–91)

Roof: Creative individuals

Main story: Social and religious conditions of art

Ground story: Technical arts

Artistic tendencies: Classical, Romantic

The written building: Der Stil (1860–63)

Materials of contemporary architecture

Materials of modern architecture

Materials of traditional architecture

Abstract procedures: Textile, Ceramics, Tectonics, Stereotomy

We could argue that the museum in Vienna constitutes the third volume, built rather than written, of the unfinished Der Stil. At first sight, the museum presents itself as a three-dimensional composition of tables whose height, length, and depth each make up one type of analysis. Actually, the two volumes of Der Stil could themselves be understood as a two-dimensional sub-table of the facade organization. As I already mentioned, in one direction we could find the technical arts, whereas orthogonally, we could find the progression from the material to the immaterial. These two directions are of very different natures. The leitmotiv of Semper is that there are a limited number of abstract procedures,[6] which is why he shows himself to be very parsimonious in counting them

Objectile, Semper Pavilion.

(table 4). Thus, metal is introduced as a material in itself and, rightly or wrongly, Semper did not associate a specific procedure with it. Metal only provides another media for the development of each of the four abstract procedures, especially that of textiles. Semper goes back to embossed Greek statuary to advocate metal as cladding or, at least, as a hollow structure that provides an alternative to the thin, cast-iron columns of Joseph Paxton's Crystal Palace. In this way, the fact that Semper fails to mention any procedure specific to this material should be taken as an indication that he disregarded it. Behind his claim for monumental columns lies a very modern conception of metal construction as hollow structure.

Table 4 Historical and traditional materials (including metal)

Abstract Procedures	Textile	Ceramics	Tectonics	Stereotomy
Fabric	Carpets, rugs, flags, curtains	Animal skin flask, ex: Egyptian situla		Patchwork?
Clay	Mosaic, tiles, brickwork cladding	Vase-shape earthenware, ex: Greek hydria		Brickwork masonry
Wood	Decorative wooden panels	Barrels	Furniture, carpentry	Marquetry
Stone	Marble and other stone cladding	Cupola	Trabeated system	Massive stonework, Goldsmith's
Metal	Hollow metal cladded statuary; Olympian Jupiter reconstituted by Quatremère de Quincy; metal roofing; articulated metal structures; curtain wall	Metal vases or shells	Cast iron columns	Forge, ironworks

In the other direction, that of materials, the number of cases seems, on the contrary, to be limitless. Not only does Semper dedicate a full chapter to metal, in addition to the four privileged materials, but there are also many references to various other materials such as glass. Therefore, the openness of Semper's theory is due to the possibility of introducing new materials (table 5). It would be very interesting to see how reinforced concrete would fit in Semper's scheme and how much his theory would be able to account for the modern triumverate of metal, concrete, and glass. Even more pertinent would be an evaluation of Semper's theory with regard to those materials that he would have called more spiritual and that we would simply designate as more immaterial, in the sense that they deal with lower energies. In this category would fall both biology and information technologies.

As for biology, I will only briefly mention the fact that Semper was in Paris in 1830, at the key moment of the debate opposing Baron Georges Cuvier to Geoffrey Saint-Hilaire. The core of the problem was Cuvier's refusal of Saint-Hilaire's establishing a continuity between his four animal categories.

If one looks closely at Cuvier's four categories – the mollusks, the radiates, the vertebrates, and the articulated – they would appear to share a common geometric structure with Semper's four corresponding abstract procedures. It would be too involved to get into this matter here, but I would like to emphasize the fact that the abstract procedures should not be thought of as Platonic ideals, independent from the materials to which they are applied. On the contrary, it would be in the nature of these procedures to look relentlessly for more "immaterials" in order to find a new occasion for their progressive abstraction.[7] Thus, information technologies would not simply be accidentally accounted for by Semper's theory; it would be in their very nature to fit into his system as the best vehicle to push the abstraction of the four technical procedures further. Far from being limited to fabrics, textiles could be the procedure of going alternatively over and under, what in terms of information technology is called modulation. In turn, distinct from pottery, ceramics could deal with revolving solids and operations in radial coordinates as opposed to tectonics, which could deal with nonrotational transformations adequately described in Cartesian coordinates. And finally, stereotomy could be the art of tiling and paving as it results from Boolean operations. Taken as a whole, we would have described the interface of a Semperian computer-aided-design software.

Table 5 Materials of Modern and Contemporary Architecture

Abstract Procedures	Textile	Ceramics	Tectonics	Stereotomy
Metal	Hollow metal cladded statuary; Olympian Jupiter reconstituted by Quatremère de Quincy; metal roofing; articulated metal structures; curtain wall	Metal vases or shells	Cast iron columns	Forge, ironworks
Concrete	Prefabricated concrete screens; light warps; curtain wall	Ruled surfaces, like: hyperbolic paraboloid	Slabs on stilts	
Glass	Thermoformed glass; curtain wall	Blown glass	System glued glass (pictet)	Glass bricks
Biology	Mollusks	Radiates, D'AT: Surfaces de Plateau	Vertebrates, D'AT: squeletons and bridge structures	Articulated D'AT: bees' cells
Information	Modulation interlacing (Eurythmy)	Revolving solid, polar coordinates	Translation, Cartesian coordinates	Boolean operation, tiling algorithms

Of course, this remains a hypothesis so long as this software has yet to materialize. And it is not necessary to offer an uncritical acceptance of the closed number of four procedures. But we can find enough interesting arguments in Semper's text itself. The definition of ceramics as a revolving operation rests much less on the technical gesture of the lathe than on the classification table that Semper borrowed from Jules Ziegler. As Mallgrave reminds us, Ziegler was a painter who worked for several years on the murals of La Madeleine church and established a classification of ceramics on the basis of the rotation and deformation of two simple geometric figures: the square and the circle. Interestingly enough, Ziegler conceived his Etudes Céramiques as 24 Cartesian meditations.

More relevant to our own practice is the concept of modulation, which is not at all foreign to Der Stil. One could even say that it is the key concept of the Prolegomena. It is what, under the name of Eurythmy, Semper conceived of as the Gestaltungsprinzip. Eurythmy was first introduced as the principle of all regular closed figures, like snowflakes or crystals, but also architectural frames and cornices. Semper articulated a more general definition: "Eurythmy consists in the sequencing of spatial intervals displaying analogue configuration." This very general definition benefited from further specification. Sequences may be mere repetition, as in the dentils on Greek temples, or an alternation, as when a minor element is inserted between the repeating major elements like the triglyphs and the metopes, again on the frieze of Greek temples. Here, the principle of alternation becomes the rhythmic repetition of unequal parts. Beyond these two sequences, the eye would accept that the simple repetition and alternation be periodically interrupted, as in the Renaissance balustrade. There Semper points out additional levels of complication used when one wants to get rid of rigid architectural sequences to achieve the delightful confusion of lace and interlacing. At that point the reader is directed to the chapters dedicated to textiles.

This suggests that a close reading of Semper allows us at least to test the hypothesis of an identification of textiles with modulation when the former deals with electronic materials instead of fabrics. This association of textiles to modulation occurs through the concept of eurythmy, which is nothing other than the description of modulation techniques (with their various parameters of amplitude, frequency, and phase), techniques which provide the basis of the algorithms that we use in our practice, for example, to design our Semper Pavilion. The Semperian eurythmy provides us with a mathematical understanding of the concept of concinnitas which, as Caroline van Eck reminds us, was the keystone of Alberti's De re aedificatoria. Renaissance aesthetics should certainly not be reduced to a theory of proportions; but the fact that the concept of concinnitas encapsulates the sub-concepts of oppositio and varietas does not preclude a mathematical interpretation of Alberti's De re aedificatoria if we understand the encapsulated specifications as oppositions or variations of amplitude, frequency, and phase. This is precisely what Semper is hinting at in the fourth section of his book, dedicated to stereotomy. Commenting on the architectural proportions of the Doric order, he underscores the fact that the interval of the interco-

lumniation decreases from the middle toward the corners of the temples as a continuous variation. Let us not forget that the word modulation comes from the Latin modulum, which originally designated the diameter of the column to be used as a reference unit in the relationships of proportion. Therefore, by reading Semper's Der Stil on an abstract plane, rather than literally, we can draw many lessons from architectural history in view of a contemporary practice. In other words, Semper allows us to confront Euclid and Vitruvius. Could we not then look at the Renaissance style of Semper's architecture outside of mere historicism?

Against all claims of Semper himself, it seems that the German architect kept the very heart of the treatises of his Latin predecessors. What is so surprising in Vitruvius is his concept of transposition. Regardless of whether the motifs in stone, such as triglyphs, have their origin in wood, as Vitruvius argued, or in fabrics, as Semper would propose, the general principle is that the forms and proportions of the architectural orders are technically determined. Nevertheless, this determination does not come from the actual material but via procedures associated with another material, which then have to be transposed (table 6). There is, then, a material determination in architecture, but it only appears through a process of transposition, a process which manifests itself in the stone pediment ending the series of wooden trusses that support the roof of Greek temples. The pediment transposes the wooden structure of the trusses in stone. The word transposition is the translation of what Semper termed Stoffwechsel in German – "material transformation" in English – which brings us back to biology, since this was the word used by Semper's friend Moleschott in describing the metabolism of plants and animals.

Table 6 Vitruvian and Semperian transposition

Abstract Procedures	Textile	Ceramics	Tectonics or Carpentry	Stereotomy or Masonry
Fabric	(Semperian)			
Clay	( )			
Wood	( )		(Vitruvian)	
Stone	( )		(transposition)	
Metal	( )			
Concrete	( )			
Glass	( )			
Information	(transposition)			

So, rather than contradicting Vitruvius's theory, Semper raised it to a higher level. The origin of architecture is no longer unique, since it comes from four technical arts, and, we might add, is no longer Greek. We could even say that there are no more origins at all, but instead a composition of several lineages of transposition by which the four abstract procedures constitute themselves by switching from one material to the other. Ut pictura architectura. **Vitruvius** invents the transposition principle, but its application to tectonics in stone as a transposition from wood is only one step within Semper's general table. Architecture emerges in the move from one technology to another. Hence, textiles would today be the abstract procedure emerging within the transposition process that leads us from primitive fabrics to contemporary modulation techniques, while continuously emulating mosaic cladding, wooden panels, and embossed metal. Technical art is a contracting memory as opposed to an engramme.

1 By moderns, I designate the architects of the 20th century who took a strong position against history and ornamentation, which in practice did not prevent them from caring about surfaces and cladding, but actually limited their ornamental design to material textures, washed out coatings (**a-plat**), and rectilinear geometric patterns.
2 Richard P. Feynman, **Lectures on Computation** (Reading, Massachusetts: Addison-Wesley, 1996).
3 Michel Serres, **Éloge de la philosophie en langue française** (Paris: Fayard, 1995).
4 Gottfried Semper, **Der Stil 1860–63**, partially translated in **Gottfried Semper: The Four Elements of Architecture and other Writings**, trans. Harry Francis Mallgrave and Wolfgang Hermann (Cambridge: Cambridge University Press, 1988).
5 In Harry Francis Mallgrave, **Gottfried Semper, Architect of the Nineteenth Century** (New Haven: Yale University Press, 1996). Generally speaking, all of our analyses rely on the considerable and remarkable work done by Mallgrave and Wolfgang Hermann to unearth the history of 19th-century architectural practice and theory.
6 It is true that in the museum, the number of technical arts is six, and that none of them is explicitly textiles, although metal is presented as "hollow metal and embossing," while sculpture in marble could be assimilated into the fine texture of Corinthian as opposed to the rough forms of Doric. Also note that casting could be understood as the imprint.
7 Up to the point of negating matter itself. See Semper in Mallgrave and Hermann: only by fully mastering the technique can an artist forget the matter.

Bernard Cache **is a visiting professor at the Universidad Internacional de Catalunya and at UCLA. He is the author of** Earth Moves **and a contributor to** Libération et Médiapouvoirs.

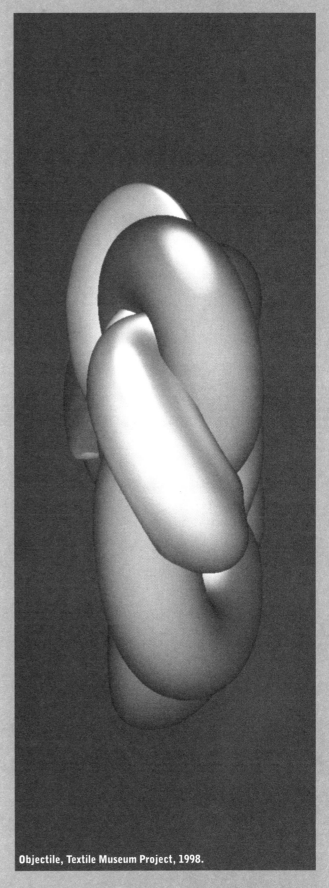

Objectile, Textile Museum Project, 1998.

The Architectural Project:
A Real Virtuality
Marc Mimram

Solfèrino Bridge, Paris, 1999.

Throughout the course of its history, the evolution and transformation of the architectural project has been linked to new developments in production and manufacturing and to the possibilities provided by mathematics. Today, certain observers would like to think that the emergence of virtual projection technology will transform our approach to architecture. I would argue, however, that this is highly unlikely. Rather than reinventing the discipline, these technologies lend a new coherence to the tools of the architectural project (in terms of architectural thought as much as architectural production), lending architecture whatever sense it has of itself. Nothing is achieved by pitting abstract form against real construction, since material, which is indispensable to the condition of architecture, allows for making as much as for thinking.

In the 18th century, indicators of progress centered on developing industries. After Brunelleschi, it was J.R. Peronnet who expanded upon the possibilities of architectural form, thanks largely to developments emerging through methods of construction. For example, the vault became more grand and expansive. In this way, new methods of construction could totally transform the architectural vocabulary, with inspiration, in this case, coming from the opportunities offered by the arch. Charting its evolution, the formal idea prevailed only after its encounter with the real in the form of new technology, the influence of which affects, rather than is affected by, the imaginative capacities of the designer. For example, consider framework and de-arching, and the cylindrical vault disappears, giving way to flattened arches. Consider the angle as the basic element of the structure, and the empty space between the two cupolas in Florence becomes the line of a resolution of forces.

In the 19th century, industry began mass-producing new materials with incredible mechanical characteristics, relocating the traditional scenes of architectural production from the stone quarry to the iron foundry. Later, by enriching iron with carbon, architecture was able to discontinue the use of autonomous girders assembled in space. But how does one separate architecture from these material developments that offer new, expansive, and transparent architectural visions? Previously unimagined formal universes were born out of these new practices – practices further enlarged upon by the theoretical possibilities emerging from the science of resistance of materials in the work recently done by L.M. Navier. From this research came whole assemblages and conditions of support: rivets and joints, laminated products, and lattice frameworks. In a sense, these new materials advertised the discoveries lent to building through science and the iron forge, allowing architecture to anticipate a greater openness of structural rigidity rather than massiveness, of articulation rather than continuity.

In the 20th century, geometry became increasingly predicated upon the rediscovery of polyhedral spaces and the potentialities of surface coverings. Platonic geometry joined differential geometry to give meaning to the "resistance of form." Forces began to appear within the material itself: prestressed by E. Freyssinet, stretched in equilibrium by Buckminster Fuller, as progress began to be measured in kilograms and meters. The architect could then marshal materials in space by abandoning traditional frames of reference; tensions could express themselves

mechanically, while double curves could provide a kind of organization to orthonormal orthodoxy, to the extent that structural designer Robert Le Ricolais could reach for the ideal of an "infinite range accompanied by weightlessness."

Over the last 300 years, the footfall of architecture has recognized structure in terms of materiality, geometry, and construction in a kind of informed formality. Nothing today would lead us to believe that our constructed reality can abstract itself from this reasoned alignment simply to reinvent itself by means of the virtuosity of the virtual. Quite the contrary, the pursuit of good sense passes through the divide between the capacity to open up the imaginary and the commitment to continually encounter the real. Construction does not follow the project; it informs it.

The Real Informs the Virtual

A project is not a linear process that transforms a mental construction into a physical one. At the École des Beaux Arts, the process used to be called "un parti," a contest, though today it is typically called a concept. Everything today seems to favor the confluence of doing and thinking rather than their juxtaposition. Our imaging machines are not isolated objects but have a long interactive history, integrating the project and the factory, the tools of prefiguration, and the tools of production.

For example, in 1989, through a project to design the structure of a passageway in Toulouse, we discovered the interaction between geometry and the shaping of a double-curved sheet of metal. It was then necessary to come up with a structure properly oriented in the landscape that would respond to the distribution of stress in the chosen material. Geometry provided an extremely powerful tool here, supported with the aid of mathematics, in order to address the potentialities of the shaping workshop. The final form arose out of this dual experiment: first, to respect the hypotheses formulated with regard to the site, and second, to work in such a way that the calculations, the manufacture, and the montage give coherence to the projected form. The separate tasks were disparate to begin with, but were then assimilated through the stabilizing influence of geometric principles. Numerical calculations were developed as the form took shape through an encounter with the capabilities of manufacture – in this instance, a sheet-metal shaping machine. It was then necessary, as is the case with a tailored suit, to identify the physical peculiarities of the "client," creating the patterns by cutting the metal in its flat state before bending and placing it in its final form in the designated space.

Ten years have passed, and the processes involved have been integrated further. Calculations are now carried out alongside the virtual project and its image, though the calculations are themselves a virtual, theoretical reality related to a planned structural schema. Today, these two stages are indistinguishable, inasmuch as the calculation tools are directly related numerically to the spatial models. The new defining characteristic is the plurality offered by modelization and integrated calculations.

In this way, this virtual solution is directly related to the process of manufacture today. In our project for the toll plaza at Eprunes, and even more recently for the Solfèrino Bridge in Paris, these same models served to produce the precise cutting of the sheet metal by an automated machine. The machine no longer subjects the project to its ability to reproduce a model, but rather integrates the parameters of the project by introducing the geometrical and structural conditions into the tools of manufacture. The whole process becomes a question of producing a unique product, yet it does so through the use of shared tools of production.

Industrial processes are predicated upon traditional thinking. Architectural and engineering works depend upon a mode of fabrication and are conditioned by its limits, although they are in no way predetermined by it. A greater sense of freedom can be rediscovered not only by the abilities of a skilled working crew, but also by the pursuit of a more craft-based way of thinking, open to the capabilities of industrial production. Integrating the devices of fabrication into the process of the project prolongs the virtual image, confronting it with the properties of the material.

In the high-tension pylons project for the Electricitè de France (EDF), we used mass production in order to construct a unique object. Machines digitally programmed to manufacture tubes — a heavy industrial process of series fabrication — were used in the production of specific elements that would have been impossible to manufacture one by one in the traditional manner. Rising to a height of 70 meters on a base of 1.25 meters, the pylons were rendered possible by the integration of the mode of manufacture, the relevant calculations, and the construction process.

Therefore, the architectural project can be seen to make use of the integration of different stages of production, putting the capabilities of industry at the service of the specific object being built. The architect can no longer take refuge in a world of virtual objects, subjected solely to the risks of form, on the pretext of refusing to abide by Taylorist methods of production. On the contrary, it is necessary for us to integrate the powers offered by the new tools of production and to adapt them to the demands of the architectural project, both in its uniqueness and in its capabilities of representing the resources of our age. Without pitting thinking and doing against each other, this modernity expresses itself at every stage of the project.

Architecture as the Art of Transformation

The purpose of architecture, like that of art, is neither formal nor stylistic. Architecture is an art of transformation. Here we are now taking another look at the production of space (space being a kind of matter), since simple construction situates space in a lengthy process of transformation moving from grand landscape to grand landscape. In effect, nothing we use can be considered outside the process that fashions landscapes and constructs architecture. If one considers that bauxite and coke are extracted from the soil, that carbon is a transformation of coal, that wood is a regenerated material, that plastics come out of petroleum — in a sense, that everything that produces the materiality of architecture belongs to the world, whether mineral or vegetable — then architecture becomes the art of the transformation of the world.

When one also sees that bauxite is extracted in Australia, transformed into aluminum extrusions in Germany, and put to use in structures in France or elsewhere, one realizes that architecture participates in this transformation of the world. And when infrastructural projects necessitate the opening of huge quarries, crushing factories, and the transformation of the Earth's topography, one realizes that in fact a territorial project of landscaping is being undertaken. The inscription of architecture into the lengthy processes of transformation not only makes us belong to a mode of socially determining production, but it makes us players in the metamorphosis of the planet.

Suddenly, this informed view renders architecture attentive, precautionary, more generous. Our work not only is situated in a geography that gives it context, it also comprises an element in the evolution of that geography. How, then, can the work absent itself from the real world and seek refuge in virtual abstraction focused on a formal quest? On the contrary, architecture stakes its relevance in the modern world on belonging to the reality of the world. Our responsibility lies there. Our attention is drawn there.

Architecture is thus rediscovering the materiality of its origins. The choices involved become reasoned, and the materials of the project go beyond any "mappings" of virtual surfaces as they rediscover the pleasures of the senses and give themselves over in lasting attentiveness to the slow process of transformation.

The Materials of Pleasure

This sustained and repeated attentiveness to the materiality of architecture does not imply a pragmatic approach to "build well." Rather, it is a matter of developing a theoretical point of view regarding the materialization of the projected space. Today this approach seems to preoccupy artists more than architects. Richard Serra instructs us as to the texture of thick metal sheeting and of its manufacture. Dan Graham allows us to experiment with the values of the architecturally ignored concept of transparency. James Turrell offers us work on light that far surpasses the plastic approaches of the Modern Movement. These artists invite us to leave behind the dreams of immateriality so that we can effectively interrogate the choices, the textures, the very light of the materials we insinuate into our work. And here we can find a whole new arena of pleasure, of tactility, of shaping, which gives architecture flesh that no virtual retreat can rediscover.

On the contrary, in the encounter between the pleasures of the material and the potentialities offered by new technologies, the architectural project takes its place in modernity. Our architecture is built upon these encounters, upon this stratification of knowledge and of time, upon the materials of our projects. Let us not pit high-tech and low-tech against each other, but rather interrogate these pleasures of the real so as to enlist ourselves in the logic of the world.

Marc Mimram teaches at the School of Architecture in Marne la Vallée. He is currently working with the Bureau of Studies and Architectural-Engineering on a new type of high-tension wire pylon for France's electric company (EDF).

From Autoplastic to Alloplastic Tendency: Notes on Technological Latency
Mark Goulthorpe

In **The Transparent Society**, Gianni Vattimo suggests that contemporary cultural production no longer relies simply on shock but on an effect of sustained disorientation – almost a suspension of shock.[1] For Vattimo the effective event/work is one that endlessly differs/defers cognitive assimilation, marking a shift that I will characterize here in psychological terms as **trauma** (the mind struggling to comprehend a lack). The term **latency** is used in psychology to describe the lack of incorporation that attends trauma – that it is founded on an insistent yet unassimilated event – which I will here consider in terms of the effects engendered by/in certain digital media.

Vattimo's text is concerned with the cultural effects of technical change, tracking shifts in the base "psychologies of perception"; here I will extend this to a consideration of architectural production/reception in its attempts at the incorporation[2] of a new technology.

Vattimo's insight suggests a marked shift in cultural aptitude – a sharp contrast to Ernst Gombrich's **The Sense of Order**,[3] for instance (subtitled **A Study in the Psychology of Decorative Art**), in which he continually asserts that cognitive disorientation cannot be tolerated and will quickly be grounded by a representative predilection (the mind short-circuiting the difficulty). Gombrich was fascinated by artworks and patterns that confound perception, but he appeared to consider this only a momentary disorientation before the mind exerts an order in absentia, as if this were somehow a preordinate and natural "representative" capacity of the mind.[4] Vattimo's suggestion that the effectiveness of strategies of shock seems to be giving way to "softer, more fluid" modes of operation (fluid in their dissolution of representative certitude) corresponds to current strategies throughout the arts. These I would characterize as being of precise indeterminacy, as precisely calibrated forms of disorientation that Gombrich, for one, might have struggled to account for.

Such thought has been provoked in large part by my attempt to register the bewildering effects of William Forsythe's Frankfurt Ballet, where he asks his dancers to "represent loss," "sustain the reinscription of forms," "capture an absent presence," and so forth – strategies of sustained and deliberate absenting.[5] Articulating this in terms of trauma draws from Heidi Gilpin's suggestive essay, "Aberrations of Gravity," in which she characterizes the charged effect of disappearance such dance engenders in terms of trauma, as "the staging of that which does not take place" (Forsythe), a traumatic **absence**.[6] But having worked with the Frankfurt Ballet in their production of **Sleepers' Guts** and having witnessed the creation of **Eidos/Telos**, I realized that both production and reception, which for Forsythe are very much extensions of one another, are traumatically implicated in that both operate with no a priori, no representational dictate. "We work free of **idea**," he suggests, preferring an open, processural, creative drift to the determinism of ideological constructs.[7] The creative process is highly implicated in the resultant effect – it embraces disorientation in its very process – a crucial aspect in such strategies of cultural latency.

As we begin to operate in a fully electronic creative environment in architecture, which offers the possibility of quite open-ended and fluid creative processes, such strategic yet nonlinear creative strategies of dis-incorporation seem prescient. The psychological shift hinted at by Vattimo requires not simply the **incorporation of** a new technology but a fundamental reevaluation of the very manner of cultural creativity and receptivity that it engenders.

Shock

Shock has long been considered the modus operandi of the modern, with writers from diverse fields such as Martin Heidegger, Walter Benjamin, and Roland Barthes, all accounting for the effectiveness of artworks in terms of "the shock of the new" and the dis/re-orientating wrench that it engenders. For Benjamin this marked the shift from "aura" to the exhibition-value of artworks: henceforth art would no longer derive its meaning by being somehow replete with preordinate significance, but rather in its capacity to actively reorient cognition through its interrogation of extant cultural pattern.[8] His prognosis seems in hindsight to have been an accurate one: that art has moved off its pedestal to come into much more direct contact with the world, deploying new genres of effectivity – most significantly (for Benjamin) as strategies of shock.

But in considering the effects of a profligate and radical new productive electronic media that is rapidly infiltrating all aspects of the current cultural field – an "art in the age of electronic de-production," as it were – one senses a general dissipation of shock-effect. For it seems that different patterns of cultural registration are emerging, engendered by an electronic medium that reconfigures the field subliminally. For shock implies reference for it to be effective, the resulting disorientation figured consciously as a strategy of reaction (frequently also as a strategy of reorientation). But much contem-

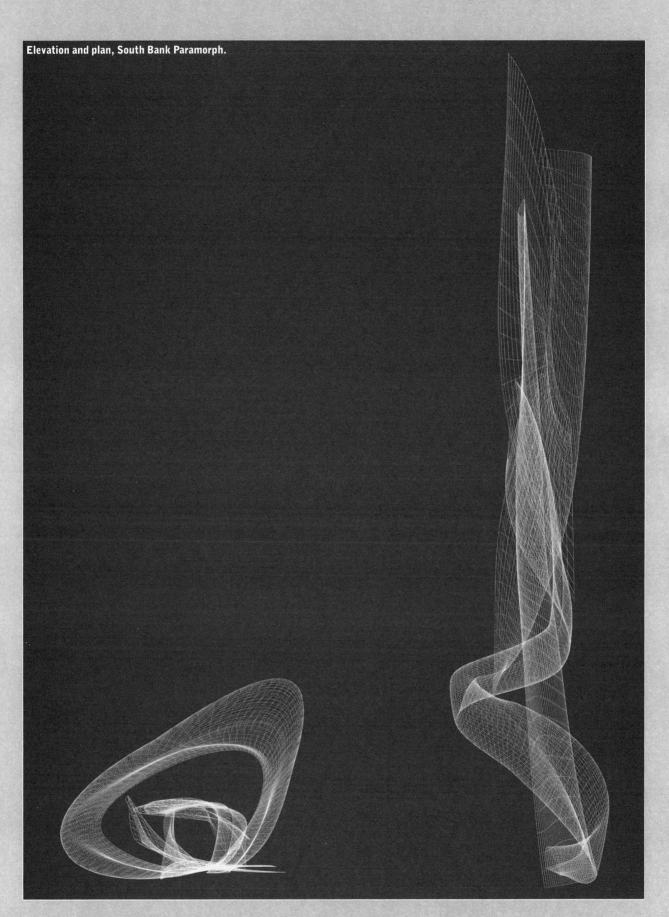

Elevation and plan, South Bank Paramorph.

Site plan and elevation, South Bank Paramorph.

porary work, in its genera(c)tive profligacy, disenfranchises comprehension in an absence or overabundance of evident reference, the trace of its coming-into-being "digitally" indeterminate.

The ensuing disorientation differs from that of shock in its very indeterminacy: no longer is it simply a strategic dis/re-orientation, but it acts as a suspension of the possibility of orientation. It does not rely, that is, on a memorialized circuit for its effect — in fact, quite the inverse — it stimulates through its very denial of incorporation. Frequently this seems to take the form of/as an endless transformation of the same, engendering a range of effects propitiated in the struggle for an endlessly absented comprehensibility. Here I am thinking of artworks such as Michel Saup's **Supreme Particles** — an endless reconfiguration of two floating objects distorted sharply by an improvisational violinist who responds to each distortion as a new reading event — a hallucinogenic patterning-in-time that sends the mind reeling in its continual reconfiguration. Such works evidently "work" according to an entirely reconfigured psychological circuit.

Trauma

Psychological accounts of trauma are varied, but generally it is characterized as stemming from a moment of incomprehension or cognitive incapacity. At a moment of severe stress, for instance, there is a frequent shutdown of the conceptual apparatus (as if for protection), which creates an **anxiety of reference**. Cathy Caruth, who has written extensively on the relations of trauma and memory, suggests that "in its repeated imposition as both image and amnesia, the trauma thus seems to evoke the difficult truth of a history that is constituted by the very incomprehensibility of its occurrence."[9]

Trauma, then, develops not as a direct response to (a) shock but through the very inability to register it conceptually — through the **absence** of its assimilation and the struggle of the mind to account for this cognitive incapacity. "While the traumatized are called upon to see and relive the insistent reality of the past, they recover a past that enters consciousness only through the very denial of active recollection. The ability to recover the past is thus closely and paradoxically tied up, in trauma, with the inability to have access to it . . . an event that is constituted, in part, by its lack of integration into consciousness."[10]

Freudian psychoanalysis is effectively predicated on trauma in its belief that neuroses are constituted as unconscious traces which are palpably "there" but repressed or forgotten, inaccessible to the conscious mind (the very conscious/unconscious divide was posited by Freud to account for this).[11] Psychoanalysis then sets itself the task of recovering such traces for consciousness, permitting their assimilation and comprehension: it works by reestablishing representative linkage and causal lineage. In positing trauma as a now effective cultural trope, one would then be working against the Freudian grain and against any simple causal sequence, creative or receptive, posing the question, "How might one learn to write the way the Wolfman spoke?" Forsythe is a creative practitioner who operates in just such a manner, working with primary memory, which he never seeks to entirely recover for consciousness: there is no ideological incorporation.

It seems incontestable that the representative indeterminacy that resides in trauma is no longer, as Gombrich might have it, intolerable: modes of productivity and receptivity increasingly seem to operate in an indeterminate (electronic) milieu where absence is deployed with cultural effect. "Understanding" here seems to be replaced by "effect." My interest is to speculate on the relations of trauma to the patterns of creativity propagated by digital technology, in order to counter the reincorporation of electronic technologies within traditional ideological frameworks.

Transformation

Evidently such technical developments can be considered through a variety of conceptual frameworks (psychoanalytic — Freud/Ferenczi; philosophical — Derrida; art historical — Benjamin, etc.), but perhaps most simply as the apparent break-up of representative strategy. I would characterize this shift as moving from a notion of **origin** to one of **transformation**, the most evident effect of which is to implicate time in an activated sense. The link with electronic production seems evident here: as we enter a mode of creativity that implicates time in multiple ways, to the extent that the generative patterns of creativity are left as indeterminate traces of that transformative process. Transformation displaces origin and disperses its vertical legitimacy to a now limitless electronic horizon. In this the notion of trauma seems redolent: cognition searching restlessly for an endlessly absented referent.

Trauma, like shock then, needs to be thought of in terms other than those of simple debilitation (even in medical terms trauma functions as a strategy of survival). In trauma, the very lack of cognitive assimilation from which it derives produces a variety of effects, such as an immediate compulsion to account for that lack (a stimulus) coupled with a heightening of bodily awareness; as if the very absence of cognitive assimilation dispersed thought throughout the sensorium. Trauma, therefore, tends to stimulate neglected modes of cognition as an intense "sampling" of experience as the mind deploys its full cognitive capacity to account for the unfamiliar pattern.

This raising of the body to a cognitive level, a **chemic** as well as **optic** mode of thought, metonymic as much as metaphoric, is characterized by Forsythe as a proprioceptive mode of production/reception, "a thinking with/in the body." The current generative environment, in which "the image becomes primary"[12] (develops a life of its own, begins to lead creative endeavor), dislocates familiar patterns of comprehension and the referential strategies they seem to imply. The turmoil this engenders for determinate creative strategy – both productive and receptive – then poses profound questions for cultural (and not simply technical) activity. Most essentially, perhaps, it forces thought back within the body, interrogating the privileging of the senses in relation to conceptual thought, loosening the hegemony of optic sense (on which the linear, causal, memorialized representative circuit largely relies).

Autoplastic/Alloplastic

Drawing from Ferenczi's analyses of trauma, one might characterize this as a shift from an **autoplastic** to an **alloplastic** mode of operation. Autoplastic is defined as a self-determinate operative strategy, and alloplastic as a reciprocal environmental modification. Classically, in trauma an autoplastic response is predetermined by the inertia and indifference of the environment: "For trauma to have effect, no effective 'alloplastic' action, (that is, modification of the environmental threat) is possible, so that 'autoplastic' adaptation of oneself is necessary."[13]

If trauma becomes culturally operative, we might then characterize it in these terms as a shift from an autoplastic to alloplastic mode, both in a productive and a receptive sense. We operate creatively within an alloplastic "space" as one begins to work in a responsive, conditional environment, sampling and editing the proliferating capacity of generative software: it is a transformative, creative medium, by its very nature. But increasingly this also extends even to physical contexts, which through the (over)deployment of electronic systems, become interactively malleable, our very

determinacy being placed in flux. In the new electronic environment there is a reciprocal negotiation between self and environment – an interactive "allo-plasticity."

Asked what his ideal theater might be, Forsythe suggested that it would be an indeterminate architecture in which the surfaces themselves would ceaselessly reconfigure, with even the floor offering differential resistance and support, compelling the dancers to continually recalibrate and reimagine their movement strategies. The physical plasticity that such a suggestion implies need not be taken literally (although this is the point of departure for the **Aegis** project described below), the essential challenge being the more general one of deploying alloplastic strategies in both creative and receptive registers. The **Aegis** project and the **Paramorph** project described here each in its own way has developed as a speculation on such alloplastic potential. As such they are vehicles for foregrounding current operative design strategies, exploring dynamic and static aspects of open-ended transformative processes.

Aegis

Aegis was devised in response to a competition for an art piece for England's Birmingham Hippodrome – specifically for the cantilevered "prow" that emerges from the depth of the foyer and extends over the street. The brief simply asked for a piece that would in some way depict on the exterior what was happening on the interior – a dynamic and interactive artwork.

The resulting project is simple in its conception: one might even say that it is **nothing**, or that it highlights **the nothing** – the everyday events which occur in the theater around it. It is a plain, architectural surface – metallic and faceted – just one of the walls of the prow penetrates from exterior to interior as a gently curving surface. But it is a surface that carries dynamic potential, and in response to stimuli captured from the theater environment, it can dissolve into movement – supple fluidity or complex patterning. As such, it is a sort of visceral three-dimensional screen, capable of a rapid and detailed surface reconfiguration driven by a matrix of thousands of electronically controlled pistons. It plays the fields of art and architecture, alternating between background and foreground states.

The resolution and speed of the wall surface will emerge from the actual parameters of the device – both physical and electronic – but subject to those parameters, it will be capable of registering any pattern or sequence that can be generated mathematically. The sur-

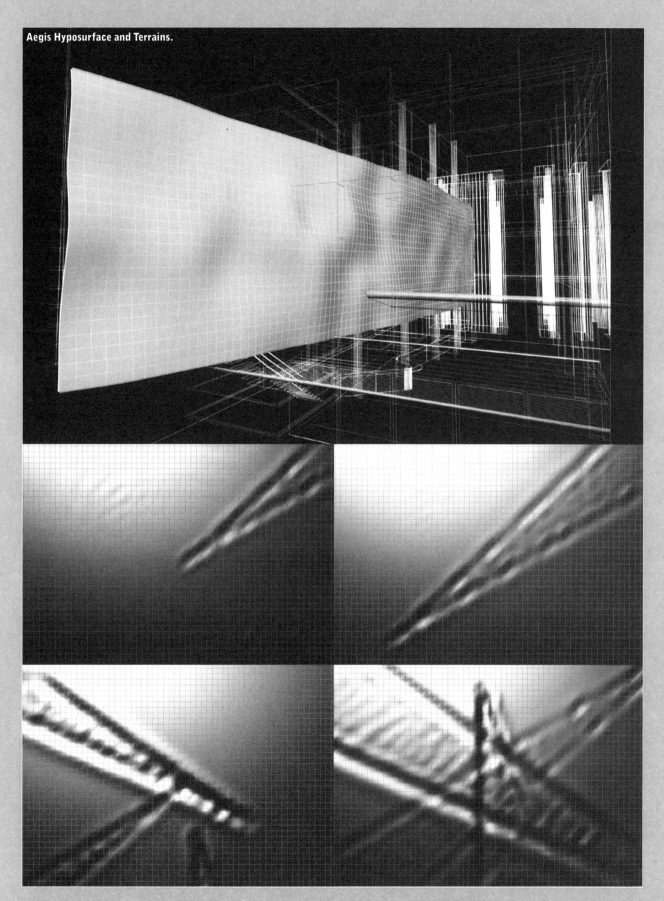

Aegis Hyposurface and Terrains.

face deforms according to stimuli captured from the environment, which may be selectively deployed as active or passive sensors. It will be linked into the base electrical services of the building, which are to be operated using a coordinated bus system, such that all electrical activity can feed into its operational matrix, allowing it to register any aspect of electronic capture. Additional input from receptors of noise, temperature, and movement will be sampled by a program-control monitor, which responds by selecting a number of base mathematical descriptions, each parametrically variable in terms of speed, amplitude, direction, etc., and producing a near infinite series of changing permutations that continually overlap, drifting in and out of sequence.

Aegis is, in this way, effectively a **translation** surface – a sort of synaesthetic transfer device, a surface-effect for cross-wiring of the senses. As a translation surface it is in principle readable, a form of **glyphism**, but now as a real-time event laced programmatically with causal triggers/disrupters. Like the hieroglyphs, it drifts between pattern and writing, proffering and deferring a promise of meaning but in a sensual and rhythmic form of tectonic electronic writing.

The surface is therefore not **designed** or determined as such: it is genera(c)ted by a random sampling, a deployment of electronic sensory-input from the immediate environment. In its creation, as in its reception, it suggests an alloplastic rather than autoplastic logic, the designer's role becoming that of editor or sampler of a proliferating range of effects. **Aegis** is perhaps, therefore, not a "form" at all, since it escapes "design" ideology, conceived rather as a matrix of the **possibility of form**: registering, in fact, the becoming/absenting of form-in-pattern.

Hyposurface

Trauma, as we have noted, is not marked by an overfullness or excess of significance but by an **absence** of conceptual registration. This suggests that the prefix **hypo-**, which is characterized by deficiency and lack, by a subliminal incapacity, might be more appropriate in considering the effect of such numerically generated surfaces than hyper-, which denotes excess or extremity. In engendering a sort of inexpressive plasticity in its languid surface distortions, **Aegis** would seem to mark a shift to the sublimity of hyposurface. As a surface of variable significance, a literal distortion of reference fluctuating between hypnosis and hallucination (the limit cases of optic sense), it will be interesting to

gauge the displacement of conceptual registration that results and to inquire as to the possibility of an emergent genre of hyposurface.

Paramorph

In response to a competition to design a gateway to the South Bank in London, we have continued to pursue this alloplastic potential. The project here is a **Paramorph** – a body that may change its form but whose fundamental property remains the same – in this case its geometric character. Here, the "dynamic" final form is static, but it has been derived from a paramorphic process inhabited by variance.

Our gateway derives from a series of different mapping strategies – sound and movement models in particular – which have each been pursued openly as generative processes (i.e., as environmental "samplings" with no particular goal in mind). We concentrated on nonvisual aspects of the site, producing mappings that revealed its dynamic rather than static character, actualizing time in the exploratory process. From this derived a constantly evolving formal solution for a gateway-in-depth, genera(c)ting series upon series of sheaths, sheets, shellforms, and so on – an open process of discovery that condensed a "final" form as a sort of collapsing vortex. The mappings were revelatory and dynamic, a series of strategies which were aimless but cogent in deriving a series of coherent and precise formal solutions, each of which propagated the next. The "final" form folds down from the scale of the public plaza (Sutton Place) to the quite constrained passageway beneath the viaduct (Sutton Passage) as a languid spatial compression.

The **Paramorph** is imagined as a series of tessellated aluminum surfaces that act as host to interactive sound sculpture, sound deployed in response to the passage of people moving through the form, morphing the site-sound. These will be "floated" through the form by temporal relay such that the generative process continues into the actual architectural effect – one of an endlessly distorted redeployment of the dynamic aspects of the site itself. Such a transformation of "nothing" – of the ambient environment registered electronically – feeds back into that same environment as a temporal condensation and a heightening of sensory effect.

Parametric Process

The developmental process of the **Paramorph** was accompanied by the creation of customized parametric models of geometric constraint – i.e., as "elastic" models of precise descriptive geometry. This effectively embeds a geometric property into a descriptive model as a sort of inviolable genetic code – in this case, that all surfaces be described by straight-line geometry (therefore, as derivatives of hyperbolic paraboloids), which then informs the various reiterations of the form that we apply. No matter how we distort the form (here 15 hoops were controlled by 157 variable parameters), the surfaces are always derived from straight-line description (and hence can be fabricated by straight lengths of extruded aluminum). In fact, the model allows us to facet, rule, or nurb the surface, offering transformative reiterations of the form, each self-similar but different.

Here again we have created not so much a form as the possibility of (a) form, embedding specific parameters which are latent within an open, creative system. It is this latent "forgotten" character that, we feel, gives the object a "precisely indeterminate" quality and stimulates, yet denies, incorporation. The form seems fluid but is highly constrained so that its tension can be somehow sensed viscerally. The form derives from and propagates the absenting psychologies of trauma, preferring an open and speculative transformative process to a reactive ideological determinism. If such forms offer a fluid potentiality for both production and reception, the liquefaction of the linearity of extant "design" processes (verification and refinement now collapsed into the base parametric description) will be suggestive of modes of fluidity to come.

1 Gianni Vattimo, **The Transparent Society** (London: Polity Press, 1992). See, for example, "Art and Oscillation": "The aim of this is not to reach a final recomposed state. Instead, aesthetic experience is directed towards keeping the disorientation alive." 51.
2 Here I use the term in the psychoanalytical sense, used by Sigmund Freud to denote cognitive assimilation.
3 Ernst Gombrich, **The Sense of Order: A Study in the Psychology of Decorative Art** (London: Phaidon Press, 1979).
4 Ibid., 9. For example, "No jolt should take us unawares . . . the most basic fact of aesthetic experience is the fact that delight lies somewhere between boredom and confusion . . . a surfeit of novelty will overload the system and cause it to give up."
5 My knowledge of William Forsythe and the Frankfurt Ballet derives from study of their work and many discussions with them over a number of years. See my essay "An Architecture of Disappearance" ("Un architecture de la disparition") in **Contredanse**, 1998.

6 Heidi Gilpin, "Aberrations of Gravity," **ANY** 5 (March 1994), 50–55.
7 These experiments were carried out during rehearsals of **Eidos/Telos**, 1995, which I studied while running Intermediate Unit 2 at the Architectural Association, London.
8 From the seminal "Art in the Age of Mechanical Reproduction" in Walter Benjamin, **Illuminations** (New York: Schocken Books, 1986).
9 Cathy Caruth, "Freud, Moses and Monotheism" in **Unclaimed Experience** (Baltimore: The Johns Hopkins University Press, 1996), 18.
10 Cathy Caruth, "Unclaimed Experience: Trauma and the Possibility of History," **Yale French Studies 79, Literature and the Ethical Question** (1991): 187.
11 The "classic" texts on trauma are those of Sigmund Freud, which deal largely with the neuroses associated with vividly disturbing events. Sandor Ferenczi offers a more subtle interpretation, extending Freud's thought to a wide range of everyday events, in effect using the discourse on trauma as a means of developing a generalized psychological theory. In my view, such "extension" does not imply opposition to Freud's basic thought – rather, a requalification – and in seeking to extend Ferenczi's thought to the consideration of cultural reception, I would note the basic similarities of both thinkers in their descriptions of trauma. A good account of their respective differences is given by Jay B. Frankel, "Ferenczi's Trauma Theory," **The American Journal of Psychoanalysis**, vol. 58 (1998).
12 This is an expression of Bernard Cache's in **Earth Moves: The Furnishing of Territories** (Cambridge Massachusetts: MIT Press, 1995), describing the extent to which the computer image is no longer a representation of something prior, but begins to develop a life of its own – to become primary, or generative, in the creative process.
13 Sandor Ferenczi, "Notes and Fragments" in **Final Contributions, 1930–32** (London: Hogarth, 1955), 221. This is the third volume of his collected notes and papers, published posthumously.

Mark Goulthorpe is the founder and creator of dECOi, a reasearch-based architecture studio in Paris. They recently renovated the Luschwitz House in London.

High-tech
in Architecture:
Of Disenchanted
Technology
Yannis Tsiomis

Temple of Hephaestus.

Working on the development of the archaeological site of the Athens Agora and the surrounding district, I began to wonder what kind of architecture could be put up opposite the Acropolis, what rapport could be established between the city and the site of the Agora, how the landscape could be allowed to speak like a history book, given not only that the topography is historic but also that the architect is a historian working by intuition.

How do we answer such banal questions? More history or none at all? More architecture in the name of history or none at all? More or less technology? I found I preferred to look at the site itself and, before reflecting on "my" abilities as an architect, to reflect on the technic/history metaphor, knowing that the Agora is the place where democracy and fire power meet — the meeting of myth and politics.

The 1932 dig of Homerus Thompson from the American School of Archaeology revealed that the Agora of Athens was a political space encircled by a cottage industry of ceramicists and blacksmiths — those who worked with earth and iron and who practiced their art and industry outside but alongside the political space.

Their god, Hephaestus, whose temple overlooks the Agora, marks the division between the two spaces. So here is one symbolic function of architecture: marking, demarcation, and segregation. It represents the tension between politics and the technical, between myth and the rational world.

Yet physically, architecturally, there is no wall to signify this limit. It is the landscape, the placement of buildings and boundaries that mark the passage from the space of the city to the space of the city-state, which is the space of the Assembly and of democracy. Therefore, in essence this void can be read as a line, but this assumes an extraordinary capacity for abstraction on the part of the Athenians of the day. Thus we find ourselves before virtuality and abstraction without a correspondingly high level of technical skill.

In reality, this signals a civilization very different from our own, one that induces another mental structure. The problem for the architect confronting this space is knowing how not to betray, through some token of contemporary modernity, a complexity that is also the modernity of ancient times.

What is at stake for technology can be viewed in two ways. We can first look at ancient technology in terms of myth and politics. Second, we can see today's technology, through our mandate as architects, as being about the need to solidify and render readable and visible the relationships between past and future. I will look at the first aspect later, but from the outset it seems useful to recall a certain number of things architects do not necessarily remember.

The democratic agora was a space born out of opposition and "invented" to resolve opposition, crisis, and conflict – conflicts beginning in the 5th century; clashes that centered on the reforms of Cleisthenes of Athens at the very outset of democracy; of the Median Wars, and so on. Democratic structures sprang from such opposition, along with the spaces and built structures in which democracy is practiced.

The notion of public space as public property and "sector" (**res publica**) also emerged at this time. This gave rise to the distinction between the city-state and the city, signifying the double dimension of the urban – political and physical. This distinction was subsequently applied to the inhabitants of the city in the 18th century, distinguishing between the status of the citizen as a political entity, master of the city-state's future, conscious of his rights and duties, and his status as a city-dweller, the inhabitant of the town going about his own business and preoccupied with his private life and his money. In this way, in the space around the Acropolis in Athens was born an urban figure who codified a dichotomy between the public and private that informed all subsequent city spaces.

Curiously, in looking at the role of technics we can unravel some of the strands of this complexity: "technics" or, rather, the manner in which tragedy, as an autonomous literary genre, treats the technical as what is at work in making architecture and the free man. Aeschylus's **Prometheus Bound** may be some help to us here.

Further discussion, involving reflections on technics today, could begin with some seemingly banal questions that take on a certain profundity whenever a designer takes on a project. What kind of architecture and what kind of development can possibly be conceived for the Agora of Athens? What kind of urban planning is appropriate for the historical center? What critical technics does one use? Independently of the concrete responses and solutions proposed in my project, which I will not go into here, I wish to discuss the aporias that history itself has presented to us – questions concerning theory, situations, and contexts. Questions about architecture.

Faced with the Acropolis, it is not a matter of making or not making an architecture that is either light or heavy, transparent or opaque, modern, high-tech, or "neo-classic." It is a matter of placing oneself in real life in relation to the city and the rapport it maintains with the archaeological space. It is a matter of the present and history. Given that this relationship is shifting, the notion of reversibility arises and demands to be transfigured into architecture. For the space of the first democratic assembly must not be killed by an architecture, as this runs the risk of physically and symbolically freezing the myth and politics of a civilization that is no longer ours but which gave birth to our own. This, of course, poses questions, yet again, about the work of the architect in relation to other disciplines, about work on the existing city and work with its inhabitants, about a relationship with history that we maintain today and reinvent tomorrow. Questions of ethics, in effect, that I will approach by way of technical considerations, since we are here to talk about technology and because technics cannot be reduced to the application and repetition of some simple savoir faire, nor to some kind of exhibitionism of assemblies of glass and metal or stone and wood.

Anymore technology in fact incites us to reflect on these ways of connecting, whereby technics – our technical methods as architects – seems to be working at the edge between material and immaterial things. This is the point of departure for my reflections, which I will present under the twin aspects of technics and technology.[1] I will be particularly concerned here with the relationship between technics and technology and their relationship with architecture, but I should specify that, though these thoughts are being offered on the occasion of the Any conference in Paris, there is nothing makeshift about them. They form part of my approach in designing the Athens Agora project.

Technology and Technics

Architecture's relationship with technology and technics remains obscure, despite the abundant literature. And the terms **technics** and **technology** are too often used interchangeably, as though there were no distinction, which only adds to the confusion. I would like to cloak this obscurity with a further layer, at the risk of making the relationship even more opaque.

When it comes to architecture and technics, we must first clarify a certain number of problems. I will deal with just three of them here by way of example.

1. The first problem is whether or not we treat technics in terms of applications of practical knowledge and overall performance serving building as an art. If we do, it is a matter of repeatedly applying existing technical methods.

2. The second problem is whether or not we speak of innovation, again technical, in the sense of the performance of new materials, or even of the application of new theories and ideas that in turn generate a new level of thinking. If we do, it is a matter of the relationship between knowledge and architecture, and the transmission of knowledge with a view to attaining a common goal. For example, if the ideal is to live better, while remaining in the same world, within the same social, emotional, and other relationships, then so-called smart houses, for instance, will or may already allow added comfort, while remaining within the same environment of culture and civilization.

3. The third problem in considering technics in relationship to architecture is whether it is a question of technic proper to architecture, or of transfers and adaptations of technics stemming from other domains, such as past innovations deriving from war machines, avionics, or naval engineering.

We will return to this issue once we have distinguished technics from technology, but from the outset we should consider this third problem fundamental to the legitimate question of whether or not architecture, in light of the new purposes it assigns itself, invents new technics by and for itself or whether, on the contrary, its particularity consists in sidetracking or stealing the innovations of others, then improving, modifying, and presenting them differently. In other words, does architecture work on the ideology of the machine or on the machine itself? The question is all the more delicate since visual and aesthetic definitions cannot, properly speaking, be considered technical questions. We should remember the British-built De Havilland Comet, the first ever commercial jet plane. Despite its superb lines, the Comet was a tragic failure, for people confused genres at the time, jumbling together aerodynamic line, aesthetics, and passengers' visual comfort. The Comet represented an ideological vision of the art of flying, and its "failure in the face of reality," to borrow Jürgen Habermas's formula, was immediate: death.

Obviously I am referring to precedents with which most of us are already familiar, especially those of us who have trained as both engineers and architects or who employ a twin approach. But I would still like to recall the subtle manner in which Le Corbusier, in **Towards a New Architecture** [**Vers une architecture**, Paris: Crès, 1923], shows that, as long as man hoped to imitate the flight of birds, he was unable to fly; the day man succeeded in separating aerostatics from aerodynamics,

Top: aerial view of the site; above: model of the Agora Project.

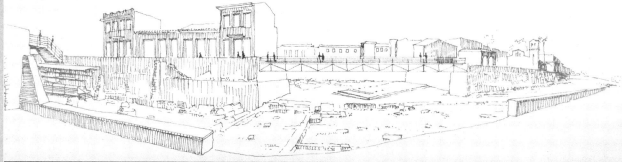

Above: existing condition and proposal for the Agora Project; left: "I am the boundary of the Agora."

that is, in separating the form of the flying object from its propulsion, he was able to achieve his goal to fly.

The same question arises today: what is the new technical goal, and what is the new approach designed to achieve it? The consequences of the goal to fly were a shift in our ways of inhabiting and occupying the Earth, and the emergence of new practical knowledge, and of new trades. Le Corbusier's delusion was, of course, to believe that architecture could follow the engineer's approach and set itself the task of inventing new, predetermined ways of inhabiting the earth for a new, equally predetermined civilization.

What followed showed that what was actually involved was a shortcut, for architecture merely transferred, or transposed, practical knowledge without engendering any actual mutations. At best, architecture simply accentuated its heteronomy without worrying about how it would reconstruct its autonomy, and so this autonomy was weakened. But it remains true that technics, as a new savoir faire and style, accompanied the quest for, and promise of, this unprecedented – and perhaps totalitarian – civilization. This required a new mental structure, a "new man." The three problems mentioned above suggest an alternative concept of the relationship between practical knowldge and architecture.

With these three problems or issues we effectively remain within an existing logical framework, within the same technical culture, and obviously within the same civilization. The goal remains the same. At best, what is involved are improvements that require no fundamental change in mental structures, only the updating of knowledge and the renewal of the business of construction for new results and nothing more.

Up to this moment, I have spoken about technics, but things change as soon as we speak of technology. What draws my attention is not the manner in which architecture develops its new applications based on new technics but how architecture thinks about these technics, old and new. This gets us away from an obsession with performance.

To put it another way: Is applying new technics in architecture what architecture is about? To what degree does architecture develop new technics and, supposing it does so at all, what significance should we give to such innovations? Can architecture be the breeding ground for the production of new technics? Can it be this nonexistent "laboratory" so desired by Le Corbusier and later so decried? Or, on the contrary, does it remain the field of application, a field of borrowing, an area that works

through transfer and that, in this sense, can only be a place for adaptation, manipulation, and tinkering – a tinkering that has nothing to do with what the engineer-inventor does, moved as he is by some new goal he sets for himself. For today we need to ask ourselves about the goals that architecture sets for itself, not only in terms of social and cultural projects but as a plan of civilization. And we can demand that such a plan not remain unspoken or that it not remain an abstract vision "of immaterial communications networks," without the contents being defined and communicated.

Myth and the Liberating Capacity of Technics in Architecture

Take Aeschylus's **Prometheus Bound**. Prometheus, as the poet describes him, is a "philanthrope" – in other words, a man who loves mankind, a humanist before the term was ever invented – bound in chains on Zeus's orders by Hephaestus, the god of fire and metalworking. Prometheus, who is tortured by an eagle eating at his liver, has given man fire and technical knowledge. Listen to the voice of the tortured man:

See with what outrage
Racked and tortured
I am to agonize
For a thousand years! [. . .]
Under such suffering, speech and silence are alike
Beyond me. For bestowing gifts upon mankind
I am harnessed in this torturing clamp. For I am he
Who hunted out the source of fire, and stole it, packed
In the pith of a dry fennel-stalk. And fire has proved
For men a teacher in every art, their grand resource.
That was the sin for which I now pay the full price,
Bared to the winds of heaven, bound and crucified.[2]

Prometheus tells the daughters of Oceanus that in giving man fire, he also offered hope, an end to the fear of death, as well as the thousands of technics that man would learn when he mastered fire. Moreover, Prometheus (who thinks before, and in view of, an act and is therefore a man of foresight, "wise-before-the-event," unlike his brother Epimetheus, who changes his mind and thinks after the act and is therefore a man of hindsight, "wise-after-the-event") proclaims that he desires his "crime" for the liberation of mankind. Postmodernity may well see in this an outdated image of the hero. I prefer the image of an intelligent god shedding his own image in time. There is a price to pay because there is a plan and so there are risks; the stakes are not technical but the freedom of mankind. In Aeschylus's tragedy, which is surely on a par with **Oedipus Rex** for daring, incest and technic meet. The message is thus implacable: there is a price to pay wherever there is daring, but wherever there is daring there is also a liberating plan. In this way, technic, to reiterate, is not a goal in itself and never was at any time, from Greco-Roman Antiquity to the 18th-century Age of Enlightenment. Without technics, however, there can be no liberation.

And so Prometheus poses a fundamental question concerning the morality of action, or rather, the ethics of action, a question I will not go into here, except to say that it concerns most specifically the political dimension of technical action.

Prometheus poses the question of power and knowledge: Zeus then punishes Prometheus, for he steals knowledge and know-how to give to mankind, thus proclaiming the end of divine power. Man thus remains free but also alone in the face of his destiny.

Prometheus then proclaims that technics will become the issue. The poet's greatness is to put us on guard against this at a time when the technical is considered an automated mirage. For do not forget that the tragedy of **Prometheus Bound** dates several years before the building of the Parthenon, from a time when the Agora and Acropolis had already set up public space as political and aesthetic space.

Aeschylus's reflection thus corresponds with the century when the distinction was being established between, on the one hand, the spaces of the city, of Myth (Keramikos, the cemetery for local Athenian citizens), and of religious worship (the Acropolis) and, on the other hand, political and civic space, public space par excellence (the Agora) – that is, spaces where architecture was given its propaedeutic and aesthetic value. This was Pericles' plan – a political, urban, and aesthetic plan combined.

Thus anticipating the construction of the Parthenon by a few years (it was completed in 432 BC), Aeschylus introduces around 460 BC this notion of the role of the technic, which becomes the place of mediation and practical meditation on the future of the world at a moment of political reform and philosophical revolution.

What did men do before Prometheus offered them fire?
In those days they had eyes, but sight was meaningless;
Heard sounds, but could not listen; all their length of life
They passed like shapes in dreams, confused and purposeless.
Of brick-built, sun-warmed houses, or of carpentry,
They had no notion; lived in holes, like swarms of ants,
Or deep in sunless caverns; knew no certain way
To mark off winter, or flowery spring, or fruitful summer;
Their every act was without knowledge, till I came.
I taught them to determine when stars rise or set –
A difficult art. Number, the primary science, I
Invented for them, and how to set down words in writing –
The all-remembering skill, mother of many arts.
I was the first to harness beasts under a yoke
With trace or saddle as man's slaves, to take man's place
Under the heaviest burdens; put the horse to the chariot,
Made him obey the rein, and be an ornament
To wealth and greatness. No one before me discovered
The sailor's wagon – flax-winged craft that roam the seas.
Such tools and skills I found for men: myself, poor wretch,
Lack even one trick to free me from this agony.[3]

Like blind ants swarming in a dark cave, men first of all learn to build walls, to become masons and architects, **tekhtones** – later **technics**; they learn to build "sun-warmed houses." They learn the different ages and astronomy; to sow seeds and become farmers; to break in their horses and have ploughs drawn by bullocks; to economize their pain. They also learn to build boats, to master the wind with woven sails and to travel. Because they are philosophers they become town planners, like Hippodamus at the very moment Aeschylus is writing. What Prometheus does not tell us is that they also learn to render the city plan systematic.

Lastly, they learn to make war, to kill scientifically. Victims or executioners, they remain masters of their fate. The difference between Hephaestus and Prometheus is not that one is ignorant of the technics the other possesses, but that one is not prepared to steal it from the gods, from the Powers That Be, in order to give it to men. One is compliant and merely replicates. The other is a rebel and inventor who loves human beings. One assures the power of the gods, the other is recalcitrant, proclaiming the death of the gods and making technics an agent of their death.

Prometheus, or technics, announces the death of Zeus on the condition that technics does not then become a god in place of the dead gods, but that it offers mankind's liberation as a project for a new civilization.

So we can read the story of Prometheus at different levels: as a discourse about politics and the liberating capacity of technics; as the moral discourse of the being who possesses technical knowledge in confrontation with the reigning powers; as a discourse meditating upon technical innovation and its aim; as a discourse on the mastery of technics by the greatest number, about skill as a democratic asset; as a discourse about awareness of new knowledge and thus of common membership in this new civilization of the **tekhnê** – art and technical skill combined.

Of Disenchanted Technology:
From Lewis Mumford to Alexandre Koyrê

And so the discourse of Prometheus, which places architecture first in man's journey from blind ant to free being, is a techno-logical discourse: a discourse about the reason for technics, a logos – reasoning and argument – about technics. This is the etymology of the word **technology**, and it indicates how we should rethink the term instead of seeing it as a simple "image" of meaningless achievements.

To put the issue another way: If the relationship between architecture and technology were reduced to turning a technological imaginary into images, from the moment we admit that architecture does not produce technics, then architecture is a mere foil, in a relationship of representation of technical production that does not emanate from it. Architecture would thus be in a dependent relationship such that even its translation into forms would be external to its own goals.

If, on the other hand, architecture participates in technic's rationale, as constructed discourse, as logos, and if architecture thereby participates in the business of technology, then it is called upon to "speak" and not to "illustrate" a future world by taking a stand in the "political," and so philosophical debate about our future.

If technics – what was known as the arts in the 18th century – is practical skill, replication, the set of specific processes, then technology refers to knowledge and so necessitates reasoning and argument in the name of some rationale (to what end do we do this or that?). In this sense, reflections about science or art, both inherent in technological thought, are obviously relevant.

Because technology is not simply a modern, state-of-the-art technic or some simple image of modernity, the observations of Alexandre Koyrê (1882–1964), philosopher and historian of technoscience, seem to go to the heart of our debate.

Writing in 1948 about Maxime Schül's book, **Mechanization and Philosophy**, published in 1947, Koyrê, in an article entitled "Mechanization and Philosophy," discusses the curve described by the relationship between mechanization (understanding the term as technics) and philosophy:

This curve can be summed up as follows: it goes from hopeless resignation (Antiquity) to enthusiastic expectation (the modern age), only to return to desperate resignation (the contemporary age). We should add, however, that it was to the absence of the machine that the philosopher of Antiquity resigned himself and that it is to its presence that the contemporary is forced to resign himself.

So why exactly do we go from hopeless resignation to desperate resignation? What attracts Koyrê's attention is actually "the evolution of human attitudes." He specifies: What interested and preoccupied the philosophers was not the machine as technic, but the machine as human and social reality. In other words, the philosophical problem of mechanization and technics does not pose itself in terms of the role of the machine in production but in terms of its influence on human life, in terms of the transformations that the development of the machine makes on human life, or might subject it to.

If the absence of robots justified slavery in Aristotle's eyes (attesting to hopeless work), if Descartes saw in the robot the end of human toil and exhaustion (attesting to enchanted hope), then Koyrê, for his part, introduces the paradox of a machine-technic that both liberates man and enslaves him in intellectual ugliness and impoverishment – repetition, dehumanization, monotony, etc. Koyrê considers these situations similar in both the Soviet Union and the United States of the postwar period.

I might not have referred to Koyrê if he himself had not referred to the fourth edition (1946) of Lewis Mumford's **Technics and Civilization**, with its division of the ages into the **eotechnical**, **paleotechnical**, and **neotechnical**. The iron and coal of the paleotechnical age (the 19th and early 20th century) is ugly and uninform (despite modern art), says Koyrê, borrowing from Mumford. From attempts at communes to the efforts of the ecologists, Koyrê goes on to list utopian endeavors to liberate man from the technical – man of the ugly, dense, and dirty town – to the benefit of technological man – man of the spread-out, tidy town:

In creating wealth, the machine seems indeed to have brought us oliganthropy and it is perhaps also the machine, which has already recreated nomadism, that will enable the redispersal of urban populations and their reinsertion, conscious this time, in nature. The machine, by which I mean the technical intelligence of man, has kept its promise. It is up to man's political intelligence and to his intelligence alone to decide to what ends he will employ the power it has placed at his disposal.

Obviously Koyrê is wrong about the "oliganthropy" brought about by wealth. The demographic data of this fin de siècle reveals, on the contrary, that "polyanthropy" and poverty go hand in hand with wealth. Similarly, the reinsertion of man in nature through the dispersal of urban populations has proven to be a mirage: dispersal and densification go hand in hand, "eating into" nature just as the eagle ate Prometheus's liver. Urban sprawl, or "metropolization," point to an "oeucumenopolis," an invention appreciably of the same era, without the illusion of the maintenance of the humanist values of its inventor, K. Doxiadis. The post-city (**metapolis** in Greek) is still an abnormally enlarged city without being the polis-city-state, and without inherent political awareness and intelligence, without civic awareness or the awareness of being part of a civilization.

Koyrê, along with Mumford and before Henri Lefebvre – though all of them after Karl Marx – understood that the urban question is not fundamentally a question of culture but a question of civilization. Whence the pertinence of the reference to "nomadism" – what is today meaninglessly labeled "mobility" – a nomadism that requires above all a mental mobility, a culture conscious of belonging to a civilization and exercisng intelligence about the good uses of technics and innovation.

Koyrê despises Vitruvius because he "has no science and is in no way a scholar," because he has a "practical" mind, "routine technical skill," and because "he copies without inventing and, indeed, restricts himself to codifying rules and listing recipes." Vitruvius displeases him because he fails to produce "the theory of practice," meaning the theory of that moment when "technology, the science of technics, and technics born of science appear."

What does any of this have to do with us? If you consider the fact that Greek antiquity, despite Aristotle's contribution to the distinction between technics and science, "did not develop a technology even though it formulated the idea of it," what we might find frightening today is the development of a technology lacking any formulation of an underlying idea, one without any civilizing purpose.

What price will we pay for this lack of purpose? In breaking the rules, Prometheus suffers "punishment based on conventional sanctions." This is the "failure before the authorities," as Habermas has written, the failure before Zeus and his discretionary power. But when the technical is transgressed in the age of rational systems, the price to be paid is all the more painful. It is, quite simply, a lack of success, a "failure before reality."

To me, the problem we are facing in regard to architecture and technics is that for centuries, before internationalization and globalization, people lived through universals, that is, values deemed general and imposed on all. We might call these Prometheus's values, humanist values. The avatar of this civilization of common values has been the internationalization of structures, forms, and styles, and the struggle between values and structures.

Marx posed the question of the relationship that might be obtained between Achilles (myth) and "the age of powder and lead" (technics), between the **Iliad** (epic art) and the printing press (the technics of diffusion). The question may be outmoded in its formulation but it is still pertinent when it comes to the relationship between the mental structures of a past age that produced various works and the technics of another age that, though it may not recognize itself in these works, imagines that it at least shares some fragments of aesthetic values with them, without denying its own.

The paradox today is that internationalization and globalization do indeed exist. Their significance may be relative – the corollary being regional backwaters – for this body is unreadable, not so much in terms of culture as in terms of civilization, because there are no longer any universals to refer to. In the face of such relativism, architecture remains in aporia as to the significance of a form that no longer travels – because it is everywhere, simultaneously, thanks to technics of representation, transmission and diffusion, because it is stripped of universal value systems managed by local cultures, that is, stripped of the capacity for interpretation. So what will be the price we pay in case of failure?

It will probably be the inability of the technical to reflect on itself, as well as the end of technology and, with it, the reduction of democracy. In other words, clearly, this would be the end of the road, the end of what has brought us together here.

1 According to the dictionary, Ancient Greek technics (from **tekhnikos**) is what is proper to art, practical knowledge, trade, and dexterity but also production, what is artificial, art understood as a work of art as much as manual art and industry. Plato contrasts science (**episteme**) and knowledge to technic. Ancient Greek **technology** signifies a treatise or dissertation (**logos-discourse**) on art as also being an exposé of the rules of art. In one modern French usage, the word signifies "the study and science of technics and technical objects" (1896).

Derived from the English, **technology** designates "modern, complex, state-of-the-art technique." The French lexicographer A. Rey notes, in regard to this definition, "the meliorative, promotional, modern, connotation" of the term. The ambiguity of its current use in architecture should not escape us, especially when applied to "high-tech" architecture.

2 Aeschylus, **Prometheus Bound**, trans. Philip Vellacott (Penguin: London, 1961), 24.

3 Ibid., 34.

Yannis Tsiomis is a professor of theory and conceptual architecture at L'École d'architecture de Paris la Villette. His books include **Athénes et Washington ou comment confondre l'origine et le progrès** and **Américanisme et Modernité.**

Architecture Between Reflections and Plans
Alain Fleischer

Architecture has always produced images and been reproduced in images – images made by others, such as painters,
designers, photographers, filmmakers. Architecture has even
thought of itself as image; as volume in three dimensions, of
course, but always transferable to a certain number of flat
images according to its different reflections and to the different points of view its photogenic properties afford. Architecture has gazed upon itself as though in a mirror, in images
reflected to it over the centuries by the visual arts. Because it
inscribes itself in the landscape, sometimes even constituting
the entire landscape – whether an urban landscape, an industrial landscape, or the landscape of the suburbs – architecture,
that functional object, has more viewers of its images than
users of its functions. A residential apartment block, for
example, is seen daily by a far greater number of onlookers
than its occupants. And more often than not, those who
admire architecture's objects are not those who use them.
Within the visual languages, architecture has even managed
to impose certain specialities, specific styles and technics,
particular conventions, in order to attract attention, and
favorable attention at that, through architectural drawings,
photographs of architecture, and films about architecture,
whose rules, particularly those associated with frontality,
orthogonality, and perspective, are extremely precise, and
often very different from those of the same medium faced
with other objects and other projects. Plans and models are
already images that generate architecture or prefigure it and,
as such, testify to an absolute legitimacy as supreme arbiters
of all other images, just like musical scores you can always
refer back to in order to check an interpretation. Drawings,
paintings, photographs, and films on architecture are so many
interpretations of an architectural score, which, although
already played as a built object, is endlessly replayed, reinter-
preted, through and in its images.

Yet, thanks to a complexity that covers the parameters of
time and movement, architecture cannot be reduced to an
image; and no image, no set of images, whether still or animated, can claim to exhaust it even if certain films, for
example, have such objectives as filming image upon image
to make visible the movements of natural light and shadow,
multiplying the number of angles, using crane movements,
(cranes became cinematic devices after having been intro-

duced as architectural devices used to construct buildings),
using aerial views, etc. Images in fact question architecture,
confront it with the idea that it creates of itself, with its purpose and function. Images also confront architecture with
other objects, architectural or otherwise. The way in which a
building is photographed or filmed, whether in the natural
light in which it basks or the artificial light needed to illuminate it (and in the most flattering way), reveals what an object
of architecture is and what it says. There is a lot to be said
about a building's photogenic qualities. Just what is it that
makes an object of architecture photogenic and determines
whether its representations will be spectacular, seductive?
Might there not be a comparison to be made between the
photogenic qualities of a building and those of a face? Any
portrait photographer knows that what makes a face photogenic resides in the relationship between the invisible bone
structure and the skin, and the interaction of these two architectural elements in the light – the way the face registers and
is sculpted by light. There is also no doubt plenty to say – critically, if not polemically – about a form of architecture that is
content with dazzling mirror reflections, as well as about
architects for whom the success of a building is judged by the
number of architectural magazine covers that feature images
of it. These same architects also seem to think that architecture should first produce plastic objects before producing
functional objects, and think of architecture in terms of its
photographic or cinemagraphic properties, forgetting that,
without leaving the same field of art and aesthetic production, architectural objects exceed the images produced by
photography or film: architecture is surely, equally, scenogra-
phy, set design, mise-en-scène, script, and plot in a living
spectacle, offering an unlimited number of live performances
and endless light and sound shows.

The kind of architecture produced by Bernard Tschumi for
the Le Fresnoy/Studio National des Arts Contemporains sometimes refers to the theory of images and, more specifically, to
film theory, with emphasis on framing effects, camera movement, depth of field, editing features, and so on. In this case,
architecture borrows by inevitably distorting certain concepts
imported from other practices. For the Le Fresnoy building,
Tschumi frequently evokes an architecture of movement, an
architecture of the event, as well as certain features of editing
and collage. And the simple technic of collage, using bits of
paper, bits of photographs, and scissors and glue, and bringing together fragments of images collected by chance and
reconfigured as new images, has provided him with hunches,
intuitions, evocations, and approaches as to what Le Fresnoy
would be according to the ideas he hoped to see at work there,
even before drawing his first sketch. In his New York office, all
of these images were accumulated on a huge wooden panel as
soon as they vaguely resembled the ideas being tossed around.
When Tschumi's building was built, or the main part of it at
least, I wrote previously of the comparison of the articulation

of the old buildings (what was once a popular entertainment center) to the contemporary sanctuary of the audiovisual and of new technologies – placed alongside and above and below each other by Tschumi – with the straightforward cut that, in film editing, is known as a jump cut. There is no dissolve, the two different historical periods are slung together using nothing but a simple void, a gap – as distinct as black to white – what Tschumi has called a residual or interstitial space. What happens is that an inner segment of an overly long, fixed plane is removed by performing a sort of ablation. The suture or join is then made – it must be absolutely invisible – between the two parts of this same plane previously separated by the removed segment. At Le Fresnoy, the segment that would have ensured real continuity between the old and the new was removed in advance and eliminated because Tschumi did not like it and so excluded it from his plan, relying on this solution of continuity. And, miraculously, the beginning and end of the plane, the beginning and end of the architecture – over a ninety-year period – join aesthetically and narratively without any sudden visual shift, without any fault in the editing, through this perfect fake-join, this sort of jump cut.

In another context, more precisely in filming two states of the interior architecture of the Musée National de l'Art Moderne at the Pompidou Center – the original architecture of Richard Rogers and Renzo Piano, supplemented by that of Gae Aulenti – I confronted the architecture with the logic of the images that look at it, in effect, with the theory that organizes these images and predetermines them as soon as filming starts. The idea was to show how the same collection of works of art, the same series of paintings or sculptures, was differently staged, distributed, and lit by two different interior architectures that are also differently articulated to the building's overall architecture. I wanted to look at how different effects of meaning are released in the individual works and the set of works as a whole – that long syntagma that becomes a collection – by the way the paintings are placed on the walls and the relationships that establish themselves between the paintings, and then between the paintings and the surrounding decor, as well as by the light the architecture distributes over them. I also wanted to show how the mode of filming induced by a space then informs that space itself, its properties and its meaning.

In the original interior architecture, and in the museography conceived by Pontus Hulten, based on the model of traditional African villages and their boxlike structures, the permanent collection of the Musée National de l'Art Moderne could be read in terms of depth of field in the relationship of foreground to background, as well as the relationship of characters – the works – to a backdrop known in film as a backcloth. These images of the distance appear at the Pompidou Center behind the huge picture windows: the real Eiffel Tower, emerging on the horizon, on the same axis as the one painted by Delaunay. The camera traveled diagonally from one work to the next, producing a reading through associations of ideas and according to transverse perspectives. It was as though the works were suspended in space with no support. The thinness, the lightness of the almost invisible partitions, maintained the illusion of the works hanging in a state of weightlessness, but as soon as the support revealed its fragility by some sort of oscillation, a vibration or reaction to currents of air, the flimsy materiality – the false immateriality – on which these masterpieces of 20th-century art were hung appeared savagely obvious. The way the works were hung took no notice of either their dangerous exposure to sunlight, something curators are normally worried about, nor of visitors' discomfort with reflections. But the camera, that ideal eye that is also an implacable judge, enjoyed complete freedom to negotiate the most favorable angle in its approach to the works.

In direct opposition, the interior architecture of Aulenti and the museography of Dominique Bozo force the camera to keep to a strict orthogonality and to seek out successive frontalities: a lateral tracking shot along the central distributor aisle is followed, at right angles, by progressive penetration into the first room of the Matisse sanctuary. This is followed by a new lateral tracking shot as we go into the second room of the artist. From there, we backtrack out at right angles, then there is a 90-degree panoramic shot as we again take the central aisle up to the new sanctuary and turn, again at right angles, to enter Picasso's domain; and on it goes, from Braque to Miro, etc.

And so the same works, the same collection, the same sets, artist by artist, were filmed in a radically different way in the structures built by Aulenti, with their massive walls that look thicker than they are, imitating the old museum of the Palais de Tokyo, with its rooms closed in on themselves, without any opening to the outside, and their somewhat solemn character. The light itself was quite different, of a different nature, of a different color temperature, and distributed differently between daylight and artificial light. In the Rogers, Piano, and Hulten area, daylight and artificial light keep crossing, conflicting and mingling, and sometimes the choice of the film stock and the filter was difficult if we wanted to avoid the cold blue light of day or the warm orange light of tungsten. In Aulenti and Bozo's space, the two different kinds of light are separate. Along the central corridor, daylight reigns absolutely supreme, delivered through the immense glass windows of the facade. In contrast, each sanctuary, each "box" dedicated to an artist, is lit only with artificial light, adjusted to suit each work. But the shooting of the film, that is, the eye of cinema, the gaze of images upon images, revealed the many deficiencies and defects of such supposedly perfect lighting, like, for example, its completely uneven distribution between the upper and lower parts of the wall.

Architecture, then, may like seeing itself in images, but it can also be seen by images, commented on and criticized by them. For architecture cannot help but have images taken of it, whether these are meant to sing its praises or have nothing to do with praise – from the least respectful, like those Jean-Luc Godard projected in filming the Louvre, which the trio of Bande à Part (The Outsiders) crosses in four minutes and 26 seconds flat, to the utterly mediocre and far worse images of everyday reality produced routinely for televised news reports, which only derive any legitimacy from their chaotic jumble when the architecture they are filming itself degenerates into chaos and becomes a pile of rubble: images of war, images of earthquakes.

Le Fresnoy, for which I drew up the artistic and educational plans as well as piloted the architectural programming that was the basis of the competition finally won by Tschumi, is a building that, in several ways, finds itself at the center and at the turning point of what remain today and what will become images of architecture and architectural images. On the one hand, the building has been photographed a lot: its photogenic appeal has not been lost on photographers and architecture critics. I myself was able to confirm its extraordinary potential in the film I devoted to it. This turned into a feature film that, at times, goes off the rails, temporarily steering the story along documentary tracks before returning to the main narrative line. Le Fresnoy looks good no matter the light and almost no matter the camera angle. At night, it is doubly lit with floodlights that illuminate the basic structures and with networks of little blue lights that mark out the space in between. But if you take the trouble to light it using powerful studio lights, its photogenic magic can reach truly enchanting heights. It is true that the architecture of the building calls for movement and catches the light; true, too, that it offers places that invite action and frameworks that invite characters to perform in them. But, by the very fact of being an artistic and educational project, and in addition to its being a trial for the architectural programming I mentioned above, Le Fresnoy is a building whose principle function is to pool all kinds of tools and to offer all kinds of spaces for the production of images and sounds – hence its title as a studio, designed to conjure up the same associations as the photographer's studio or film studios.

The architecture is photogenic because the function of the building is the engineering of images – in the sense in which we speak of civil engineering for the production of works. Le Fresnoy is thus caught between the images produced of it and the images it produces and displays – for it also comprises vast exhibition spaces as well as two cinemas. Among the images Le Fresnoy produces, there are the now classic ones of the silver supports of photography and film, as well as the magnetic-electronic ones used in video. But images in which it is presented as a sanctuary – as in "The Bauhaus of the New Technologies," or "The Villa Medicis of Hi-Tech" – are computed, digital images, whose referent is no longer necessarily visual reality – either of nature or the built environment. These images have lost the status that photographic and cinematographic images once had as prints. They are captured and altered; they are purely computer-generated, produced by sophisticated software and run on powerful computers; tales told in interactive images, virtual reality – urban or architectural spaces that can be traversed through movement computed in real time; simulated images of spaces or objects called upon to be produced in reality.

Perhaps because it has stood out as a remarkable piece of architecture and as the work of an important contemporary architect, Le Fresnoy has a significant proportion of postgraduate and graduate architects among its students. This seems to me to be a sure sign of Le Fresnoy's preeminent position, not only as an educational project and a place where images are produced, but as a building and an aesthetic object within the enormous field of images that is rightly its working terrain.

Today, as has been eloquently demonstrated by the contributions at this Anymore conference, architecture is no longer merely an object in search of images that it might permit photography, film, or video to capture; it is no longer merely a stage waiting for the role that might be conferred upon it in some story, some scenario, some mise-en-scène; it is no longer merely an object that may be large-scale but is nonetheless reducible to an object of design – one approached via pathways, corridors, ascents, commissions, and so on. Architecture has become its own scenario, its own principle of narrative and plastic generation, its own mise-en-scène, lit, played out, interpreted, then filmed and edited by itself – and this, from the outset, from its initial conception. Today, architecture has stopped waiting for the images it might manage to provoke once it is built. It seeks itself in advance. It bases itself and thinks of itself in images, within images. Architectural plans are developed in computerized images that take the script wherever inspiration carries it and according to a minimal synopsis: images of organic or mineral forms, images of flowers, shells, animals, whatever. Architecture thereby short-circuits the previous processes in which its own images once emerged, as well as the laws governing discovery of its photogenic quality.

That photogenic quality is somehow integrated, it is what is in play at the heart of any architectural project, it is what regulates the program, the software. Architecture's "point of view" – concerning a model, for example – is no longer a physical place from which the building is to appear, from the front or the side. "Point of view" is now a computed place, and this endlessly computed place radiates outward and spreads, controlling the future architectural organism. We are living in the age of computed, machine-generated forms that are just as likely to clothe a building as a car or a lamp or a refrigerator. Not only can the same family of forms, deriving from the same production processes and the same plastic genealogy, provide images of objects whose functions and sizes are extremely varied, but this aesthetic mold can also determine the object itself in its totality – that is, at the same time, its function as an image, its image as a function, the image of its image.

Perhaps this will give architectural, industrial, and other objects produced today a sort of common, identifying style; a signature marking the plastic and aesthetic kinship of a washbasin and a skyscraper, or of a car and a bed, a motorbike and a vacuum cleaner. Then again, a Louis XV cabinet and a carriage of the same period are surely objects belonging to the same aesthetic family. And surely it would be easy to imagine the transfer of the function of one to the other through hybridization and vice versa, achieving a sort of functional communication of forms created by the same period, in the same part of the world. In the 18th century, families of forms depended on the state of technology, on taste, and, above all, on practical skill. The hand that created the form also created the space. Time too depended on the hand: manufacturing time, finishing time – the time it took for the hand to work on the form also allowed for the form to be thought out. Analagously, the action of traditional film editing takes place within this same time frame – using a physically present film reel that is handled physically and looked at against the light, then cut and pasted. In digital editing the hand is almost absent, it has no space, no material support to handle, and so the time of the hand, the time that allows for thinking, has disappeared. The time of gearing up needs to be imposed on the neutral impudence of machines that are ever more powerful, ever more contemptuous of time, ever more productive of immediate spaces; machines that do not progress, that do not evolve within any temporality, that do not result from history, but are strictly synchronic with their generative formulae. The complexity of the shapes that architecture requires of computing machines gives these machines a bit of time. This is the revenge of the aesthetic dream, of theoretical speculation about the mechanical production of forms, however complex and sophisticated they may be. But such computing time is diminishing every day, and the hand continues to remove itself from human constructions. We can counter the question, "Anymore technology?" with another question: "More or less time for thought within the instantaneous space of machines?"

As I have said, my primary relationship with architecture has been as a filmmaker. I have also worked as a project leader, invited to translate the spatial requirements of an art project into the language of architecture, involving image invention and production. At Le Fresnoy, we train young filmmakers to reflect on such questions as how to film contemporary art, how to film theater or dance or opera, how to film architecture. But we also train young architects to become scriptwriters, producers, and directors of objects of architecture that start off as images and will in many cases remain so. No doubt this is currently one of architecture's most exciting gambits – to be at the crossroads between its reflections in time-honored images and its projection as a screenplay using images that it itself has already exhaustively, and ideally, filmed.

Alain Fleischer is the dean of the Fresnoy School of Contemporary Arts and a documentary filmmaker. His films include Le Louvre imaginaire and Le cow-boy et l'indien: quelques rendez-vous.

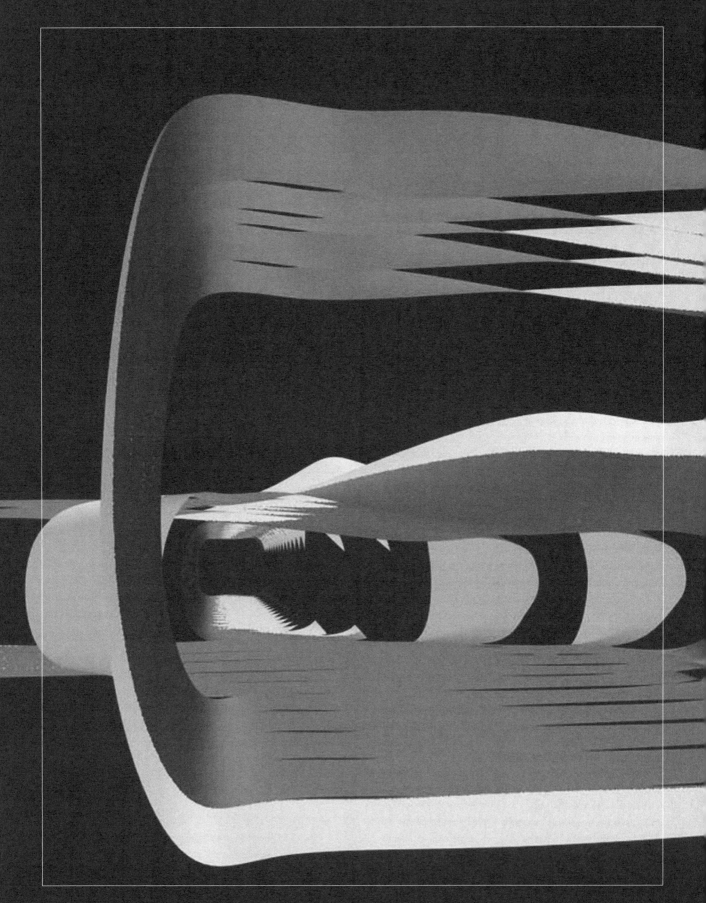

Surface Effects
Greg Lynn

Dining hall wall study, Korean Presbyterian Church, New York, 1999.

I want to address the principles and design techniques of surfaces. I will slice through several projects very thinly and focus on surface characteristics rather than on those of volume. Many issues already discussed at the Anymore conference are implicit in this presentation, so let me briefly articulate some of them.

The first is the reemergence of **Gesamtkunstwerk**, or total design. The connection between this 19th-century notion of totality and the shift from point-based definitions of architectural space to deformable vector surfaces is one that is easier to describe with surfaces than it is with points and lines. This implies that there is less reductionism, purity, and essentialism in deformable surfaces than there is in defining a point. There is also something contemporary and accessible about design with surfaces, in that one can more easily describe, for example, an athletic shoe with surfaces than with a plan and section. This also implies a connection, at the level of tools, with other areas of design. Suddenly, then, architecture shares techniques with other fields and can more freely migrate into other disciplines. Inevitably, when this happens, these other disciplines are carried back into architecture. So to further the analogy, we might be able to design the shoes for our occupants, and thus extend the idea of the architecture that encloses them.

Second, issues of brand and variation have been discussed. Due to the needs of both change and continuity, products demand a constant identity in media culture and at the same time accelerated degrees of variation and change. This problem is a marketing and mass production phenomenon and is provocative to architecture – a design field based on timelessness and uniqueness rather than production and development. Contemporary identity must be both stable and fluid. In the world of products, unlike architecture as we understand it, there is a need for techniques of variation and identity.

The third discussion occurring at this conference is a theme that links the first two. The scope of design is expanding as more and more of the world is being designed. There will be an increasing need for architects to interface with design and manufacturing. Here the term **architect** is expanded to describe not only building design but also the management, invention, and conceptualization of production and assembly processes. To return to the discussion of athletic footwear, one could then need an architect to design a pair of shoes. This is distinct from having a cobbler make a pair of shoes because it involves customizing a generic product.

Clockwise from top left: cross-section study; administration wing study; floor study; roof surface study, Korean Presbyterian Church.

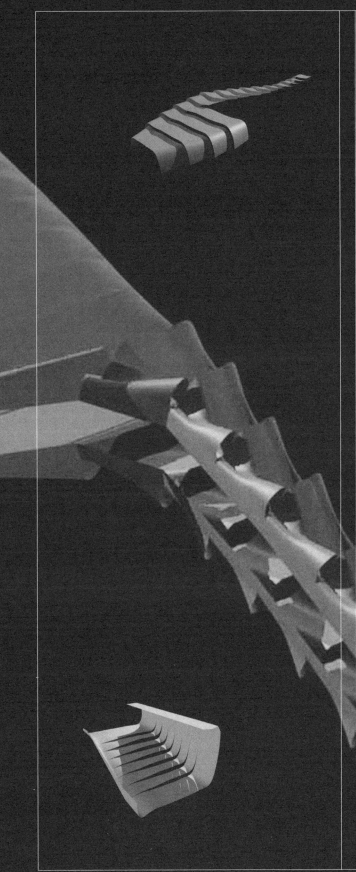

Nike™, Adidas™, Puma™, Converse™, and perhaps even Prada™ could turn to professionals resembling architects to control the color, shape, materials, and dimensions of their product lines in direct contact with consumers. As an increasing number of products are designed in a generic fashion, with an increasing number of options, soon there will be a need for architects at car dealerships, fashion boutiques, appliance stores, etc. In order to organize these types of processes there will be a parallel need for new techniques of managing variation and identity.

One of the many uses of surface is for the production of special effects. This is related to a shift from typology, which is fixed, to traits, which are variable and interchangeable. Special effects not only imply film techniques but also the addition of features and contours in a surface continuum. Traits can be manifest without respect to the typologies in which they occur.

This discussion that I have prepared unashamedly focuses upon style. Unashamedly because I blame Winy Maas, who at the Anytime conference in Ankara accused me and several of my fellow panelists of constituting a **neo-Jugendstil**, or perhaps a new art nouveau or even a new Secessionism. I think Winy voiced this accusation as an extreme condemnation, but I found it enlightening. The Jugendstil, art nouveau, and Secessionist styles are often portrayed as premodern. Occurring at roughly the turn of the century and involving new technologies of production and design, the Jugendstil is interesting to examine in light of the transitional character of these premodern styles. Nikolaus Pevsner, Sigfried Giedeon, and others argued that these styles were modern in two senses: first, to the extent to which they rejected classical orders in favor of the abstraction of nature; and second, for their use of new techniques for production and fabrication. An instance of the abstraction of nature would be both the vegetal abstraction of nature linked to Louis Sullivan's "seed germ" studies by the Brussels school and the reptilian abstraction of surface and skin by the Viennese Secessionists. Despite these modern characteristics, Pevsner and Giedeon exclude these transitional figures from the modernist canon in part because of the use of these new technologies for ornamentation and the decoration of structure. But their primary reason for excluding art nouveau, Secessionism, and Jugendstil was that the designers behind these movements were seen as architects of surface rather than as architects of space. The dichotomy between volume/decoration and space/surface was, however, naively for-

mulated. The progressive increase in the use of design and fabrication technologies based on a geometry of inflected surfaces suggests a new spatial sensibility rather than the disappearance of spatial qualities altogether. Today, surface and space are no longer opposed to one another; volume and envelope are being formed through the manipulation of continuously curved surfaces rather than through volumes defined by discrete points. In other words, Winy's critique was valid on a number of counts: yes, there is a resonance today with the premodern interests in industrial fabrication, in decoration, and in surface. But I disagree with him in one important sense: that the work of Bernard Cache, Mark Goulthorpe, and others is not neo-Jugendstil, because it treats surface as a space-producing medium.

Unlike my texts in previous Any conference publications, this discussion focuses more on the disciplinary issues and history of architecture than on the medium of surface-geometry tools. The necessity for discipline-specific discussions has already been called for by Rosalind Krauss. This paper focuses primarily on the spatial and material properties germane to architectural design that emerge from the use of topology, and not on the mathematical and philosophical issues inherent to digital surface design itself. The first trait one notices in an architectural surface – rather than in a point-based volume – is that surfaces tend to be voluptuous, in the sense that they are curved and inflected. Surfaces can also torque; they can strand and shred; they can aggregate; they can gastrulate; they can louver. These five special surface effects emerge from the unique problems of architectural design and the need to enclose space while allowing visual and physical transparency, movement, and modulation.

The first example of these spatial effects of surfaces is that of aggregation. For the Korean Presbyterian Church in New York, a project designed in collaboration with Michael McInturf and Douglas Garofalo, we generated massing and volume through the blending together of a collection of bubbles or blobs. The properties of this type of modeling produce a continuity of envelopes with distinct bulges or features that are the residue of the generating primitive volumes. In order to modulate the view and entry into this continuous form we employed a technique of offset surface louvers. The first instance of this surface effect is in the outdoor entry, where movement into the building occurs through what is a seemingly closed volume due to the overlapping panels. Movement in the other direction, out of the building and

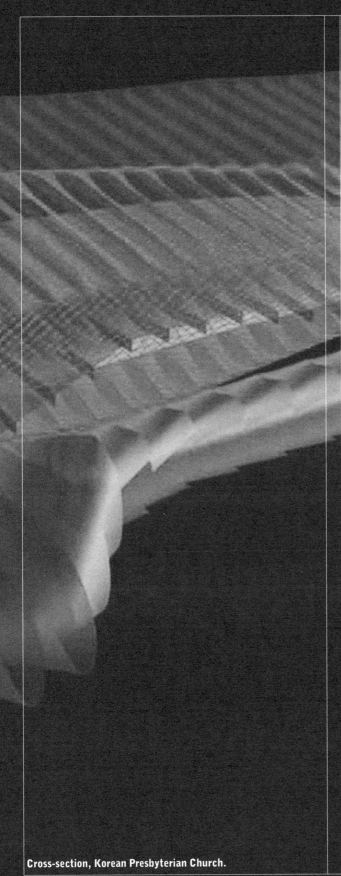

Cross-section, Korean Presbyterian Church.

down the stair, reveals the openness rather than the overlap between louvered surfaces and provides a modulated flicker effect of views toward the skyline of Manhattan. One trait of louvered surfaces is their ability to orient motion and view through overlap and alignment. Similarly, in the interior space of the sanctuary, the directionality of the volume is conditioned through manipulations of surface rather than volumetric focus. There is no axis or terminal point in the space, but there is a general drift organized by the differential offsets of the ceiling and walls. Any view from the altar toward the seats yields a crenelated volume; ceiling and wall surfaces, disrupted by cuts and slivers of frontal surfaces, blend and disappear toward the middle of the space. When one looks from the seats toward the altar, these cuts smooth out through overlaps, so that the volume enclosed by the ceiling and wall surfaces appears more continuous with blurred bands of light. A rotary movement around the space transforms the interior from a continuous smooth space to a flicker surface of segmentation. Another quality of this kind of spatial effect caused by manipulations of surfaces is a manipulation of space that is by definition vague. There is no point or location, just a blurred directionality and dominant orientations. The transition between looking forward and looking back is a gradient and not a line or edge.

These torque effects are also evident in the design studies we made for an unbuilt house project, where the relationship between surface, ornament, and structure emerges through the bending of tubular surfaces, producing curvilinear pockets and volumes. The intersection of tubular surfaces through torquing captures volume in pockets, crotches, forks, bends, and elbows. A similar special effect of surface deformation is stranding, where surfaces are slivered along their controlling curves, called isoparms. By tearing a surface along its length and in different directional grains, biases and striations can be defined. Similar to the effects of a point-based grid, stranding is an organizational technique that is vaguely modular. Unlike a grid of points, this modular stranding occurs through the splitting and bending of a surface.

Both the installation in the Encore Gallery, Brussels and in the h2 House Visitors' Center in Vienna use bidirectional shreds to produce louver effects much like those in the church but through the torquing of surfaces. In the upper sections of these surfaces there are openings oriented in one direction, while on the lower sections the orientation flips to the other direction. A

volume is opened in two different directions through this bidirectional shredding. There is a catalogue of the effects of these flipping shreds in the schematic design studies that I worked on for the Cincinnati Country Day School, designed primarily by Michael McInturf. Similar to the Korean Presbyterian Church, six volumes are nested within an undulating roof surface, defined by baglike surfaces that Michael refers to as the programmatic organs. These organs are defined by a series of iterative surfaces that vary along their length. These elements can continuously mutate between different architectural traits, for example, between a stepped or a sloped floor. In the administration wing, surfaces are oriented toward natural light, neighboring views are modulated through offsets to the dining-hall wall surfaces, and the single volume of the information center is divided into two zones, library and computer center, through twisted ceiling surfaces oriented both east and west. The volume of the auditorium was generated using an E-shaped sequence of surfaces in the longitudinal section: the stepped floor plates turn into the wall, ceiling plates then return to the opposite wall, folding over to produce a balcony floor above. In the cross-section a similar E motif was reproduced to effect a nested volume of self-intersecting surfaces where the space is continuous even though the surfaces pass through themselves.

Surfaces can self-intersect, or fold over on themselves, to produce volumetric gastrulations, polyps, and herniations, as they do in the design line of Embryonic Houses. These surfaces are shredded along their isoparms and unfolded into fronds so that the surface geometry is never violated by a fenestration or opening. One of the most critical issues in architectural design is the management and design of openings like doors and windows. It is important that these elements emerge from the same thinking about surface rather than being imported from another sensibility about frame, structure, and opening. These surfaces are not intersected by another type of space and geometry but are instead fenestrated using their own logic of composition. These landscapes contain 64 panels within their surface that can be cut out and reassembled to generate a closed volume. There are two techniques for fenestrating these volumes, one by louvering and another by shredding; neither adds geometry to the surface, but both use the surface geometry to generate the apertures.

My closing contribution to this discussion on contemporary surface geometry and the decorative surfaces of the previous century is an installation that I am working on at the Secession Building in Vienna with the painter Fabian Marcaccio. Fabian and I are both interested in the fusion between surface and figure, so we began this installation with a mutation and regeneration of the famous cabbage dome of Joseph Maria Olbrich's building. The cabbage dome is a primitive that we duplicated down the face of the building and into the gallery space, letting it drift through the building while sweeping a surface that became the volume of the installation. I would attribute Winy Maas with putting his finger on something here, which is the fusion of ornament and structure through techniques of surfaces rather than through mere decorative techniques. In this existing building it is important that the surface belongs to neither architecture nor painting. We articulate the surface of our installation as both a painter's canvas and a rhythm of ornamental structural frames. The specificity of architecture and painting is maintained; it is clear that I am nowhere near making a painting, just as it is clear that Fabian is nowhere near designing a building. But the two of us are working with very similar themes in terms of surfaces of pictorial activity and spatial activity, and we are collaborating to produce a set of flowing effects in space. If you were to ask Fabian to present the project, he would say it was a giant painting. When I present it, it is architecture. For both of us, it is an interest in the ability of modulated surfaces to create special spatial effects.

Greg Lynn is founder of the studio FORM in Los Angeles. He teaches at the School of Architecture at the University of California in Los Angeles and is the author of **Animate Form**.

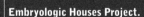
Embryologic Houses Project.

Discussion 5

JEAN-LOUIS COHEN In the wake of Bernard Cache's presentation, we seem to be discussing Anymore History rather than Anymore Technology. I'm fascinated by this reemergence of history as something clearly fundamental and construed as both subjective and technical.

HUBERT DAMISCH I would like to say a few words on the relationship not only between this morning's session and history and theory but also yesterday afternoon's session, Anymore Architecture. There seems to be a continuity of some sort. Yesterday we heard how movement can come into architecture. Rosalind Krauss raised the issue of specificity, based on fixed, still images, and then we saw architects like Peter Eisenman debate the issue of movement in architecture. Rosalind questioned how one can actually make movement with something that is still, how you can animate still images. Today, we saw another theme emerging – that of continuity, of surfaces, changes, and of a lineage, as Bernard Cache said, between cyberspace and the past, since this all has to come from somewhere. Looking at the virtual through history (not because history offers an answer – history never offers an answer – but it does at least raise the question) the interesting thing for me is: can we still work in a continuum with computers and video? In answering this, perhaps we should look back to the idea of construction in architecture. At the end of the 19th century, the real novelty of construction was to combine what is continuous with what is discontinuous, and vice versa. There is a direct link between these two sessions, with ideas of movement, continuity and transformation.

BERNARD CACHE Computers don't invent anything. I mean, processes and procedures working with continuity existed long before circuit boards made them accessible to everybody. The interesting thing is that man himself has lost quite a lot of knowledge – look at any treaty on descriptive geometry of the 18th or 19th centuries, or at the intricate design of cupolas – this is something that most architects today don't really understand or know. But now we have other types of help – computers. It was the same in the past. Viollet-le-Duc could not actually think about architecture in continuous terms. He needed a material to make this continuity possible. You can see the same type of operation with cinema and video. Cinema is basically making something continuous out of something discontinued. You can always use a computer to generate any type of interpretative image, and so images today are computed.

AUDIENCE Listening to the first three speakers this morning, it seems that new technology implies or involves a new type of thinking about architecture, and what seems commonplace here is the emergence of new models of construction – based on folds, inflections, and more broadly speaking, a kind of baroque problematic. Modern art and architectural styles have been called an elaboration of abstracts – abstracts of materials and formal shapes. It seems to me that we are shifting from the model of the box, or the mold, to a space that presupposes deformations, discontinuities, disjunctions – a new typology in the mathematical sense of the term. This change seems to me really quite revolutionary. But how does technology affect these new ways of thinking about architectural space, from the small scale to something as big as cities?

GREG LYNN Your question could generate a whole other conference. But the one issue that I think is most interesting is how one reads technology. It's already been said today that the computer was theoretically a baroque invention, and only now is it an instrumental technique. This relationship to the baroque – more to baroque mathematics than to baroque architecture – is very interesting, and probably the best way through which to understand abstraction. The only thing I want to avoid in shifting the panel toward history is the idea that an understanding of history would also allow us not to repeat it. One of the issues would be not to site the architectural techniques in a baroque moment, but to extract from that baroque moment the theories and concepts that have only manifested themselves 200 years later. This is the thing that makes me a little nervous.

MARK TAYLOR There is another way, it seems to me, to elaborate Damisch's point about continuity and discontinuity and the relationship between the panel yesterday and this morning. It is through the issue that was at stake yesterday, with the debate between Peter Eisenman and Lars Spuybroek about individual criticism and individual critique. If one looks, for example, emblematically at Peter's Staten Island project and Greg's Korean Church project, the relationship between interiority and exteriority is significantly different. It has to do with a certain kind of criticality (as Peter was explaining it) – that the interior is discontinuous with the exterior in a way that allows a discontinuity that can function critically. For Greg, there's a convoluting and involuting of interiority and exteriority that does not have the same kind of disjunction, as I understand it.

I also want to come back to a category Mark Goulthorpe introduced that I found very interesting. He used the term *pleasure* repeatedly, but did not emphasize it theoretically, along with the category of trauma. How does the category of pleasure relate to the kind of criticality that Peter was arguing toward, and in what way is trauma not discontinuous? In other words, how does it relate to the kind of interrelation between interiority and exteriority that differentiates Greg's church from Peter's Staten Island project?

LYNN Mark, I think that your observation is right on the money, but I don't know that I would make the boundaries so coarse. There's never an absolute condition. It's really a question of scale; with both Peter's Staten Island project and our Korean Church, you see a kind of macroradicality between the interior and exterior. The real test for the church will be when they get 3,000 people in there and see how they respond to it. If the congregation responds to it as a conventional church, then I think we've failed, but if there are microscopic disturbances, then I think we have succeeded. It's not an absolute condition, but the relationship between interior and exterior was one we tried to blend microscopically. It still has a lot of edginess to it – I mean a literal, formal edginess – but this happens at a finer texture.

MARK GOULTHORPE I introduced those terms only through my own difficulty in understanding contemporary art works and events that have really moved me, in particular in relationship to the Frankfurt Ballet. It was Heidi Gilpin who introduced the notion of trauma in trying to comprehend the cultural experience of the Frankfurt Ballet. I've thought about it more and more, and it seems to me that what characterizes most architectural conferences, and certainly this one, is that everybody is saying we're in a new environment, that there is a paradigm shift of some sort. But everybody seems to flounder at giving examples of, and articulating, what it is that's new. I think that the two architects you mentioned, Lars and Greg, are the only architects who simply put their hands on their hearts and say that there's something new here. At the Morph conference two years ago, Greg said that working in a time-force environment gives potential to move people in new ways. This needs qualification, but it certainly stimulated me over the last couple of years. Are there really new potentials of form and space? It's just going to take a while to qualify what we mean by these terms.

MICHAEL NUROCK The terms *shock* and *trauma* appeared through a 19th-century understanding of technology, more specifically with the incidents of railroad accidents, and it was from those accidents that Charcot and Freud came up with their theories on trauma and shock. It also involved a shift in the understanding of memory; a memory that is now some-how repressed, somehow removed from consciousness. I'm wondering to what extent technology, and more specifically, technology with respect to architecture, might be playing into new understandings of what is mind, what is body, and what is memory.

CACHE What I was trying to show in my presentation, was that textiles, as a procedure, is best applied to fabric – to a physical warp and weave. But the same technique can also be used on new materials – electronic, intangible materials. The word *textiles* has such significance now because it encompasses and embraces the multitude of processes operable on all these different materials. The technique was not preexistent as an abstract idea but emerged from working with the materials themselves. As the scope of these materials is broadened, we can implement different techniques, changing, in the process, the nature of the technique. It's very similar to Bergson's theory of a memory that contracts instead of a memory that is inscribed or imprinted.

I also want to reassure Marc Mimram that there are people in this room who are interested in materials. Simply because we deal with computers and virtual technologies every day it does not mean that we have lost contact with or interest in the physical materiality of the architectural site. Last week, for example, I was busy dealing with these kinds of textual/architectural issues for a hotel in Hong Kong. I am making this point not to create an argument but rather to put an end to one before it starts. You see, on the one hand, you have the Americans and their simultaneous embrace of both computers and imported French philosophy. On the other hand, you have the French with their feet planted firmly on the ground, and then all the clichés reverse themselves – the Frenchman as a kind of Eastern cowboy, and the American as a kind of weary rive gauche intellectual. It might be time for us to abandon all these clichés – to think of architects as using computers not simply to illustrate virtual images – I'm speaking not only about me but about Greg Lynn and perhaps Marc himself. Marc is involved in a restoration process, so it's something quite material. You can also use computers without being totally uncultured. You're thinking even when you are using a computer. It happens you know.

MARC MIMRAM You're quite right, Bernard; caricature is not an end in itself. We have to go beyond these clichés. But I can't see the moral of this story – your idea of building well/correctly, or building badly. For a long time now we have been using computers because it is impossible to do what we do without a digital program directly related to production. But when we make a mistake in our projects, obviously it is directly reflected in the construction.

IGNASI DE SOLÀ-MORALES I have an advantage in that I am not French and I am not American. As a result, when I read Foucault I don't feel I am reading a French philosopher. I'm just reading a philosopher. But I'd like to ask a different question. This morning's panel was particularly interesting in terms of the represented models of both complex and renovative ideas – but the two models are two totally different paradigms. On the one hand, you have analytical geometry qualified as baroque and related to a problem that I think is very important – that is, to what extent can you find in the cyberworld a kind of formal determinism? The other paradigm is related to praxis, to pragmatism rather than theory. For example, the idea of textiles is not a mathematical model today but a pragmatic model, a model that takes effect in the decision-making process. When you make a textile, you have to follow rules and procedures, but at each stage a decision has to be made with regard to the ornaments, to the fonts, and so on. This opens up a whole new set of questions that are related to something very important for architecture, and that is the traumatic aspect. So these are totally different types of discourses, but it is absolutely essential to see what they share because this is really the core of the issue. This same comment can also be directed to Yannis Tsiomis. I think that his presentation was very elegant, but he did not specify enough the pragmatism of urban archaeology, of memory, and of the management of a city. It seems that he was speaking about technique, not as in excavation or drawing techniques, but the technique of a present-day city with all its tensions. This pragmatic aspect, Yannis seems to be arguing, has to be supplemented by technology or techniques – not a deterministic technique, but rather a kind of decisive technique.

CACHE We have always used tools in architecture – tools such as a square or a rule, and a computer is really just a more sophisticated tool. Through these devices, there was no deterministic concept in ancient architecture, and there is still none today. But what is interesting is to bring together fields of knowledge that are totally different – both deterministic and others that are more pragmatic. For example, if you look at Semper, you can see that he wrote a whole mathematical text on the form and shape of arrows fired by bows. Semper was somebody very pragmatic who had a kind of nonnegligible mathematical knowledge – it took him over a year to write the study – yet if we look at the formula he comes up with, it's really high-tech. The interesting thing, then, is the bringing together of two approaches.

LYNN I think that there are some facts about computation and factory production that architects don't really want to digest.

For instance, I read in the newspaper the other day that in the United States, 45 percent of single-family houses are now built in factories. There are no architects designing these houses but rather engineers, who use computers for their design and computer-controlled robotics for their construction. If architecture doesn't digest this fact, then it's not going to be able to engage in contemporary problems. The real task for us is to theorize computation and to develop some kind of intuition, expertise, and finesse with the use of these tools, so that we still have relevant cultural activities. I have a sense that a lot of this discussion is academic in the worst sense – it's already been decided for us. The issue then is not whether or not architects should use computers – all architects use computers. The questions are who's using them differently and what kinds of decisions are people making with them.

YANNIS TSIOMIS What is interesting for me and my work, regarding the theme of technique and technology, is the issue of archaeological space. Each day, I'm confronted with a vacuum. An agora is a void – it contains no object, it's empty. In trying to deal with the architecture of this absence, I have to look further afield at what is available in the city, negotiating with the authorities as to the best way to organize this empty space. There is, then, a kind of reflection between the technical object, which was once spectacular, and the issue of the relationship between the city and the archaeological space, the urban and social fabric, and an intangible heritage and archaeology. This is a negotiation that has been going on for two years now. I don't want to go into the details of these extremely complex relations, but what I think is fascinating is that the issue of technology has extended across time, from the agora to today. Innovation influences, and has to influence, civilization – this is where one can say that we can reflect on technique without technology.

I also have the feeling that we are engaged in a false polemic, especially when we refer to the fear of America, the fear of Europe, of Kosovo, and so on. A few months ago, Jean Baudrillard made a speech at UNESCO, where he said that we do not suffer from abstraction today but from an excess of reality. He argued that in the precomputer, previrtual society it was impossible to have an exchange because everything was open to the imagination – everybody had their own vision as to how to recreate and anticipate the world. With the virtual world, he argued, comes the realization of the perfect double, the double of the world that through virtual technology can actually be there and exist – cloned man usurping real man. This is not a hypothetical issue but a real situation today.

CACHE Concerning the question of anticipation, when we create architectural surfaces we trust completely what we see on the computer screen. Typically, we send these images to the factory, wait for the sample to come back, and then make a final decision. By this, I mean to suggest that computer science has its own actuality — an actuality that does not really apply to all other material things. Computer science is in effect an ideology.

TSIOMIS But you are philosophizing about a reality that is not your own.

CACHE No, I think there is an ideology of information that would have the world reduced to a series of ones and zeros. Looking at these numbers, you don't hear a sound, you don't see an image. For these ones and zeroes to turn into words and pictures you have to have a membrane to render it — this is something extremely material. Without this membrane, computer science does not exist. Information is a completely physical thing.

BERNARD TSCHUMI Twenty years ago Manfredo Tafuri wrote that there is no theory; there is only a history of theory. In the debate this morning and yesterday, we have seen that this opposition between theory and practice is being questioned again. A hundred years of dialectics disappear, and all of a sudden there is a new way to produce — in terms of both intellectual and material production. So there is a short circuit here that really puts into question all the categories that I, for one, am working with in the context of a university, an American university, where scholars, historians, and theoreticians are separated from architects and designers. This separation is no longer possible. We are in a new system of coordinates.

6. Anymore Mores?
Throughout the 20th century architecture has both reacted and capitulated as the seats of power proliferate and disperse against a background of information economies and accelerating corporatization. How might architecture position itself to serve not only clients but patrons in a larger sense, from local to global communities? How can architecture's relationship with collective purpose and social action navigate trends toward nationalist protectionism and cultural hegemony?

Any Mores
Anthony Vidler

Misreading the publicity handout, which I received before the detailed program, and not alerted to the Latin skills of the organizing team, I had thought that this session was about "Anymore **mores**," as opposed to "Anymore mores." Thus I was prepared to speak on the question, perhaps already addressed in previous sessions, as to whether there was "any architecture, anymore." A question that seemed to imply that, indeed, there was a distinct possibility that there was no architecture anymore. But the question "Are there **mores** anymore in architecture?" is of course deeply related to the first, "Is there architecture anymore?" Since the 18th century, generations of critics have linked the fundamental characteristics of architecture – structure, style, function, technology, social purpose – to its ethical and moral role.

It is not surprising that the question arises once more in the context of a digitized fin de siècle, which seems to have substituted surface for structure, arbitrary form for function, technological hubris for social values. Calls for a return to the fundamentals of "tectonics," stemming from a deep-rooted sense that the principles of modernism are being undermined, or for a commitment to a "New Urbanism," out of a sense of loss – of community, of place, of neighborhood – in the face of indiscriminate development, are reminiscent of earlier reactions against modernism itself, and before that against the first age of industrialism. Architecture, since its first definition as a profession dedicated to serving the private and public realms of bourgeois life in the Enlightenment, has always cherished its fundamentalists and its revivalists, whether they were Greek, gothic, classic, modern, or postmodern.

The question that arises in the moment before Y2K, however, is of a different order entirely to those relatively confined reactions and responses to industrial production and society. It is whether we should see the advent of universal digitalization as simply one more shift in the modes of production and consumption, to be absorbed or criticized in the same way as glass and iron, steel and electricity; or whether the transformation it proposes is in the process of developing an entirely new world order, demanding new epistemological instruments, and thereby new models for its representation and manipulation.

In architectural and aesthetic terms, we are certainly witnessing a change in the modes of representation that alters, if not entirely replaces, the perspectival frames through which we have been viewing since the Renaissance. The difficulty of representing perspectival space in "virtual reality" crude wireframe models seems to point to the foreignness of traditional "reality" to the digital world. Perhaps we might frame the difference in terms of the place of the subject in space. Simply put, where perspectival space presumes a viewer's eye, a station point and a vanishing point, digital space knows of no such restriction. Its auto-generated characteristics privilege no vertical or horizontal dimension; its internal and external are subject-neutral. The subject in animation software is rendered as a robotic instrument of three- and four-dimensional exploration and rendering; the spaces it produces are delineated, in principle, for similar nonhuman subjects.

Equally fundamental would be the seamless relations, in digital modeling, between modes of representation and modes of production; this holds not only in the realm of biological and genetic reproduction, but also in the more primitive domain of architecture, where the complicated surfaces and structures developed by animation and morphing programs can be transposed digitally to the factory floor, thereby completely transforming the notion of mass production and standardization. It is at least ironic that what the arts and crafts nostalgics saw as the fatal separation introduced by industrialization between delineation and manufacture has now, in this way, been overcome by industrialization's next stage.

All of which raises the question of mores once more, but in ways that can no longer resort to "authenticity" of structure or materials, form or style. Where, as Walter Benjamin noted, the first era of industrialization introduced for the first time materials that could be shaped in multiple forms — iron and glass — setting off the call for a rigorous morality of structure and style as a "control" mechanism, so to speak, now, in principle at least, the formal and the material have been themselves subsumed within the digital. Further, the literal disappearance of the human subject in digital space, one, interestingly enough, already anticipated by psychoanalysis and philosophy, provokes a series of questions about the role of this "architecture" in society.

Even as we must look on these changes with a certain optimism — for nostalgic reaction, as has been demonstrated by the fate of all such reactions in the recent past, will have little effect on the inexorable processes at work in the technological sector — and seek to tie them to our own interests, social and aesthetic, it must be admitted that the early results of digital application have demonstrated a number of tendencies that run counter to the verities of modernist morality. First, the

ease and speed with which form can be manipulated in animation points to a logic of endless morphological transformation that even an uncritical celebration of process finds hard to arrest: how to determine a stop point, a termination for interminable analysis and generative iteration? Second, the existing software seems to privilege formal transformation of outer surface rather than inner space; as in the imaging of dinosaurs, once patiently built up from skeleton to outer skin, modeling is now worked from the scanning of a three-dimensional solid and its subsequent surface animation, leaving the interior to chance. As Greg Lynn has noted, occupation of such an interior might be compared to inhabiting the Statue of Liberty, possible but not predicted by the form of the outer skin.

Here, all the traditional truisms of modernist ideology — "the plan is the generator," the outside skin as transparent to the space of the inside, the structure as exposed — are not simply reversed but denied or blocked. These considerations have impeded any unqualified acceptance of the new media, and certainly call for very different criteria of form and function, to use these somewhat outdated terms, than those of modernism.

But perhaps the overwhelming difficulty of working to formulate a new moral code for the new architecture is the resistance posed by our conceptions of history, to which are bound our beliefs in, or against, progress. For the question of whether architecture is anymore alive has been the continuing problem, not simply of modernity but of historicized modernity: from Hegel and Hugo in the 1830s to the present. Such questions, whether from the left or the right, have taken their place in broader terms in the set of those that posit the "death" of cultural practices and beliefs — the death of God, the end of art, the end of history — questions in a vulgar sense derived from a mechanistic but compelling reading of Hegel and, later, the sense of an ending/beginning that emerged in the fin de siècle. They were given intellectual force by the feeling of radical disenchantment, as Max Weber put it, brought on by rational, systematic, bureaucratic, modern thought, as it rejected all myths, faiths, mysticism, in a second, postromantic wave of neo-Enlightenment thought.

For Weber, "disenchantment" meant literally that — "de-mythologized" — no more enchantment, no more fairy tales in favor of rigorous social science and materialist critique. From Weber to Manfredo Tafuri, intellectuals, both liberal and left, have held onto this axiom of reason. Alberto Asor Rosa, as we know, characterized

Tafuri as the most absolutely disenchanted of historians. But, while the Weberian/Tafurian model of disenchantment (often masquerading as skepticism and unbelief, if not cynicism) generally wants to hold onto a progressive, demasking, truth-seeking ethic, the term has also served conservatives as an ideology to prove their own negative characterization of the present — no more faith or belief, and thence no more ethics, morals, at least as we have known them in the good past. For conservatives, disenchantment was an indication that a stage of history had been reached that was beyond history; history had for all intents and purposes stopped. The modern epoch was characterized as a **posthistoire** site, where all good things had come to a close. As formulated by interwar and post–World War II thinkers such as Arnold Gehlen and Hendrick de Man (Paul de Man's uncle), the end of history was signaled by the end of movement, of progress, and evolution. As Hendrick de Man wrote:

The term post-historical seems adequate to describe what happens when an institution or a cultural achievement ceases to be historically active and productive of new qualities, and becomes purely receptive or eclectically imitative. The notion of the post-historical would fit the cultural phase that, following a "fulfillment of sense," has become "devoid of sense." The alternative then is, in biological terms, either death or mutation.

More recently, the Italian philosopher Gianni Vattimo has resurrected the term **posthistorical** to, as he puts it, "prove" postmodernism in a book that, in quasi-Nietzschean terms, explores the question of the "end" of history and art. There is a profound immobility in the technological world, which science fiction writers have often portrayed as the reduction of every experience of reality to an experience of images (no one ever really meets anyone else; instead, everyone watches everything on a television screen while alone at home). This same phenomenon can already be sensed in the air-conditioned, muffled silence in which computers work. Here, extrapolating from Vattimo and less concerned with his notion of postmodernity, we might want to imagine at least one possible version of the digital world as posthistorical. Something like that flattened out, gray-screened sky above the world of William Gibson's **Neuromancer**. Gibson's cyberpunk "disenchantment" would then be one side of the Weberian coin, one that sees in the absence of faith, myth, and belief, in modernity, the collapse of human values, and that understands the present only in terms of a dystopian nightmare. **Posthistoire** would

be, in these terms, a real ending, with hope for little more than, as de Man believed, "death or mutation."

This was the end predicted by de Man's contemporary and fellow believer in **posthistoire** fatalism, Hans Sedlmayr, an art historian whose strictures against modern architecture, outlined in his **Art in Crisis, The Lost Center** (1945), were the result of his hatred of the democratic, socialist, and avant-garde heritage of the French Revolution. For this historian of the baroque, architecture ended with 1789. "The events to which we refer as the French Revolution are only a fractional part, even though they are the part that is most patent to the eye, of that huge inner catastrophe . . . this climax of history . . . our concern is direct and personal and immediate . . . by the light of it we know ourselves." Sedlmayr's method was pseudopsychological, his pathological subjects, buildings, seen as "manifestations, not merely . . . historical facts, but . . . symptoms [help] in forming a diagnosis of the malady that affects our time . . . this our age is sick" (**Art in Crisis**, 1). Here Sedlmayr was the self-appointed doctor, a parodic and vulgarized Freud, or perhaps a Reich, offering small comfort to an age already lost: "Just as in psychological disturbances it may help towards the restoring of a lost balance if we assist unconscious thought to rise to the level of consciousness and so bring it under control, so an analogous examination of our age, as reflected in its art, may not only prove of theoretical interest" (**Art in Crisis**, 2).

These etiologies of modernism were advanced between 1939 and 1945, in response to his calculated withdrawal from enthusiastic participation in the National Socialist Movement and his shift toward a general sense of nihilism in the face of modern culture. His architectural villain was Claude-Nicolas Ledoux, accused of projecting a house in the form of a sphere — a groundless and rootless form not worthy of the name **house** and destructive of a humanist architecture conceived as premised on vertical walls, deep foundations, and principles of beauty ostensibly derived from Vitruvius:

Such a radical new form, for instance, is inherent in the idea of using a sphere as the basic form of an entire house. Most people have treated this notion as nothing more than a bad joke or a very ordinary piece of lunacy, while the more charitable have looked upon it as an experiment with form. The thing is certainly insane enough, but if it were no more than that, we should hardly be justified in wasting much time over it. A nonsensical idea, however, need by no means be wholly without significance . . . such abnormalities reveal very specific characteristics.

Ledoux was the more criminal for Sedlmayr, in having made possible similar substitutions of geometry for architecture in the 1900s, including the reprehensible avant-garde designs of Melnikov, a favorite of Rem Koolhaas, who had the audacity to propose a transparent sphere. Here it is interesting to see Sedlmayr's resistance to modernism as an opposition to its supposed dematerialization of architecture, its "reduction" of architecture to geometry. As he noted, where formerly architecture had been a question of real architectonic elements — walls and other physical elements rooted in foundations — now it was not only uprooted and without foundation, but also its essence was no longer physical but geometrical. Moreover, it was, in the sphere, given over to a nonhuman, non-ground-based subject — something like an alien from outer space. Architecture had become its forms of representation, which in turn were ignorant of human subjectivity and physicality — a question that, as we have indicated, is raised in an even more dramatic form today.

The pertinence of Sedlmayr's observations, however, rests not so much on this parallelism but on his reliance on a historical model of change that inevitably led to his conclusion of death and ending. For as a student of Riegl, he had early on incorporated Riegl's historicized optical theories into his own analysis of architectural space. But if Riegl had seen the history of spatiality moving from Egyptian hapticality, through Greek "normal" vision, to Late Roman ambiguity (of figure and ground), Sedlmayr projected these intuitions into the baroque period, which, with Wölfflin, he understood to be the last, great evocation of humanist spirituality, which, in its manipulation of space for religious effect, had nevertheless exhausted all the resources of architecture as traditionally conceived, and thereby literally "blown apart" architectural stability. Piranesi, then Ledoux, and then Le Corbusier were the unhappy results of this explosion, which seemed to mimic the sickness of industrial and mass society as a whole. History here was a motor, an instrument, if not of Spenglerian decline, of humanist collapse, and architecture was to be seen as the (pathological) symptom of such a history.

The opposite pole of the debate saw a happy outcome for historical development — the Hegelian "positive" ending was, of course, the utopia of modernism, a vision of "ineffable space" transcending time at the end of time, a history-less world once and for all constructed for the good society. It was Sedlmayr's contemporary, and in some respects his nemesis, Emil Kaufmann, who represented this pole of architectural interpretation in the Vienna School of the 1920s and '30s. Indeed, most of Sedlmayr's crucial architectural examples had been literally stolen from the research of this former colleague, cocontributor for a time in the influential Viennese journal **Kunstwissenschaftliche Forschungen**, edited by Otto Pächt. Kaufmann, the Jewish student of Riegl and Schmarsow, was never to gain entry to the academic establishment in anti-Semitic Vienna, and was forced instead to take up a bank-teller's job until his equally forced emigration to the United States in 1941. Writing, not accidentally after Kaufmann had left for the States, Sedlmayr belatedly acknowledged the source of his own epochal conclusions:

Sedlmayr's cowardice was equaled only by Kaufmann's bravery. In 1933 he published his little book with a large title: **Von Ledoux bis Le Corbusier**. Most commentators have simply remarked on the fact that Le Corbusier, together with other modernists such as Richard Neutra, only appears in the last three pages of the book; only Hubert Damisch has recognized the special valor needed even for a coded defense of modern architecture at this juncture. With epigraphs from Rousseau, Kant, and Montesquieu, Kaufmann's essay was a spirited plea for Enlightenment values on the level of that launched by Ernst Cassirer in his essays on Kant and Rousseau that same year — the year, we should remember, of Hitler's putsch. For Kaufmann, Ledoux's special quality was that he had, in an age of reaction, welded an idea of social justice with a practice of ideal forms, the kind of utopia, Kaufmann stated openly, that characterized the Modern Movement's attempt to join the new society to the new abstract forms. He was also well aware of the fragility of this utopia:

In architecture, just as in politics, the reactionaries were to triumph over the inspired, though not sufficiently realistic modernists. But the temporary victory of the conservatives should not lead us to believe that the achievements of the progressives lacked significance. Having lived in the atmosphere of growing political and social discontent, the revolutionary architects wished to realize, for the common good, the ideals of the time by contriving architectural schemes such as had never existed before. They did their part in the double task of the period: tearing down the old and building the new. Like others who served the same cause, they were not spared the ordeals of their times and were menaced by its fanaticism. In the end, they themselves became disillusioned and reactionary (**Three Revolutionary Architects**, 434–35).

For Kaufmann, however, as opposed to Sedlmayr, this did not mean a loss of hope – indeed, his last pages evince a utopian faith of his own that it would be in California, under the aegis of Richard Neutra, that these ideals would finally be realized. Eventually, three years before his death, Kaufmann succeeded in reaching the West Coast, and it is perhaps symbolically right that he was to die returning to Los Angeles by train, at the station of Jackson Hole, Wyoming.

In the silent discussion between Sedlmayr and Kaufmann, we are presented once again with all the complexities of "disenchantment." On the one hand, a disenchanted conservative against modernism in all its forms; on the other, a proponent of neo-Kantian disenchantment as progressive modernist.

It is here that this discourse is deeply connected to the "are there architectural mores anymore?" question and, it turns out, precisely in the context of the Sedlmayr/ Ledoux argument. After all, it was Ledoux who was the first "modern" to include the word **mores** in the title of his treatise, **Architecture Considered in Relation to Art, Mores, and Legislation** (1804). He had chosen this title as a response to a Revolutionary competition, which asked the question, "What does art do to improve the mores of society?" His idea of mores (in French, **moeurs**) was inherited from an Enlightenment sense of progress, of inevitable improvement over time, of the essential role of the **philosophe** in the development of social justice, and of the critical role of the architect/engineer in the construction of a new and enlightened society. As we know, his architectural hubris anticipated that of the modernists in the 1920s, and seems, from our contemporary standpoint, to be indissolubly linked to the

impossible, if not utopian, dreams of modern architects to change the world, dreams shattered by World War II and, despite a brief revival in the Paris of the late 1960s, definitively dashed by consumerism and capitalism. It would indeed be possible to write the history of the disenchantment debate through the reception of Ledoux – in modernism or even in postmodernism. (Could one find anyone more complexly "disenchanted" in the Weberian sense than Philip Johnson himself?)

I have introduced this abbreviated history of a debate between two historians, heirs to historicism and Weberian disenchantment, not to propose a solution for thinking through the architecture of the new digital era, but rather to expose the rooted nature of our thinking about history, temporality, and change within modernism. If we were to follow the same models of thought for the present fin de siècle, as many have proposed, we will certainly fall into the difficult trap of "ending" or "future," pessimism or optimism, no more or more, posed by the terms in which the question "anymore mores" has been set. I would argue that this trap is only avoidable if we develop alternative approaches toward history and spatiality – approaches already sketched by Gilles Deleuze and others – that refuse to see time and space as distinct, separate, and potentially opposed entities, and that understand the processes and forms of digitalization as integral to the development of the very interpretative schema that we need to work with and control these processes and forms. We are, in this sense, bound to think digitally to work digitally. Anymore **mores** in architecture depends on this.

Anthony Vidler is chair of art history at the University of California in Los Angeles. His books include **The Architectural Uncanny** and **Architecture, Revolution and Restoration: The Politics of Monumentality, 1799–1989**.

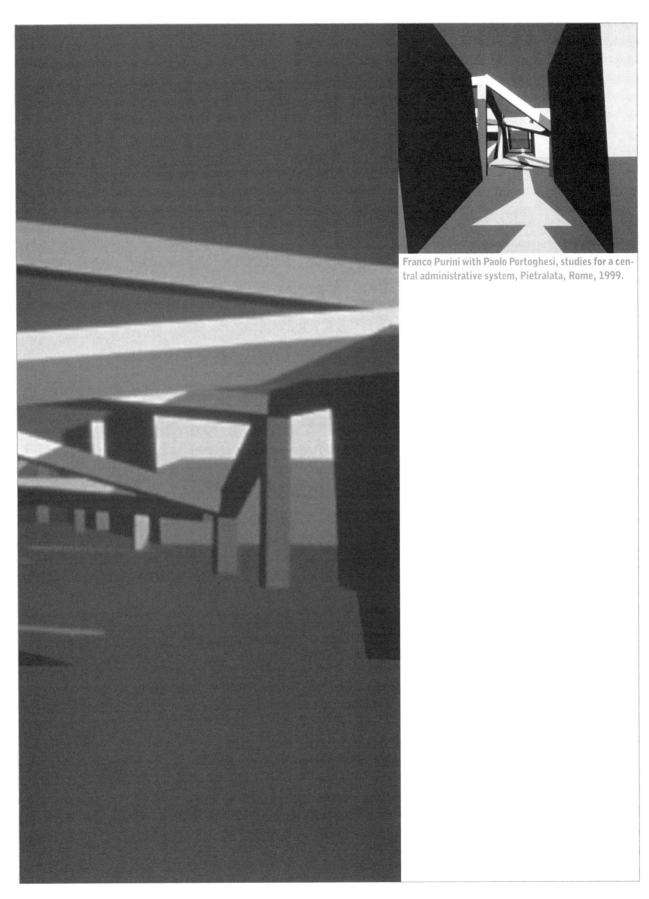

Franco Purini with Paolo Portoghesi, studies for a central administrative system, Pietralata, Rome, 1999.

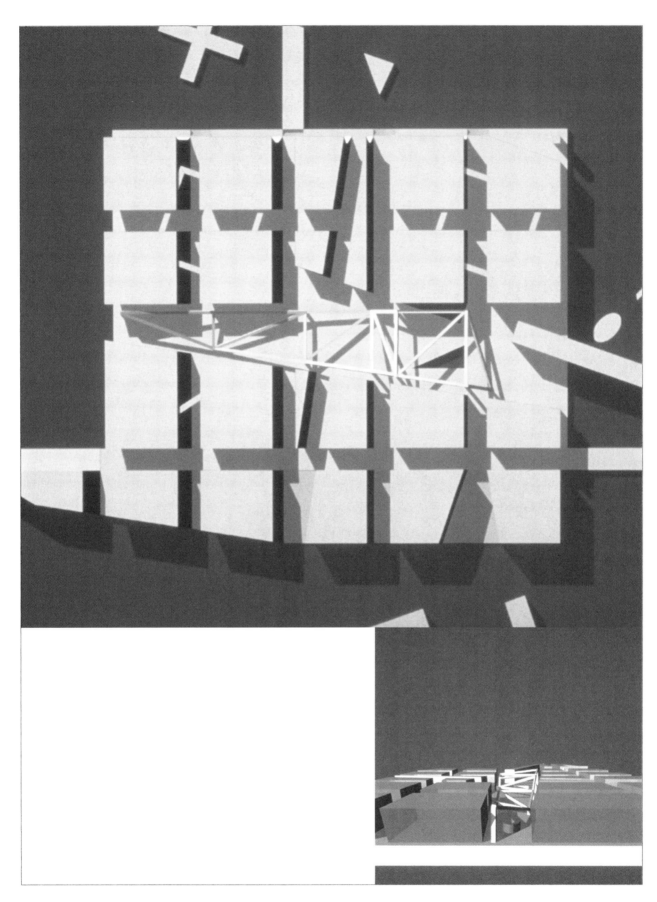

The Scalpel and the Axe
Franco Purini

There are things that vanish, states that disintegrate, assembly lines that shorten and interact with lines of other countries. This is what desire seems to demand. A production mode that satisfies the cultural and personal needs, not the depersonalizing ideologies of the cold war. And the system pretends to conform, to turn more flexible and enterprising, less dependent on rigid categories. But as soon as desire tends to individuate itself, becoming intimate and persuasive, the force of the converging markets produces an instantaneous capital that darts away towards the horizon at the velocity of light, pointing to a certain furtive uniformity, to a flattening of particulars involving everything, from architecture to free time, to the way of eating, sleeping and dreaming. – **Don Delillo**, Underworld

From America to Europe, from Australia to Japan, architectural culture has undergone an unprecedented transformation in recent years, comparable to the most contested years of modernism's avant-garde. Such transformation is the result of a series of complex phenomena, barely decipherable, and of many structural and superstructural processes that have followed one another with such speed as to render unclear their comprehension and consequences. In the form of a schematized, hypothetical list, one is able to review the principal aspects in order first to chart a map of the situation entangling the discipline today – a situation presenting itself in such radical ways as to make Bruno Zevi think we are witnessing something entirely new. At the heart of this issue are the general submovements that have irreversibly changed those societies participating in the economic, political, and cultural dimensions of globalization, i.e., the West in its entirety and the most advanced areas of the East. I will discuss these transformations only as they relate directly to architecture.

As a kind of prologue to this discussion, I want to introduce the dichotomy of full and empty as a visual emblem of the opposing sensibilities of planning today. The Millennium Dome, an immense full, is about to be completed in London. In Rome, on the occasion of the 2000 Jubilee, is Tor Vergata's big empty, a boundless residual space of the Campagna Romana, offered as a testament to history, and which will welcome two million young people gathering around Pope John Paul II. The London presence appears somehow less evident and involving than the Roman absence, which poses itself as an enigma. Maybe emptiness today is the real meaning of architecture.

Within those countries constituting the various pieces of a global, geographic mosaic, architecture ceased a long time ago to satisfy primary exigencies. All the gigantic, urban construction problems posed by modernity have more or less been solved. Infrastructure now extends under and across the land; cities are complete entities, and now require different, if not opposing, strategies to those governing their often abnormal growth; and the housing question – a theoretical and physical construct inherited from the problems of late-19th-century industrialization, and central to the heroic visions of the Modern Movement – today no longer exists. This transformation, manifestly complete today, renders architecture, for all intents and purposes, superfluous. This new condition brings architecture closer to art – the superfluous thing par excellence. From this apparent evolution, the architect now perceives himself as a visual artist, like a painter or a sculptor, free to work in any (unexpected or even inappropriate) direction. It is exactly this passage of architecture – from an absolute devotion to the creation and inhabitation of hardware to the pursuit of superficialities – that explains the discipline's move toward the ornamental maintenance of the city.

Developing within this transformation, figures such as Peter Eisenman and Frank O. Gehry have reinvented themselves as brilliant, plastic performers, whose large urban sculptures, or gigantic installations, only secondarily fulfill the functions for which they were conceived; functions essentially contingent and ultimately interchangeable. Nonetheless, not everything in these operations is a mundane game. The spaces of the Guggenheim Museum in Bilbao appear as organic cavities. They remind one of the interior of a human heart; the pulsing lining of the aorta, the vibrating curved surfaces. By way of this anatomical dissection, architecture reveals itself today largely through analogy and metaphor. Responding to this disconcerting architectural marriage of expressionism, the baroque, and a distended physiognomy, Eisenman has produced a divergent, equally cruel and scientific, dismemberment with his Staten Island museum. But this time it is not a radical disarticulation of languages; on the contrary, here it is the disarticulation of the history of architecture as defined through architectural form in time. And it is precisely time, in the end, that is finally annulled in a Promethean impulse impeded by a totally and sensationally subjective existential alarm. Moreover, beyond their intrinsic architectural value, the unquestionable merit in these works is the way in which they compel the observer or the inhabitant to acknowledge them as edifices, priming a process of creative self-consciousness that turns out to be the reconstruction of a new intelligibility of architecture. In any event, the fact remains that the deconstruction of every interpretative code is the premise of its reconstruction. In this we cannot but notice an obvious contradiction.

Allied with these trends is another, more defining condition. Globalization is not only a condition of a totally aesthetic society but of an integrally artistic universe. The inhabitants of the economically strongest countries, educated and sufficiently motivated, have somehow become artists themselves; not, however, exclusively. They have also turned into demanding consumers of an art that, as Franco Rella has written, declares itself today as the new metaphysics. Modern art seems dead in its residual, elitist preciosity, realizing in this way the Hegelian prophecy that in order to achieve something genetically different, it must organically immerse itself in the physiology of the mass culture, which can be called an art of deferral and of delegation, an art which primarily exists without uniqueness. Extended further, such a demand forces the architect beyond well-known linguistic modules, however advanced, and turns him instead to everything (superficially at least) nonarchitectural. He sees himself deprived of an exclusive right to the domain of form, a form he is constrained to pursue into the unknown. The specificity of the architect's profession has dissolved into a diffused confusion of roles, which combine the talk-show model, competence, and operative rituality. Art, an immaterial value by definition, the product par excellence of the global society, becomes therefore an extreme competition, the milieu of a power negotiation in epochal terms. Once it becomes the most coveted consumer commodity, the work of art irradiates its precious uniqueness over all aspects of life. Removed from the preceding aesthetic-literary atmosphere, from rarefied and exclusive contemplation, the fruition of art is oriented toward a historical-scientific level, so as to exorcise an internal contradiction that occurs the moment it enters the mechanisms of global consumption.

The image just described needs to be qualified further. During the 20th century, art existed as a hidden discourse, distinguished by invisible boundaries, out of reach for the majority of people. Even for those who succeeded in penetrating its sacred perimeter, the work displayed itself through an enigmatic system of continuously renewed signifiers – semantically revealing many levels of meaning but nonrepresentative of the work itself. Today the statute of the object or of the artistic event has literally been overturned. In order to exist as an object or an event, the work of art has to be spectacular, funny, infused with the spirit of advertising, and therefore immediately comprehensible like a slogan: familiar, surprising, attractive, fundamentally compatible with the media. This does not mean that it lacks any kind of profundity, but this depth is, so to speak, driven to the surface. This is a matter of a new constitution for art, breaking the romantic image that portrayed the true artist as a tormented and misunderstood individual, compensated with acknowledgment and devotion only after death. Art, rather, is the primary expression of the market, and appears to us through the communicative modalities that govern today's information society. If it is true, as Marshall McLuhan wrote, that the medium is the message, then communication represents

something, even if it fails to communicate anything. The more art reduces itself to its most simple, communicative function, the more it represents a pure, empty vehicle, and the more it is understandable.

It is not possible to effect an ideological censorship on the condition sketched out above, which sees the visual as asserting itself by pitting the earlier conception of an obligatory, moral finality of art and architecture against the ephemera of spectacle and the redundancy of communication – a finality that turned out to be premeditated, ruled by understatement, oriented more toward the construction of collective expressions than to the disclosure of personal responses, to an absolute signature. And it is indeed the difficulty of accepting the irreversibility of these mutations that seems, for instance, to prevent Vittorio Gregotti, in his recent discussions on the present condition of architecture, from capturing the real heart of the matter. For his part, the young critic Pippo Ciorra – antagonist of the master from Novara and supporter of that distorted style which arouses so much interest between Rome and Pescara – so involves himself with this panorama of adventurous mutations as to forget the fact that, in whatever field one may choose, the problem of the quality of writing is posed. A quality that can never be aligned with the single program in which such a choice is inscribed.

The situation summarily described so far requires the use of the scalpel and the axe. The axe serves to prune architecture of all those branches of ramifications, diversions, and complications that conceal the essence of the architectural tree, and in which neo-Vitruvian academics meet with major or minor recoveries of a too-explicit descriptiveness, where the fundamentalism proposed by the intent admirers of the typology enters into an alliance with the impetuous theoreticians of a tectonic consent in the definition of a restoration of the nobly arcane and fundamental notion of the long duration. The scalpel is the perfect device to dissect single, specific problems, to move among the resistant and intertwined fibers of a relativism that is increasingly becoming an equivalence of each thing, in an opportunistic and ultimately conformist agnosticism. The more the scalpel and the axe are necessary, the greater the speed in the production of events interferes with seeing them in sequence, causing the need for a new meaning, a swift and piratical instinct, which determines one's proper place inside a condition of synchronicity with the events themselves, at the exact juncture of the current debate in which one wants to be. As critical distance from these events is no longer possible, it is necessary for the architect to develop both feelings of instinctual navigation, preventing him from making directional errors, and a sense of difference as a keen sensitivity for variation. This new situation is also accelerated by that exasperated devotion to the present, which, by reducing events to a daily standpoint, thwarts any temporal perspective and any idea of process. Things do not follow one another, but dispose themselves in a sort of frontal-

ity that denies or hides the relations between phenomena and objects. A frontality is revealed as authoritarian at exactly that moment when it decentralizes the author's role.

This leads to the conclusion that the problem architecture faces today does not actually consist of replacing the goal of modernism – the hard and totalitarian ideal – with the manifold goals of postmodernity – various and sophisticated software for the existing city – or even of finally negating such a succession. The issue is always how to employ the new resources offered by the vision just described, always keeping in mind that, in more ways than one, this multiplicity is nothing more than a new version of the eclecticism that characterized the last two decades of the 20th century. This transition occurred at the beginning of the 1980s, but the awareness that it had happened actually prevented any recognition of the characteristics of this rite of passage for a long period of time. Obviously, a superficially spectacular way to create a spectacle is there – one only has to think of the latest high-tech offerings, clearly lacking that essential, neo-Gothic structural mysticism that had characterized earlier work. In a more inward and compelling mode, one could alternatively cite Alvaro Siza's Portuguese Pavilion at the recent world exposition in Lisbon – a work that shines with an epic architectural poetry. Let us also consider Henri Ciriani's diaphanous spatial harmonies, leading the majority of the contemporary world and its eccentric character to the projective reason of a ray of light polarizing the chaotic and the diverse; and David Chipperfield's aesthetically correct stylistics, a ready-made linguistic formula, effective but entirely defuse, lacking the capacity for autonomous propulsion. And again, there is Gehry's urban communication, and then Richard Meier's rhetoric and almost completely spent communication – for years a hostage of himself and his own ability to fabricate dazzling media icons. We can continue with Oswald Mathias Ungers' sublime superficiality – his obsessive net in which are deposited the ascetic but never aphasic effects of his geometric furor, distilled from the heart of composition, the superficiality of which becomes dramatically decorative, as in the latest works of Robert Venturi and Denise Scott Brown. Paolo Portoghesi's expressive work is positively festive, exalted by a participatory empathy with things, consumed with rapt attention, while Michael Graves's hyper-declamation of the sign intellectually lingers in the surroundings of a devitalized kitsch. Norman Foster's demiurgic obsession should also be mentioned, behind which it is not difficult to see the danger of a schizophrenic vision of the relationship between man and nature – building as a danger to the environment and to man; and Jean Nouvel's technological classicism, an intrinsically static composition turned into an aulic traditionalism of the modern, visibly referencing the grand siècle. In Foster's case, the edifice behaves with ambivalence. On the one hand, it does not have to disturb the ecological order, while on the other, it has to defend itself from it. Indestructible manufac-

tured goods are derived from it, which do not share anything with the environment, in a worried and worrying autism. Conversely, Nouvel's functional program is magnified in a savant rhetorical orchestration wherein the architecture's materiality celebrates a collective gratification of symmetrical and isolated spaces, an authoritative yet distant image, obliquely accepting the contaminations of fashion. Then there is Coop Himmelblau's acidic and cruelly self-destructive violence, inconceivable except within a culture of the cold Freudian reticence of an eccentric Austrian capital; and Steven Holl's postgrammatology, whose morphemes, once truly provocative, have today settled into a sort of statistical dimension that neutralizes them within a nervous and individual, plastic sleight of hand.

Prior to this somewhat superfluous, extended parenthesis on global architecture, there were to be two essential aspects to my argument. The former, as already described, rests on the equation of architecture and art. The latter, described here, tends to revive a primary need for the discipline to exaggerate the difficulties of construction and function in order to render essential the architect's role; a role seen as the repository of an extremely complex wisdom, whose knowledge, as in the cathedrals of the Middle Ages, is the object of an arduous rite of initiation, performed in secrecy and served by an encrypted jargon. Rendering a manufactured product more complex than it is supposed to be is the basic misunderstanding of high-tech architecture. As Paul Valéry has written, the structural constitution of the architectonic object is simple by nature, at the frontier of schematism.

The problem is in the embrace of the new architectural horizon without criticizing its acceptance, as others do, in the prospective exorcism of invalidating it. This is the limit of Gregotti's otherwise enlightening analysis, whose predilection for cold, simple, and controlled forms (always justified by a thorough order of composition) does not succeed in hiding an expressive tension, which invalidates rigidity in a feverish writing of the deferral. The final result of negating the legitimacy of the project also appears to escape his lucid analysis, which has been ongoing for years and distinguished by several distinct phases. The project was first considered as an authoritarian device, expressive of a totalizing and generic, abstract and pervasive modernity. Subsequently, it was noticed, or rather determined, that the project had exhausted itself and had therefore to be exchanged for a narrative practice capable of establishing itself as an inner exercise of multiple writings. Consequently, this new image for architecture corrected the modern idea of interdisciplinary work in a multidisciplinary environment, intended as some kind of competitive game, a beneficial, revealing, and educational congress, a therapeutic assembly of insights that do not discuss themselves as much as they show themselves. As a direct result of society sanctioning the decline of the project, architecture has been socially relieved of responsibility.

Architecture is no longer asked to solve general problems, as much as it is asked to address (as pure formalism) essentially individual milieus. The technical dimension of architecture has consequently been disconnected from the aesthetic environment (see, for example, the relationship between the engineering firm Ove Arup and the proliferation of high-tech), or claimed by the power of politics (for example, with issues surrounding the environment and its preservation).

It is not necessarily pejorative that architecture has been relieved of the responsibility of a discipline charged with any kind of institutional tasks, and that the architect is today a communicating artist. It depends on how architecture interprets its new superfluous condition and what the architect intends to communicate. There will always be a considerable difference between the production of conceptual and poetic values, perhaps explicitly or implicitly opposed to one another, and the simple repetition of conformist stereotypes, between a narcissist and adulatory gesture and an authentic, Baldessarian inclination to the fluidity of the impromptu gesture, thrown into space like an ethereal bridge. Freedom from the project, therefore, for the benefit of a new freedom of interpretation and modification of the world (a world much more limited today, but also much more important), gave architecture a new libertarianism. This freedom is principally a political freedom, as the diminished responsibility mentioned above may actually be experienced as an increase in the artist's only real responsibility; i.e., overthrowing the foundations of societal codes, namely conventions of communication, where power and its liturgies are created. No polemics with formalism, then. The only thing left to be understood is whether a certain form, even the most arbitrary of forms, is humanly and artistically convincing; if it renders people happier or simply more aware; if it gives to those with whom it connects even the smallest and most transitory sense of immortality.

Cities are naturally the theater for this new architecture. Being command points, as Le Corbusier said, cities are the most advanced laboratories in the search for a new existential name under the guise of art; a renaming that would surpass the opposition between the culture of conservation (imposed by indisputable reasons in a country such as Italy) and an innovation enthusiastically dedicated to the thematic illustration of chaos. The game is so much harder now. Globalization instigates the territorial deprivation of the world – a world, furthermore, hyper-surveyed and reduced, a haunting desertification that voids places and nonplaces. This territorial deprivation is certainly an effect of globalization. It is also an entirely new phenomenon, consisting of the erosion not so much of the atomization of points within the world as of a new generic identity, a simulated identity. This annulment of identity would, in fact, still be something which works against the absence of a contrived, synthetic identity. This simulation is not, however, an immediate one. It is the condition that makes Massimo Cacciari regret the real Venice over the Las Vegas Venice, today presumably more real than the authentic original. There is nothing wrong with the fact that the relationship between the original and the copy is inverted. It already happened during the Renaissance and in the neoclassical period. The problem is that the territorially deprived simulacrum is situated on a significant ground, representative of the earthly district on which it was constructed. Belonging and relevance have disappeared. Global architecture looks like a translated text, but translated from Esperanto, a fake, composite language, a pure artifice lacking any semantic significance. In respect to this nonspecificity – prophesied by Pier Paolo Pasolini, whose death unfortunately kept him from deciphering it; and subverting Kenneth Frampton's notion of critical regionalism – all those elements that do not correspond to the canon of a substantial extralinguistic equivalence, a form of neutrality, are confined to the range of an ethnic architecture, bearer of a localism and read as an anachronism. A desperate confusion arises as a result, rendering tragic the surreal science of its associations. Hence, globalization creates sorrow and makes ground hostile after being denied habitation in all its ancestral aspects and in its most extreme and secular manifestations. There are neither secret areas nor hiding places anymore; no places where one has the chance to accumulate and conserve something, to hold it as unique only as long as it is sheltered from exposure. The last reserves of the original landscape have been plundered; the hail of a meaningless and hopeless uniformity has rained down on all of the desolated lands that all the parallels and meridians uselessly hold together. The lines marking the cycle of the sun, the alternation of darkness and light, and therefore the consecution of irrational obscurity and clear reason, have been almost entirely discharged by the parallels, trajectories of the exchange between cold and warm. The vitreous high-tech architectures, azure and translucent, lightened by unexpected golden sparks in remote points, are nothing but immense icebergs descending along the meridians, alert and frozen blocks announcing an imminent, new glaciation. These silent routes cross still-lives of anxious fragments, emblems of an aesthetics of decay looking to ennoble the infinite metropolitan deserts with an interrupting presence.

Before this scenario, art could only throw a net of recognizable points across the planet, visual goals of a human landscape recreated from its origin. In order to comply with this role, which sees the museification of the city, and elevates, as in Bilbao, the museum to a symbol of a millennial rebirth, architecture has to find the courage to redefine itself as a unitary art, to relegate the decayed interventions among its useless memories – principally the urban, which too often became, and becomes, other than space and form. Architecture cannot but split into a difficult but inevitable duplicity, between subtlety and schematization, between the tendency

to generalize and the tendency to seize the lesser particular of things, between the scalpel, which with infinitesimal pietàs investigates the identity of the most imperceptible appearances of reality and imagery, and the axe, which knocks down the obstacles making the horizon clear to see and accessible to approach.

Precisely because of its definite and total character, territorial deprivation irradiates an extreme appeal. Imagining a world deprived of the net of the points that, by their measurement, facilitate orientation and navigation throughout that world constitutes an extraordinary challenge, because territorial deprivation deducts its own reality from architectural language. This happens because architecture, no matter what type of architecture it might be, no matter what style it might be designed and built in, is the art of staying, which therefore implies earth as the prevalent material, and instead makes earth its own goal. The act of remaining is the only strategy in accord with the extremism of this new condition. It is an action through which the existing, which does not exist by itself, but which receives its existence from a movement of will that has become real, appears, so to speak, to the architect and to architecture.

Territorial deprivation also touches the threshold of the sacred. The eradicated, earthly architecture evokes a mental vertigo, opens wide to the imagination of anguishing depths, stimulates dramatic urges that deprive the project of the same condition that makes it possible: time. Through the epiphany of the sacred, the myth returns with an unknown appearance, denying itself to vision. In front of the sacred – the void as an unthinkable void, as the colonization of each mental region, even the most concealed – the technological exorcism does not have any power: only art, once stripped of any referential commitment (representative, cognitive, expressive), can face the devastation preparing the return of the unique, the unrepeatable, the real. And architecture also, becoming the art of emptiness, the art of distance, celebrating the absence of meaning, can oppose the nihilism accompanying the domain of global communication in all of its aspects. In order for this to happen, architecture must, perhaps, betray its own essence in every hypothetical conformation of itself.

Twenty-first-century architecture arrived at least twenty years ago. Postmodernism regenerated the modern preoccupation with the manipulation of utopia at the same moment it was evoking the presence of the past, permitting the measurement of its distance (which was, by the way, completely reinvented). Architecture will have to reconstruct itself as an art by denying itself to art. At the same time, it will not be able to go along with territorial deprivation but rather must assign human and posthuman meanings to new points in the world, as formalistic hyperbole turns buildings into artificial geographies. This is the action of renaming already discussed – its relationship with power will be engaged in this pursuit.

Today global power is invisible. It is an imperialistic and abstract power, atypical and unclassifiable, Oedipal and utopian. But with the invisibility of power, the architect's glance has lost a visual layout. Only the infinitely distant and the extremely close can be observed (Faraway, So Close, as Wim Wenders might say). Furthermore, this glance is rigid, fixed by an expressionless face, and consequently excluding any context. It is, however, too banal to assert that we have to conquer that lost glance again; breaking the spell that restricts the movement of the head, and lending architecture a false sense of solemnity. Architecture has to give itself a new vision whose power to create the world will clash with those forces turning the world into a white concrete surface, where nothing can be born and only neutral things may be placed. And this vision can only be anonymous, because anonymity is the emblem of the next millennium, after having been the poetical cipher of the last century. Renaming the nameless – this is the paradox, rising sphinxlike in the face of the future's architecture.

Franco Purini practices architecture in Rome and teaches in Venice. He is author of Alcune forme della casa and Dittico siciliano.

Architectures of Excess
Elizabeth Grosz

The transition to a new age requires a change in our perception and conception of space-time, the inhabiting of places, **and of** containers, **or** envelopes of identity. **It assumes and entails an evolution or a transformation of forms, of the relations of** matter **and** form **and of the interval** between: **the trilogy of the constitution of place. – Luce Irigaray, "Sexual Difference,"** An Ethics of Sexual Difference

1. Spatial Excess

Anymore has provided a wonderful opportunity, once again, to think carefully about a new "any," another conceptual indeterminacy, another proliferation of possibles that all anys entail; this time, not any-body or any-time but the concept "more," in its resonances with architectural theory and practice. This final session of the conference, "Anymore Mores?" asks us to look at the question of social action and how architecture may address not only its clients but also larger communities and nations. In contemplating this topic, I was attracted to the idea of "more" as excess, as abundance, proliferation, or profusion, as that which has been left out of social collectives, as that which, on the one hand, glues the collective together while, on the other, finding its existence outside of that collective, marginalized, existing only in and as the set, the collective or community of those who have nothing in common. This concept of a community of the lost, of strangers, of the marginalized and outcast, is borrowed from the work of Alphonso Lingis, and especially from his concern with community, not as that which is united through common bonds, goals, language, or descent, but as that which opens itself to the stranger, to the dying, to the one with whom one has nothing in common, the one who is not like oneself. Lingis is concerned with the community that is possible only with an alien, that is, an otherness that cannot be absorbed into commonness:

Community forms when one exposes oneself to the naked one, the destitute one, the outcast, the dying one. One enters into community not by affirming oneself and one's forces but by exposing oneself to expenditure at a loss, to sacrifice. Community forms in a movement by which one exposes oneself to the other, to forces and powers outside oneself, to death and to the others who die.[1]

Communities, which make language, culture, and thus architecture their modes of existence and expression, come into being not through the recognition, generation, or establishment of common interests, values, and needs, and the establishment of universal, neutral laws and conventions that bind and enforce them (as social contractarians proclaim), but through the remainders they cast out, the figures they reject, the terms that they consider unassimilable, that they attempt to sacrifice, revile, and expel.[2] There are many names for this unassimilable residue: the other, the abject, the scapegoat, the marginalized, the destitute, the refugee, the dying, etc. I will propose here, in keeping with the con-

ference theme, to call it "more" or "excess," as long as it is recognized that this more is not simply superadded but also undermines and problematizes.

Excess is a concept that itself has a long and illustrious philosophical history, being the object of reflection from at least the time of Aristotle – the great theorist of moderation, to whom I will return. However, the greatest theorists of excess arguably must be understood in the lineage of philosophers that follows in the tradition from Nietzsche: most especially the tradition of French Nietzscheans – Marcel Mauss, Georges Bataille, Pierre Klossowski, René Girard, Jacques Derrida, Gilles Deleuze, Julia Kristeva, Luce Irigaray. This conception of excess as that which outstrips and finds no stable place in orderly systems, or within systematicity itself, as that whose very systematicity defies the laws of system, can be identified – as I will here – on the one hand, through the dramatizations of Bataille, of the excess as the order of the excremental; and on the other, in the writings of Irigaray, where this excess is cast as the maternal-feminine.

For Bataille, dirt, disorder, contagion, expenditure, filth, immoderation – and above all, shit – exceed the proper, what constitutes "good taste," good form, measured production. If the world of the proper, the system, form, regulated production, constitutes an economy – a restricted economy – a world of exchange, use, and expedience, then there is an excess, a remainder, an uncontained element, the "accursed share" – a "general economy" – a world or order governed by immoderation, excess, and sacrifice, an economy of excremental proliferations, which expresses itself most ably in "unproductive expenditure: luxury, mourning, war, cults, the construction of sumptuary monuments, games, spectacles, arts, perverse sexual activity."[3] There is an economy of production and consumption that constitutes an ordered and measured system of circulation; and there is another economy preoccupied with conspicuous and disproportionate expenditure, with consumption and a logic of crippling obligation. This distinction runs through not only social, cultural, and economic relations; significantly, it also underlies a distinction between types of art, and within particular forms of art, the arts or crafts of use and reference, and those of proliferation, the superficial, and the ornamental.

On the one hand, Bataille claims that architecture itself may function as a measured, calculated economy. Indeed, in his earlier writings, he develops a rather banal, quasi-psychoanalytic understanding of the skyscraper and of architectural functioning as phallic symbols in an aggressive access to the feminine sky they "scrape."[4] As he defines it in early writings, architecture is that which places man midway between the monkey and the machine: "Man would seem to represent merely an intermediary stage within the morphological development between monkey and building."[5] It represents an intermediary between the animal and the mechanical, retaining some of the traces of its inhuman, animal origin, as well

as the anticipation or movement toward the fully mechanized, the reign of authoritarian control. In this sense, architecture, as he provokes it, represents not the physiognomy of
the people, or of culture as a whole, but of its bureaucratic
and petty officials; and the spirit of excess is perhaps best
represented in the destruction of monumental architecture
rather than in any positive architectural production:

In fact, only society's ideal nature – that of authoritative
command and prohibition – expresses itself in actual architectural constructions. Thus great monuments rise up like
dams, opposing a logic of majesty and authority to all unquiet
elements. Indeed, monuments obviously inspire good social
behaviour and often even genuine fear. The fall of the Bastille
is symbolic of this state of things. This mass movement is difficult to explain otherwise than by popular hostility towards
monuments which are their veritable masters.[6]

If rage and destruction – the fall of the Bastille – are the
provocative response of the masses to the increasing functionality and bureaucratization of interwar architecture, Bataille
suggests that perhaps a return to expenditure, to the animal,
to the excessive and the redundant, to tread a path already
explored in painting (one imagines here a reference to dada
and surrealism) in the architectural may pose an alternative
model: "However strange this may seem when a creature as
elegant as the human being is involved, a path – traced by the
painters – opens up toward bestial monstrosity, as if there were
no other way of escaping the architectural straitjacket."[7]

As Bataille identifies it, architecture must seek its own
excesses, its bestial monstrosity, its allegiances with forces,
affects, energies, experiments, rather than with ordinances,
rules, function, or form. We must ask, following this understanding of the place of the excessive as transgression, how
to engender an architectural "bestial monstrosity," a radically antifunctional architecture, an architecture that is anti-
authoritarian and antibureaucratic. An architecture that
refuses to function in and be part of, as Deleuze names them,
"societies of control." This is perhaps a more powerful provocation today than when Bataille first raised it. It may provoke
a "politics of the impossible," the only kind of politics, as
Lingis recognized, worth struggling for. For Bataille, what is
"more," "excessive," is that which has no function, purpose,
or other use than the expenditure of resources and energy, is
that which undermines, transgresses, and countermands the
logic of functionality. The ornament, the detail, the redundant, and the unnecessary: these may prove provisional elements of any architectures of excess (instead of the Bastille,
Winchester House?).

2. Spatialized Femininity

If Bataille is perhaps the best representation of the excremental pole of the beam of excess, then it could be argued
that the other pole, its counterbalance, is the feminine or
femininity. The excremental and the excessive cannot simply

be identified with the repressed or unconscious elements of
oneself and one's collective identifications (indeed, it is only
a certain concept of a pure and clean masculinity that renders
the anal, rather than the feminine, as its other). Its most crucial condition is its otherness, its outsideness to the systems
which it exceeds and outstrips. If cultural excess is, on the
one hand, represented (in Bataille) in the animal, the bestial,
the bodily, and especially in bodily waste, it is also represented (in the work of Irigaray and other feminist theorists)
by that which is othered, rendered as a kind of human representation of this waste, Woman and femininity. Bataille himself makes clear the associations and connections between
the excremental, the fluid, and femininity.[8] But it is not clear
that we can accept or share in Bataille's vision, derived as it is
from psychoanalysis, of femininity as wound, blood, loss, and
castration. Instead, we may see the place of femininity as
that which the architectural cannot contain within its own
drives to orderliness and systematicity, its own specifically
architectural excesses. For this concept, Irigaray's work may
prove immensely suggestive, even if, like Bataille, Lingis,
Deleuze, and others, she actually has written very little that is
directed specifically to the question of architecture. It is this
labor that architectural practitioners must undertake for
themselves – a specifically architectural understanding of
excess, of more, of that which exceeds the architectural.

Her work, like those of the others, is directed more to
philosophical concepts of space, place, and dwelling than to
architectural, social, or communitarian projects. Nevertheless, like Bataille, her philosophical positions regarding the
excessive, innumerable, and unmappable territories that
make the very notion of territory, possession, and self-con-
tainment possible remind us clearly that any notion of order,
system, community, knowledge, and control – including and
especially those involved in the architectural project (from
conception through to planning, building, and inhabitation)
– entails a notion of excess, expenditure, and loss that can
be and has been closely associated with those elements of
femininity and of woman that serve to differentiate and distinguish women as irreducible to and not exhausted in or
consumed by the masculine and the patriarchal. It is Irigaray's consistent claim that the question of difference –
which is lived most vividly and irreducibly, though not only,
in sexual difference – entails a rethinking of the relations
between space and time: "In order to make it possible to
think through, and live, this difference, we must reconsider
the whole problematic of space and time."[9]

Such a reconsideration would involve at least three major
factors: (1) a reconceptualization of space and time as oppo-
sitional forms (one the mode of simultaneity, the other the
mode of succession); (2) a reconceptualization of the ways in
which the space/time opposition has been historically and
conceptually associated with the opposition between femininity and masculinity, that is, the ways in which femininity

is spatialized, rendered substance or medium to the interiority and duration attributed to the (masculinized) subject of duration;[10] and (3) a reconceptualization of the modes of inhabitation that each has and makes on the other, a concept that Irigaray defines as the interval, the envelope, the passage in between, but which we could also describe as the excess or remainder, the "more" left over between them. The interval, undecidably spatial and temporal, insinuates a temporal delay in all spatial presence, and a spatial extension of all temporal intensity; it is the site of both their difference and their interchange, the movement or passage from one existence to another. The inscription of a different kind of space may provide the possibility of exchange between and across difference, space, or spaces, become as a mode of accommodation and inhabitation rather than a commonness that communities divide and share. It is her claim that until the feminine can be attributed an interiority of its own, a subjectivity, and thus a duration, while it continues to provide the resources for masculinized subjectivity and time by providing them with space, it has no space of its own and no time of its own. It is not that Irigaray is seeking a space/place or time for women alone. Quite the contrary, she is seeking modes of conceptualizing and representing space – preconditions to occupying and using it differently – that are more in accordance with the kinds of space, and time, repressed or unrepresented in the conventional structure of opposition between them.

If sexual difference requires a reordering of space and time, then what must be reordered? Irigaray suggests that the surreptitious association of femininity with spatiality has had two discernible if not articulated effects: first, woman is rendered the enigmatic ground, substance, or material undifferentiation, the place of origin of both subjectivity and objectivity, that is, of masculinity, and the objects in which it finds itself reflected. Femininity becomes the space, or better, the matrix, of male self-unfolding. Second, the feminine becomes elaborated as darkness and abyss, as void and chaos, as that which is both fundamentally spatial and as that which deranges or unhinges the smooth mapping and representation of space, a space which is too self-proximate, too self-enclosed to provide the neutrality, the coordinates, of self-distancing, to produce and sustain a homogeneous, abstract space. A matrix that defies coordinates, that defies the systematic functioning of matrices that propose to order and organize the field.

Irigaray argues that the very constitution of the field of space-time, with space as the field of external and extended positions and connections, and time as the field of internal and subjective positions and connections, is already set up in such a way that space is defined as smooth, continuous, homogeneous, passive, and neutral, as that which has no folds, no complexity, no interior or intensity of its own. It is already set up such that it morphologically reproduces the passive attributes of femininity. It is Irigaray's claim that woman has represented place for man, and more than that, the kind of place she has provided is a specific one: she functions as container, as envelope, as that which surrounds and marks the limit of man's identity. This is a paradoxical relation: woman comes to provide the place in which and through which man can situate himself as subject; which means that she represents a place that has no place, that has no place of its own but functions only as place for another.[11]

The maternal-feminine remains the place separated from "its" own place, **deprived of "its" place. She is or ceaselessly becomes the place of the other who cannot separate himself from it. With her knowing or willing it, she is then threatened because of what she lacks: a "proper" place. She would have to re-envelop herself with herself, and do so at least twice: as a woman and as a mother. Which would presuppose a change in the whole economy of space-time.[12]**

Irigaray discusses a perverse exchange at the origin of space, and thus, as the archaic precondition of architecture itself: in exchange for the abstract space of scientific and technological manipulation that man extracts from the maternal-feminine body from which he comes, he gives woman a container or envelope that he has taken from her to form his own identity, and to ensure that she continues to look after and sustain it. The container: the home, clothes, jewels, things he constructs for her, or at least for the image of her that allows him to continue his spatial appropriations with no sense of obligation, debt, or otherness. The exchange: she gives him a world; he confines her in his:

Again and again, taking from the feminine the tissue or texture of spatiality. In exchange – but it isn't a real one – he buys her a house, even shuts her up in it, places limits, unwittingly situates her. He contains or envelops her with walls while enveloping himself and his things with her flesh. The nature of these envelopes is not the same: on the one hand, invisibly alive, but with barely perceivable limits; on the other, visibly limiting or sheltering, but at the risk of being prison-like or murderous if the threshold is not left open.[13]

The maternal-feminine (indeed, the feminine as wrapped up in the very space, commonly described as "confinement," of the maternal, so a space that is always doubled up on itself, self-enfolded in itself) becomes the invisible, spaceless ground of space and visibility, the "mute substratum" that opens up the world as that which can be measured, contained, and conquered. In Irigaray's conception, the attribution of a more or less porous membrane to the feminine, the refusal to grant it its own interior, means that the space of the inside becomes the ground or terrain for the exploitation of the exterior: "Don't we always put ourselves inside out for this architecture?"[14] she asks, which is why it is so hard to find one's place there: space itself is erected on that very place covered over by construction and thus rendered impossible for habitation!

Lost in your labyrinth, you look for me without even realizing that this maze is built from my flesh. You have put me inside out and you look for me in retroversion where you can't find me. You are lost in me, far from me. You have forgotten that I also have an interior.[15]

It is the conceptual turning inside out of the maternal-feminine, as if it had no interiority, and thus no time of its own, that facilitated and enables the cultural universe that replaces it to expand and present itself as space, as spatiality, as that which is to be inhabited, colonized, made of use, invested with value – as that which can be calculated, measured, rendered mappable through coordinates, made into a matrix, the space of temporal planning. But this maneuver is not without its own ironic costs: in taking the world, nature, the bodies of others, as the ground or material of speculation (in both its economic and conceptual senses), man as explorer, scientist, or architect has both lost the resources of his own specificity (those limited resources provided by his own corporeality), as well as those which nurtured and grounded him.

Bataille is right to suggest that monumental and memorial architectures are the architectures of totalitarianism, the architecture of societies of control, of phallic consumption; his work clearly anticipates Irigaray's understanding of architectural and other constructions functioning as a restricted, phallic economy which overcodes and territorializes the more general economy of sexual difference and exchange, an economy of containment that envelops an economy of expenditure, or, in Derridean terms, an economy of gift. Following the logic established by Aristotelian physics, place is reduced to container, to the envelope of being; one being becomes the receptacle of another, the building or housing for another (in a sense, being becomes fetalized, and place, maternalized).[16] It is this that makes place a concept that is always already architectural insofar as it is conceived as container, as limit, locus, and foundation. But this origin, and the historical fidelity of philosophical and architectural discourses to it, marks Western conceptions of place, space, and measurement with the irremovable traces of that whose being becomes backgrounded as neutral space to be taken up, given form and matter, by objects, identities, substances. Irigaray calls this the maternal-feminine, for she claims that the characteristics and attributes of the maternal-feminine in Western culture – passive, receptacle, neutral, fluid, formless, lacking, empty or void, requiring filling, containment, measure – are precisely those also attributed to space, not because woman in any way resembles space, but rather because the treatment of the maternal-feminine is the condition for and template of the ways in which space is conceptualized and contained:

A certain representation of feminine jouissance corresponds to this water flowing without a container. A doubling, sought after by man, of a female placedness. She is assigned to be place without occupying a place. Through her, place would be set up for man's use but not hers. Her jouissance is meant to "resemble" the flow of whatever is in the place that she is when she contains, contains herself.[17]

3. Monstrous Architecture.

The concept of excess, or more, on which the Anymore conference has focused, has enabled the question of the superabundant, that which is excluded or contained because of its superabundance, to be raised as a political, as much as an economic and an aesthetic, concept. This excess, that which the sovereign, clean, proper, functional, and self-identical subject has expelled from itself, provides the conditions of all that both constitutes and all that undermines system, order, exchange, and production. What both preconditions and overflows that thin membrane that separates the outcast from the community, the container from the contained, the inside from the outside, is the embeddedness of the improper in the proper, the restricted within the general economy, the masculine within the feminine body, architecture within the body of space itself.

What, then, might provide a remedy for this constriction of space into manipulable object/neutral medium, which aligns itself with the erasure of the maternal-feminine and/or the excremental? Are there any architectural implications to be drawn from Irigaray's and Bataille's reflections on the role of those who constitute a noncommunity, a community of those who do not belong to a community? Is it possible to actively strive to produce an architecture of excess, in which the "more" is not cast off but made central, in which expenditure is sought out, in which instability, fluidity, the return of space to the bodies whose morphologies it upholds and conforms, in which the monstrous and the extra-functional, where consumption as much as production, act as powerful forces? Is this the same as or linked to the question of the feminine of architecture?

Here I can only make some broad suggestions, possibly wild – even excessive – speculations:

a. If space and Aristotelian place emerge from the surreptitious neutralization and rendering passive of the maternal-feminine, then the solution to this unacknowledgable debt is not the creation of women's spaces (or queer spaces, or the spaces of subordinated or excluded identities) – these create mere social islands within a sea of the same – but rather the exploration (scientific, artistic, architectural, and cultural) of space in different terms. If space is grounded in a spatial complexity, a necessarily doubled up and self-enfolded space providing the ground for the smooth, flat space of everyday existence, space is primarily defined by its modes of occupation, by what occurs within it, by the mobility and growth of the objects deposited there. This notion of space as passive receptacle or nest requires either to be doubled over again – so that the nest is itself further nested without being displaced from spatial location altogether; or, more provocatively and with considerably more difficulty, space itself needs to be reconsidered in terms of multiplicity, heterogeneity, activity, and force. Space is not simply an ether, a medium through which other forces, like gravity, produce their effects: it is both inscribed by and in its turn inscribes those objects and activities placed within it.

b. Transformations in conceptions of space are fundamentally linked to transformations in the conception of time. While they are considered a singular unified framework – a space-time field – and while they are understood in terms of binary oppositions, each providing what the other lacks, they remain intertwined as active and passive counterparts (in some discourses, particularly in the natural sciences, time is rendered the passive counterpart of the active space; in other discourses, particularly in the humanities, time in the form of history is the active force that ranges over passive geographical and social spaces, effecting transformation), and they inadvertently reproduce the structural relations between masculine and feminine. Space and time each have their own active and passive modalities, their modes of intensity and of extension: they must be considered neither complements nor opposites but specificities, each with their own multiple existences.

c. Architectural discourse and practice must not forget its (prehistoric or archaeological) connections to the impulse to shelter and covering first provided by nothing but the mother's body. The very concept of dwelling is irresolvably bound up with the first dwelling, itself a space enclosed within another space, and its materials – wood, metal, concrete, glass – are residues or after-effects of the placental and bodily membranes. Rather than return to more primitive materials, or to openly avow these primitive maternal connections, establishing a parallel between the placental universe and the social space in which housing provides shelter (a parallel, much beloved in political philosophy, that inevitably leads to the cultural and social space taking over the placental and natural space), architects may well find something else of this maternal origin of value: that of immense expenditure, an economy of pure gift, of excessive generosity, which, even if the architect cannot repay this gift, could perhaps produce it elsewhere, in design and construction.

d. This idea of gift is fundamentally linked to the notion of the monstrous and the excessive (those which are given "too much"), which defies the functionalism, the minimalism, the drive to economy and simplicity in much of contemporary architecture. I don't want to elevate the idea of ornament for ornament's sake, or the idea of a merely decorative architecture, or any particular element within current or past architectural practice as somehow an inherently feminine or feminist practice; but simply to argue that the gift of architecture is always in excess of function, practicality, mere housing or shelter. It is also always about the celebration of an above-subsistence sociality, a cultural excess which needs elevation not diminution. (Indeed, the very idea of function-

ality is itself another product of the cultural luxury of reflection that surpasses need.)

e. To produce an architecture in which "women can live" (to use Irigaray's formulation) is to produce both a domestic and a civic architecture as envelope, which permits the passage from one space and position to another, rather than the containment of objects and functions in which each thing finds its rightful place. Building would not function as finished object but rather as spatial process, open to whatever use it may be put in an indeterminate future, not as a container of solids but as a facilitator of flows: "volume without contour," as Irigaray describes it.

f. And finally, an architecture of excess must aim not at the satisfaction of present needs but to the production of future desires, not simply at the catering of pragmatic consumption but at that future consummation that transforms all present intentions and purposes. Architecture is not simply the colonization or territorialization of space, though it has commonly functioned in this way, as Bataille intuited; it is also, at its best, the anticipation and welcoming of a future in which the present can no longer recognize itself. In this sense, architecture may provide some of the necessary conditions for experiments in future living, experiments in which those excluded, marginalized, and rendered outside or placeless, will also find themselves.

1 Alphonso Lingis, **The Community of those who have Nothing in Common** (Bloomington and Indianapolis: Indiana University Press, 1994), 12.

2 René Girard has presented highly persuasive arguments to suggest that the structure of the scapegoat provides a means by which social collectives retain their cohesion during times of crisis: the scapegoat is the one, marked by some difference, onto whom the violence of the group is enacted and through whose sacrifice the group resolves its own internal differences and impulses to violence:

The signs that indicate a victim's selection result not from the difference within the system but from the differences outside the system, the potential for the system to differ from its own difference, in other words, not to be different at all, to cease to exist as a system. This is easily seen in the case of physical disabilities. The human body is a system of anatomic differences. If a disability, even as the result of an accident, is disturbing, it is because it gives the impression of a disturbing dynamism. It seems to threaten the very system. Efforts to limit it are unsuccessful; it disturbs the differences that surround it. These in turn become **monstrous**, rush together, are compressed and blended together to the point of destruction. Difference that exists outside the system is terrifying because it reveals the truth of the system, its relativity, its fragility, and its mortality.

René Girard, **The Scapegoat** (Baltimore: Johns Hopkins University Press, 1986), 21.

3 Georges Bataille, "The Notion of Expenditure" in **Visions of Excess. Selected Writings 1927–1939**, trans. Allan Stoekl (Manchester: University of Manchester Press, 1985), 118.

4 Bataille links the tall exotic skyscraper with the Tower of Babel, and with the oedipal struggle between father and son: We find here an attempt to climb to the sky – that is to say, to dethrone the father, to possess oneself of his virility – followed by the destruction of the rebels: castration of the son by his father, whose rival he is. Furthermore, the coupling, rash though it may be, of these two words, the verb "scrape" on the one hand, and, on the other, the substantive "sky," immediately evokes an erotic image in which the building, which scrapes, is a phallus even more explicit than the Tower of Babel, and the sky scraped – the object of desire of the said phallus – is the incestuously desired mother, as she is in all attempts at the spoliation of the paternal virility.

Georges Bataille, "Skyscraper," in **Encyclopædia Acephalica. Comprising the Critical Dictionary and Related Texts edited by Georges Bataille and the Encyclopædia Da Costa**, Robert Lebel and Isabelle Waldberg, eds. (London: Atlas Press, 1995), 69–72.

5 Bataille, "Architecture," in **Encyclopædia Acephalica**, 35–36.

6 Ibid., 35.

7 Ibid., 36.

8 Bataille: "When in a dream a diamond signifies excrement, it is not only a question of association by contrast; in the unconscious, jewels, like excrement, are cursed matter that flows from a wound: they are a part of oneself destined for open sacrifice (they serve, in fact, as sumptuous gifts charged with sexual love.)" From "The Notion of Expenditure," in **Visions of Excess**, 119.

9 Luce Irigaray, **An Ethics of Sexual Difference**, trans. Carolyn Burke and Gillian C. Gill (Ithaca, New York: Cornell University Press,1993), 7.

10 As Luce Irigaray claims:
In the beginning there was space and the creation of space, as is said in all theogonies. The gods, God, first create **space**. And time is there, more or less in the service of space. On the first day, the first days, the gods, God, make a world by separating the elements. This world is then peopled, and a rhythm is established among its inhabitants. God would be time itself, lavishing or exteriorizing itself in its actions in space, in places.

Philosophy then confirms the genealogy of the task of the gods or God. Time becomes the **interiority** of the subject itself, and space, its **exteriority** (this problematic is developed by Kant in the **Critique of Pure Reason**). The subject, the master of time, becomes the axis of the world's ordering, with its something beyond the moment and eternity: God. He effects the passage between time and space.

Irigaray, **An Ethics of Sexual Difference**, 7.

11 If traditionally, and as a mother, woman represents place for man, such a limit means that she becomes a **thing**, with some possibility of change from one historical period to another. She finds herself delineated as a thing. Moreover, the maternal-feminine also serves as an **envelope**, a **container**, the starting point from which man limits his things. The **relationship between envelope and things** constitutes one of the aporias, or the aporia, of Aristotelianism and of the philosophical systems derived from it.

Irigaray, **An Ethics of Sexual Difference**, 10.

12 Ibid., 11.

13 Ibid.

14 Luce Irigaray, "Ou et comment habiter?" **Les cahiers du Grif**, 26 (March 1983). Issue on **Jouir**.

15 Ibid., 270.

16 In her commentary on Aristotle's **Physics, Book IV**, Irigaray argues that place is a maternal containment for the object which it houses: "It seems that a fetus would be in a place. And man's penis for as long as it is inside the woman. Woman is in the house, but this is not the same type of place as a living bodily site. On the other hand, place, in her, is in place, not only as organs but as vessel or receptacle. It is place twice over: as mother and as woman." Irigaray, **An Ethics of Sexual Difference**, 52.

17 Ibid.

Elizabeth Grosz **teaches philosophy at the State University of New York in Buffalo. She is author of** Jaques Lacan. A Feminist Introduction **and** Volatile Bodies: Toward a Corporeal Feminism**.**

Previous pages and below: Redevelopment of the SMN Site, Caen, 1995.

Elementary Dispositions
Dominique Perrault

Contemporary architecture is very objective. It is nonhierarchical. It avails itself of all elements of an earlier architectonics and rearranges these according to a deliberately conceptual logic. A whole set of procedures, from design to realization, is thus overturned.

The architect seizes upon all the moments that make up the sequences leading to the conception and realization of a building – the process, that is – and from them makes the enduring material of an intervention. Behind these skills, these decisions, and the complex study and development of the idea (defining the architect as a creator), it is time itself that is undoubtedly the object of the architect's whole attention, his only preoccupation, the permanent restlessness of a present he tirelessly seeks to actualize.

Indeed, contemporary architecture challenges the idea of time, forming the very essence of architectural culture; an idea that turns every building into a monument, a memory; an idea that founds, that historicizes, that would like architecture to possess a historical rationale, a truth. Architecture must have its own validity and effectiveness to be experienced by all, to have an instant rapport with all of us.

It is Enlightenment reason that has to be attacked, a reason that has fueled classicism, and modernism, too, a reason that seeks for rules and laws, a reason that looks to determine the principles that legitimate and control architectural form. Principles derive from praxis, from an ongoing research in which the specificity of space is endlessly reinvented, of a form, of an intervention. Architecture is an activity that constantly renews itself, a consistently original act and a set of decisions that organize a singular, unique situation. Architecture is no longer the result of a composition but of a state of mind, which calls equally on forms, materials, and the abilities of all who participate in the elaboration of a project.

This implies, then, an architecture lacking in reference; neither modern nor postmodern, it functions with urgency, is immediate in nature, and rejects history. It would therefore be illusory, when grasping, when trying to define this work, to seek models or analogies drawn from superficial comparisons. Certain objects are present, but one can no longer speak of forms and the a priori devices of cubes and parallelepipeds common to the architect's work.

Given its lack of syntax, of obvious linguistic elements, we cannot easily scrutinize this architecture for principles or referential images. This architectural culture does not possess ineluctable authority, it has no set method; instead, it is a material, a resource, a tool like any other. The architect insists on architecture without style, without expression, not requiring definition or the precedence of any language. His work does not respond to a constant syntax, applicable according to the appropriateness of the situation, the program; it is not organized as an aesthetic project, which holds knowledge, norms, and a morality of practice in check. The project's definition is a direct consequence of the context, of the determining factors present in it, which are analyzed, put forward as a resource, a particular richness that must be interpreted by means of the tools of architecture and thus transfigured, reconverted.

Context means literally "with the text" – to supplement what already appears to make sense, or to reveal what is not immediately legible. This idea of context is not historicist, it does not dwell on the memory of a place, of an extant building, rather it is tectonic, it takes physical hold of the territory. The traditional diagnosis of use and function is only one of the aspects of the work, which is henceforth also built around an environmental analysis of defined or defining areas. The sum of the elements that define and organize the specificity of a site – its history, social use, its topography – is assimilated to a force-field, which, in order to optimize its use and management, is addressed by the architect in its entirety.

In opposition to a sociologist, who looks for traces of the sedimentation of human praxis in the city or the territory, the architect strives to be a geographer or a geologist; he rejects the authority of a past age, of an external time, of history, and retains only its current, active elements. Space does not possess its own ontology; there is no antecedent, essence, or primary nature that would rule over the built domain and that would have to be opposed to human praxis.

There are "different natures," extending from the most pure to the most artificial, natures which coexist in a simultaneous whole. This materialism, this veritable physicality, redefines the world as a complexity in which man rediscovers his capacity for definition, for intervention.

Nature is no longer the domain of indeterminacy but is asserted as an object of knowledge. Nature is submitted to the laws of regulation and industrial production, is exploited, exhausted in the extreme, but is also available for mastering anew; nature can be developed, it is the object of specific study and development.

To cultivate nature is to produce nature; it is to avail ourselves of all the various kinds of knowledge we have at our disposal to induce the natural. Behind the apparent violence or arbitrariness of these interventions, an actual mutation in the relationship

Olympic velodrome and swimming pool, Berlin, 1999.

between nature and architecture articulates the logic of design. Such a brutalist use of nature allows its phenomenal and sentient force to express itself freely, counter to any overly cultural or architectural understanding of the garden, of green space. It is the landscape as a whole that is under scrutiny. The architect must generate the effects of spatiality and, by using simple gestures, must create an order that rejects all mediation, a unique and immediate layout that does not strive to be a system, an organizing principle. Space must be concretely apprehended, brought into being according to a factual system, a unique open-ended experience. Architecture must stick to this economy of layout in which space is defined through the sort of simple interventions: encrusting, weaving, enclosing, engraving, installing, anchoring, sectioning, blending, splicing, extending, flooding, concealing.

In a word, the œuvre is without style, without expression; it does not encumber itself with affectation, any code, or presupposed knowledge. It invites a sort of unknowing, a refusal of any supposed meaning, of architecture as a defining principle. Architecture must accept the principle of its own disappearance.

The gesture is not new: the end of humankind, the end of philosophy, the end of history – in the past, structuralism had made declarations of this kind familiar to us. What it dissimulates is the refusal of typologies, of a preexisting language that could be applied to any definition of space. Its minimalism does not lead to the phenomenal truth of a purer space being elaborated from a new purism, which balances light and materials. Architecture strikes at the very heart of a structuralist vision of creation.

This conceptualism is no longer simply analytical and critical; it has an operative function, it shows disposition to be an authentic constructive principle. Like a neutralization of architecture, an architecture in act, a manifest architecture of "ecriture blanche."

Dominique Perrault is an architect in Paris. His buildings include the Bibliothèque de France in Paris and an extension to the European Community Courthouse in Luxembourg.

Olympic velodrome and swimming pool.

Discussion 6

KRISTIN FEIREISS Dominique, you spoke about experiments, about geography, changes, and nature as building materials, but what is the most important issue? What are your mores?

DOMINIQUE PERRAULT Well, my mores are always changing. I tend to see whatever is around us as a material – the landscape and also more abstract elements such as emptiness or absence. The extent of this embrace is something unfamiliar to most architects. Conventionally, architecture is seen to use only certain elements. But architects can refer to other elements in order to develop their own language and to expand the field of architecture.

ANTHONY VIDLER What if one has nothing more to say? I thought you were going to say that your more was *moins*, that your more was less, because, as you know, Mies van der Rohe said that less is not just anymore. But anyway, on to Liz's presentation. One of the things I love about your work, Liz, is that you are an optimistic philosopher as opposed to a philosopher of optimism and hope, as opposed to a philosopher of disenchantment and despair. Maybe because I'm trained as a critic and a historian. I always imagine questions to have a negative answer as opposed to a positive answer. It's very nice to have a sense of optimism.

But my comments really concern your joining, or your doubling or pairing, of these two moments of excess – the excess characterized in a scatological way by Bataille, and the excess characterized by the leftover, by the remainder, by the excluded, and, in a sense, by the feminine. And then you posited a third, concluding question as to what would be the monstrous architecture that gives a new kind of home, in a more or less optimistic way, to this kind of excess, and how that can be reconciled with the notion of Bataille's excess. That no monument, in fact, is better than any monument. It always seems to me that when questions of gender are raised, when questions of the other are raised, when questions of ethnicity are raised, when questions of identity are raised with respect to architecture, that the world divides between those who analyze the behavior and the relationships of the subjects and the subjective within and outside and around architecture. In other words, what happens to the subject in architecture? For what subject was architecture built? (By subject I mean the Renaissance subject that builds a perspectival space, that constructs the space for that subject, and the use of that space by other subjects for whom it was not constructed – the way in which they live, so to speak, in the cracks of that space, in the recesses and the interiors of that space.) The world, you said, divides itself between those who study space as subjecting and subjectivity as subjection within architecture, and those who believe that one can build a space proper to and out of the subjectivity of difference, of otherness. I am always slightly skeptical of this second proposition, and I'm wondering to what extent the abstract formulation of the space of otherness can be coordinated with the literal formulation of a space of otherness. This would be the terms with which we could conceive monstrosity as a literal, visual artifact, as opposed to a way for otherness to be a true and living subject within an architecture that both responds to and houses it. It is basically a difference between the cartoon that literalizes, or, in an expressionist sense, expresses a subjectivity, and a subjectivity that is at home in a kind of neutrality that it then adopts and reshapes to fit itself.

ELIZABETH GROSZ I think you're absolutely right. I also think that this is the problem with conceiving of architecture as simply the expression of subjectivity. But any notion of subjectivity always entails a notion of otherness, and this is the problem with the concept of the subject – there can be no subject unless there is someone who is a subject who isn't quite equal to being a subject. This, of course, is precisely the problem with the Enlightenment concept of subjectivity; a concept that is supposedly universal but, in reality, is not. So in a way, I'm not concerned about building an architecture that's more egalitarian – an architecture, in other words, that includes more subjects – because it seems to me that the very category of subjectivity is based on the necessity of some kind of exclusion. For me, the task is how we can build an architecture to which the derelict is also attracted. The answer is, we can't. Rather, the question is, how we can build architecture that understands the depths and obligations it owes to those it can't house? This is not a question of how can we improve architecture but rather one about its inherent limits. Sorry, this is a little more pessimistic.

VIDLER A pessimistic conclusion to your optimism.

GROSZ Well, it's pessimistic in that one can't have a global or universalizing architecture that includes everyone equally. But what we must have is an architecture that's highly experimental and that modulates the subjects to whom it's directing its efforts. The idea of a park, for example, is a concept of a space that is quite different from the concept of an apartment. They both have their exclusions, and in a way this is my point: you can't have a position without an exclusion. The exclusion is a political exclusion, but it's the condition of one's existence –

the most noble way of excluding is to give another time to those excluded.

FRANCO PURINI I think it is impossible not to accept the superfluousness of architecture. But in accepting it, there are three possible responses. The first one is architecture as an art. The second response, as we can see in Dominique Perrault's work, is an architecture infused with artistic research, bringing about change, but only as specific to architecture. And the third avenue forward, and this is my position, is simply to realize that the existing can exist only if an action makes it exist, and that this action for architecture consists in giving a new name to things. It's not an issue of being pessimistic or optimistic, of being desperate or happy. I think we have to rename the world through architecture. Architecture is vital and necessary when it is opposition architecture, but you have to make opposition architecture only by making architecture.

Superfluous architecture was the architecture Palladio developed around the San Marco lagoon. There was no reason why there should be three churches there, but it was the response that Venetian society had at the time to an architecture that had lost its significance and meaning. I think it's important and beautiful to have superfluousness in architecture, because it enables us to avoid continuing along this rather pathetic course of running after technological icons, reinventing the curves of baroque architecture. It's interesting, but I think that the real, core issue here is what name to give things.

PERRAULT Well, as to opposition architecture I totally agree with you. But what is it? If it is the opposite of conventional architecture, it's interesting, because the problem of architecture is indeed this kind of determinism, this predetermined dimension. Think about ethics. If we say that this person has got an ethical architect, well, good for him. But if we say that a process has started from an idea, developed for a time, then given rise to something, produced something that we'll call architecture, then this is much more interesting, because it means that you're in a situation where production is not determined. Everybody has an ethical position. What's interesting is that from this position, this diversity that you were talking about, you can develop a process which is in fact the material. It is the process that is the proof of the quality of a project – the distance that has been traveled, the information that has been gathered together. That's an ethical position, and I think this is the real opposition architecture.

HUBERT DAMISCH Dominique is really quite assertive with this proposal. You know, a child doesn't dream of becoming a critic, but a child can dream of becoming an architect, and the presentation that Perrault made of his process was typically critical. So how do you become a critic? It's not a role you dream about. But if you want to become an architect, you have to become a critic. What does that mean for an architect, though, to be critical? It means you have to criticize the reality that you're confronted with, the context in which architecture is being built, and it also means being critical of architecture. There are several ways you can do that: you can criticize your own architecture, or you can criticize architecture in general. We had a few remarkable examples when Greg Lynn showed us how, as an architect, he can invent new ways of analyzing architecture through surfaces rather than elevations. So would you accept that to become an architect is to become a critic of architecture, a critic of the world in which architecture takes place?

PERRAULT If to be critical or to become a critic means asking oneself questions, then yes.

DAMISCH It's not about questions, not about the positing of questions, but about analyzing.

PERRAULT Yes, I know, but it is through this that the architectural realm defines itself.

DAMISCH No, no. Capitalist society gives us instruments to understand the past. The past does not understand itself. There is a kind of critical becoming of society, and to become a critical architect means being able to think of your own history, your own practice, or the theory of your practice, and the articulation between theory and history.

PERRAULT But there is no ambiguity, no debate as to the definition. It's not ambivalent in any way. What is interesting is how you actually criticize – the modus operandi for criticism. I think there is an emotional aspect to architecture, and this emotional dimension is something you can bring into the field of criticism inasmuch as it has been perceived, experienced, tested, verified, and provoked. What I am interested in is the phenomena that create this emotion, this situation, as a result of which the situation is no longer the same. Since the situation is different, my analysis of the situation becomes different, and it is around this difference that criticism develops. This is my position with regard to criticism, and this is what I think is so fascinating about architecture: it cannot, in critical terms, simply be reduced to structural fields; there is an emotional field as well, and a physical field. I'm interested in thinking differently about architecture in relation to emotional and physical dimensions – something that perhaps can be analyzed, perceived, experienced, and measured more rationally, but only after you've perceived it and experienced it and experimented with it. This approach is to effect a real change in the relationship we have with architecture.

PHYLLIS LAMBERT Dominique, I can't see how a refusal, a rejection can be an ethical position. You seem to be leaving a void, an abyss even, and I don't see how this can be emotional. Talk about emotions – Hitler went to Warsaw and systematically demolished all the buildings to annihilate the feeling of belonging, the feeling of pride, the peoples' feelings for culture, by burying them in a hole in the ground. So I don't know how refusal can be an ethical act.

PERRAULT It's not a refusal. It's never a refusal. It's a total acceptance of a situation. You see, what I find interesting is that what we do is just one element. It's not complete; it's incomplete and never owned in its entirety. And this is something that does change our relationship with architecture. If you could give more, you would. If you could allow more, you would. This revealing of a new and different possibility is very often linked to paradoxical situations. I'm not saying that what we are doing has total and absolute value – these are fields of research that change one's common perceptions. But it's not a refusal. Quite the contrary – it's a present; it's a gift.

VIDLER I want to respond quickly to Hubert's comment: as a child I dreamt of becoming a thinker – not a critic, not an architect, but a thinker – and then I became a critic and an architect. Intellectual things are extremely emotional to me, and emotional things are very intellectual, too. In terms of our aspirations, our hopes, we think and therefore we live – there is no separation.

JEAN-LOUIS COHEN I would like to take up a point raised by Elizabeth Grosz and Franco Purini. Elizabeth spoke about Bataille's analysis of unproductive expenditure, the cursed share, and monuments. Then Franco told us at length about the superfluousness of architecture. As part of this debate about the issue of ethos in architecture today, we should question whether this superfluousness is really the single, prevailing condition of architecture today. What is lacking in this conference, I would argue, is the element of social science, with its roots in the analysis of the commonplace of the societies in which we live – issues of habitation, urban landscape, refuges and hostels in cities, and how this necessary condition can be approached by architecture. I'm not trying to disqualify the beautiful architectural objects that we've seen in various presentations, but we have to look at these things with a critical distance. In this regard, I would like to insist again on the transatlantic differences that have been talked about so much here. There is a very clear difference between the U.S. and parts of Europe today. Despite what has been said here about the tyranny of modern capitalism, there are social policies in Europe that deal with housing and town planning that offer a real challenge and a radical field of experiment for architecture. I feel that the areas where it would be interesting for architecture to get mobilized today are exactly where this critical function has to be exercised. In a confrontation with this ill-formulated social requirement, perhaps architecture could bring a response through an object that could meet these expectations. Then, perhaps, we could say that architecture is superfluous.

PURINI We can debate forever the interpretation we each have of architecture, but on one thing can we agree: that architecture is a thing or an event that has a single function essential to our daily life. It makes it possible to orientate oneself. It is a way of establishing oneself with a certain spiritual dignity. It means that I can go back to some places in the world and find myself again, which is exactly the condition that binds these relationships. But we have to rename this thing, architecture, from the outset. There is an obvious difficulty in this. The discernable limit to our world is anonymity. The only poets who have a human dimension are anonymous poets – violent and absolute and radically anonymous. Despite the apparent contradiction, I think it is very easy to name things in a field where everything is necessarily anonymous. I don't want my discourse to sound pessimistic. There is a terrific energy in this issue, that is, the destruction of the very reason for the existence of architecture. This is what architecture is going to have to face in the future, yet it is this very destruction that will allow us to continue through the next century.

GROSZ The idea of the superfluousness of architecture is a really interesting idea, but it's an idea that I'd want to generalize much more, rather than relating it specifically to the architectural sphere. Franco suggested that there are three responses to the superfluousness of architecture: one was the elevation of art; the other was to resort to high technology; and a third was a renaming. What strikes me about these three alternatives is that they're equally superfluous. I mean, if architecture is superfluous – and I'm not sure I agree with this – then art is more superfluous and technology is even more superfluous still. This superfluousness, it seems to me, is exactly what we need to revel in rather than anguish about – that all of cultural production, all of scientific production, all of artistic production comes from precisely the excess of energy that we have over and above the need of subsistence. This is why I think Jean-Louis's point is a crucial one – that until we have an adequate system of housing, until we have an adequate mode of habitation for everybody, we can't generate superfluousness in the whole community. It's when the whole community has what we call leisure, or the luxury of time, that all artistic production can regenerate itself, remake itself, rename itself, and open itself up to a new future. So it's precisely this superfluousness that strikes me as the most exciting element of our understanding of architecture and art and technology. They're all superfluous. And that's the good news.

YANNIS TSIOMIS All these oppositions and debates this afternoon are in effect all about ethics and morals, individuals and the collective. If we say "mores," it is a question of culture, but if we say "ethics," we have to think in terms of civilization, and in this regard, I have a number of comments to make. The first one is that of sanctions. In talking of morals, there is necessarily also a sanction. Habermas said that in an irrational system before the Enlightenment, failure was always a failure before authority. Rationally speaking, failure is failure before reality. This is a question I often ask myself – what is failure when faced with the situation we have called globalization? I'd like to know what common value we are talking about, because if we can't define these common values, then we have to redefine them. Then there is the problem of legibility, of art creating legibility, of social and spatial legibility as applied to the city. The city was absent not because nobody thinks of the city but because it's difficult to speak of the city beyond a certain established urban project. And finally there is the question of utopia. I think that in discussing utopia, one tends to forget the work of historians on utopia. In fact, utopia is an antireality term – if Plato had constructed his Atlantis, then he would have done it on the basis of an anti-Athens. I'd like to know how antireality could be made from illegibility. Not only do we have to recreate the system, but we have to configure systems in which there are identities that can live precisely in our architectures.

GROSZ I'm very happy to talk about the question of ethics because I think it is the most pressing issue, and it's the issue that's the most contentious and the least thought about at the present time. For me, the question of ethics is closely linked to the question of where one takes one's resources from. The ethical questions are the debts that one owes; not economic debts but moral debts – the debts that one owes from the place one gets one's resources from. This is why architecture is always an ethical question, although it's rarely conceptualized in these terms. Where did the concept come from? Where did the

energy come from? Where did the labor come from? Where did the possibility of this particular building come from? This, I think, is exactly analogous to the kind of ethics involved in interpersonal relations. What is my obligation to you? What is your obligation to me? How much does it cost me to do this? How much does it cost you to do that? This is the ethics of architecture – where does one come from and to whom does one owe an obligation? How you answer these questions, I think, puts you into one category of architect or another.

VIDLER I just wanted say, as an aside, that Utopia of course was written by More, not just any More, but Thomas More. I also think it's very hard to summarize, within a short panel of this kind, the very complicated relations of ethics, politics, architecture, and the forms of architecture. In the political discussion of the relationship between society and architecture over the last thirty years, we've seen many vulgarized and mechanized versions of those relationships, and so I hesitate to make clear or strong divisions between architecture and its mores or its ethics. I think that there is in the end a very subtle relationship between what we used to call the autonomy of architecture and its formal consistency; its internal practice as a kind spatial art and the externality of that spatial art as it relates to patronage – where it comes from, who gives it, who uses it, who takes it, who abuses it, who remakes it, and so on. But for a certain kind of critical attention to where it comes from, and another kind of critical and formal attention to where it's going, an architect can be in some way deeply responsive to both her practice and to the practice of the society in which the object is inserted. Generally, of course, I'm on the side of ethics, except if they are bogus, nostalgic, romantic, over-emotionally conceived, spiritual, mysticizing a fairy-tale romance of the good ol' days – the kind of ethics that ought to be put in a basket and shipped out to utopia. The ethics that I'm interested in are the ethics of a very pragmatic and practical kind that respond to contingencies and sites.

FEIREISS What about the architects?

VIDLER Well, you could put half the architects in the basket, too! I said half.

AUDIENCE More than half!

VIDLER More than half? Okay. But really, I don't think an architect's ethics in relation to every context are the same. For instance, I don't believe in the globalization of ethics in that sense, and I don't believe in the vulgarization of ethics in a kind of neoconservative sense, or an emotional-idealistic sense. I believe in the practical application of certain ethical responses to site, context, and community at a certain moment in which the object is conceived. After that, the object casts itself in a basket and society does what it wants with it, you know.

PERRAULT Ethics and ideas of identity, legibility, and a kind of enlightened pragmatism can be taken together to constitute a position. But as I see it, the idea of ethics is linked to a certain way of looking at things, or how one is disposed to certain things – my ethical position will change with my physical position, my vantage point, how I perceive things. As I see it, every place has something that is of greater or lesser importance, but at least there is something everywhere, in every place. The question of ethics ties directly into the way in which I will be able to identify this something, and then once I've identified it, the ethical outlook can then be changed.

PURINI I'd like to talk not so much about legibility but about visibility. The task of an architect is to see that the whole becomes something that is visible and understandable. I know ethics are not "visible," but I think that what we have to do is rebuild ethics, the ethics of the gaze or the way we behold things. As I see it, the gaze is about looking from very far away, whereas ethics is about looking at something up close. As some kind of intermediary, architecture is perceived at a middle distance. I think that we have to move ethics and gazes closer to this middle position.

AUDIENCE I have a question for Mark Taylor. I think that what Mark said on the first day of this conference about a complexity of differences has some relevance to this discussion. I raise this because it seems as if a lot of the discussion today has been characterized by a very strong sense of continuity, and Mark's idea of discontinuity has not been really addressed.

MARK TAYLOR I think it's more appropriate to have the panel focus on this. I would, though, like to say two brief things. I tend to find discussions about ethics frustrating, because there is a certain inevitable vacuity about it, to use Dominique's terms, and I'm just not sure it's very productive to have an Anymore discussion about mores in this kind of context. It's fundamentally impossible to distinguish the ethical from the political, and I think this is what Tony was also saying. I speak as a philosopher trained as a theologian, and I'd rather just bag the question of ethics. In response to your question, however, I do think that the issue of discontinuity has been raised in a variety of ways. Part of what I was trying to say the other day

was a way in which one can articulate discontinuity and heterogeneity without getting rid of the notion of some kind of relational whole or holistic kind of structure. It doesn't have to be an either/or opposition but a disjunction that enhances, rather than subverts, any kind of relational whole. Too much of the critical debate recently has cast ideas of holism or disruption, homogeneity or heterogeneity, as an either/or that I feel is unproductive.

GREG LYNN Massimiliano Fuksas's planned Architecture Biennale in Venice makes a statement that one could also take as a question: "Less aesthetics, more ethics." Maybe Jean-Louis would disagree, but it's kind of a statement that the aesthetics of ethics is minimalism. In the United States you have an aesthetics of the minimal offered as a lifestyle decision about spareness. You can see it in all of the boutiques along Madison Avenue, designed as minimalism, and advertising an ethics of modesty. The truth of it, though, is about selling very high-end products. There was a very funny quote the other day in the *Los Angeles Times* by a woman who is spending several million dollars renovating a modernist house. She said, "Well, we decided to spend millions of dollars renovating this house because our taste is to have a good minimal ethics." So I take that Fuksas statement as a statement. It's not a question; it's simply that the dominant style these days in the aesthetics of ethics is minimalism.

VIDLER It's true that less costs more, especially if it's wrapped in titanium.

CYNTHIA DAVIDSON Mark Taylor has provoked me into throwing away the final remarks I intended to say here about the Any project. I actually was going to ask a question if the discussion hadn't moved toward the issue of ethics, because I was very interested in Franco Purini's idea of renaming, which I linked to Tony Vidler's recalling of Ledoux's sphere as emblematizing a crisis of the age. I think that Franco is absolutely right. We are facing another crisis of an age and we've got to think about renaming architecture. Perhaps this is where the undecidability that has been the framework of the Any project over the last nine years really comes into play. I felt challenged yesterday by Rosalind Krauss when she talked about the promiscuity of undecidability and the need for specificity. Maybe renaming is part of that pursuit of specificity, figuring out what we're going to do. Mark Taylor was an early participant in the Any conferences. He hasn't been to a conference in several years, and he was saying to me today that he thought the nature of the discussions had really changed since he last attended in Barcelona in 1993. This sense of a changing discussion is particularly interesting to me, because working so closely with the project, it's hard to get the critical distance necessary to see clearly what's happening. When we were in Holland for the Anyhow conference (1997), we began to hear from a new generation of architects who are trying to feel their way along the new technologies affecting the production of architecture. This set up a generational debate that challenged the norms we've had about architecture, about all the issues of architecture that have been talked about today – history and theory, technology, ethics and mores. And renaming. This is a really exciting thing, perhaps even a crisis, but a crisis, in Liz's terms, that's very positive.

DEAR ANY,

Since their beginning in 1991, one of the recurring dimensions of the Any conferences at each stop along their sinuous world-wide circuit has been the discovery of institutions, of urban cultures, and of local articulations of architectural discourse. In every city, the meetings have revealed overlooked design strategies and laid bare intellectual contradictions. From this point of view, the potential of Paris, a seemingly hitherto hostile location, was highly anticipated for the opening of a discussion that continued those held at previous "stations."

The dynamism of French architectural practice is visible at the moment of arrival in the new Roissy terminals, where most participants arrived from abroad. But, beyond the most recent public buildings, the Paris conference site had a particular meaning for the discourse promoted by many founding members of the Any meetings, as it has been the point of origin for scores of interpretations essential to the emergence of the intellectual view of architecture that they uphold. Much more than the designers, theorists, and critics involved at a particular moment in the changing Any context, like Jacques Derrida or Hubert Damisch, the remote radiation of writings by Roland Barthes, Jacques Lacan, Michel Foucault, Jean-François Lyotard, Gilles Deleuze, Paul Virilio, and several others has had an in-depth effect since the 1980s on architectural thought and, in a lesser measure, on design in large parts of the world. Also, some of the frequent participants (or frequent flyers?) in the Any conferences have had in their nomadic lives a more or less permanent Paris mooring.

It was therefore tempting to measure on the occasion of the ninth meeting what kind of interaction could develop between patterns of thought constructed at the international level and on the French scene. It is precisely from this perspective that the originality of Anymore had to reveal itself, and in a way, it succeeded, though in an unexpected fashion.

If the relationship between what is sometimes called "French theory" and architecture has been, at least in the United States, as productive for intellectuals as for designers, while not remaining exempt from multiple second thoughts on both sides, the configuration of the interaction has been extremely different in Europe at large and in France itself. By certain aspects, many of the discourses presented under the sign of novelty – if not subversion – in the Anglo-Saxon world were part of what I should call the cultural "bath" in which French architecture had floated at least since the second half of the 1960s. This earlier experience explains the astonishment of not a few Parisian architects and scholars in front of the sometimes naive enthusiasm triggered by discourses with which they have been familiar for some time. The long ignorance of the books of Henri Lefebvre in the United States before they were finally translated and celebrated

in recent years – a neglect in sharp contrast to their lasting reception in France over three decades – is an example of these discrepancies. The immersion in a different "bath" explains – at least for the older architects – the absence of explicit references to discourses that are constantly mentioned elsewhere but have been to some extent interiorized by former generations of Paris architects.

At Anymore, Fiona Meadows and Frédéric Nantois captured with a misunderstood irony the patterns of what I should call, to paraphrase Aloïs Riegl, the cult of modern intellectual monuments in their name-dropping presentation. In fact, to put it historically, at the time of the collapse of the École des Beaux-Arts, when much of the contemporary scene was shaped, there were two essentially alternative survival strategies. The first was to attend seminars held by Roland Barthes, Julia Kristeva, and others at the École des hautes études or lectures by Michel Foucault at the Collège de France. This was the choice for many young architects and students, sometimes arriving from far away, such as Antoine Grumbach, Bruno Fortier, Diana Agrest, Mario Gandelsonas, Christian Hauvette, and Patrick Berger, to name a few. The second was to attend the evening lectures held by Jean Prouvé at the Conservatoire des arts et métiers, where, every week, he would graphically construct a new metallic structure. Only a few would cross the Seine and share both the more theoretical and the more practical experiences.

In parallel to these two places devoted, respectively, to verbal and to visual production, new frameworks for exchange appeared, for instance with the Institut de l'environnement. Created in 1968 by André Malraux's Ministry of Culture in order to weave together programs for the training of young faculty and for the development of research, it fostered history, social sciences, and early computer-aided investigations. New approaches to architectural culture were shaped in this short-lived laboratory.

Both the exposure to other discourses and the participation in the Institut's programs contributed to the emergence not only of new schools but also of new types of designers, who were profoundly reshaped by the interiorization of theoretical issues. Figures as diverse as Christian de Portzamparc and Christian Devillers, to name just two survivors of the Beaux-Arts ateliers, typify this group. Simultaneously, schools were transformed through the action of architects aware of questions and methods at work in the social sciences, as well as through the contribution of sociologists and psychologists willing to work not so much on architecture as in architecture. No single academic discipline ever achieved a monopoly over the discourse held in this context, but a new culture in which they all converged, encompassing philosophy and anthropology, was shaped.

The changes in culture were echoed by a complete redeployment of public programs previously geared toward quantitative goals. With the emphasis put on quality and innovation, new horizons were opened and a wide range of experimental projects were supported. Often overshadowed by the hype of Mitterrand's *Grands Travaux*, these policies still form the framework in which most projects shown by France-based architects have been developed.

However remote, these founding episodes still have a powerful impact on the current articulation of the French scene, although State policies are no longer the only factor in the emergence of an experimental architecture, with the appearance of local and private programs active in this direction. The gap between architects and intellectuals that characterized the French scene (despite the pioneering actions mentioned above, and which I had already discussed in 1976 as evidencing an illuminating parallel with Italy) has been reconfigured. This sort of ditch doesn't follow the previous direction, and has been erased in certain areas as it has widened in others. And it is precisely the shape of this lasting gap that Anymore revealed and, to some extent, modified. I don't perceive therefore the Anymore episode as a "shameful" experience, to use the words of Christian Girard (see "Letter from Paris," ANY 25/26: 2000), but rather a cruel one.

The exercise was a complicated one, as the very thematics of Anymore were somewhat elusive. The issues at stake were undoubtedly more difficult to grasp than the ones of any- place, time, or body, as the metaphorical range of the term *anymore* was significantly wider. As the image of despair (if we understand it as ruins) or of hope (if we understand it as construction in progress) associated with the communication of Anymore suggested, the question raised between a war in Kosovo and one in Chechnya was straightforward: In today's world, how pertinent is architecture as a professional practice, and also, simply, as a practice of observation revealing the texture of reality?

The least one can say, and the texts included in this volume bear witness to it, is that no structured, choral answer to this question was given. A certain bias in the preparation of the conference, for which I am probably to be blamed, has led to the absence of speakers representing the convergence of intellectual discourse and architecture in the realm of concrete social issues in a program that was delicate to shape. In the understandable absence of patented representatives of "French theory," probably unwilling to be associated with architectural issues in their homeland, and despite the seminal contribution of Hubert Damisch, other profiles of scholars and theoreticians engaged in the definition of architecture in France were not mobilized. These profiles are original, and here I would disagree with Girard's somewhat pessimistic view. It is vain to look in France and in other parts of Europe, such as Italy, for "theory" as it has been defined in North American academic and critical writing, projecting eastward the model of what has been the development of an architectural discourse tailored to specific institutional and professional configurations. What has been and is still the contribution of a somewhat different articulation of thought and design achieved in Europe is what I would call "theorization," i.e., an interpretation of issues at work in housing, landscape, history, and technology, that uses concepts from the humanities reconfigured in the architectural field. Bringing forward the evidence of the cross-contamination of architects and (other) intellectuals in the research programs developed in the past twenty years in France is perhaps what Anymore has missed to a certain extent.

Despite these limits, and despite the wide differences that appeared perhaps more between age groups than between architects operating in geographic contexts whose difference seems less meaningful every day, what remains as the main legacy of the debate was precisely its very existence. In front of the threatening narcissism and deafness of most current architects to the work of the intimate others that are their contemporaries, Anymore has established the possibility of a dense *conversation* between designers and critics from every origin and inside the two groups. At the center of the *mores*, the question of which concluded the conference, lies this condition of dialogue, which has, I believe, been solidly recreated in Paris by a thrilling conference.

JEAN-LOUIS COHEN
PARIS

A belated thanks for Anymore, which stimulated taste buds and intellect! My thanks also to Jean-Louis Cohen, since I regard his initiative to hold an Any conference in Paris as a bold one, and which I hope will open debate a little – or open space for debate, which seems restricted here. There has been a progressive hardening of the arteries in France despite the fluidity of new technology, and I hope this allows for a loosening of discourse. It will be good for the Institut français d'architecture to head that, since it fulfills such an important role in France.

All Any conferences seem to drift in and out of focus, but I was surprised to find the very different focal lengths at Anymore, a by-product of evidently national traits. Although the visiting architects (American and Dutch) placed great importance in being able to articulate a critical platform for their work in terms of cultural references, the French architects seemed to frame their work to a great degree in terms of the immediate concerns of practice and experience. With respect to dECOi, poised on the fringes of French practice, I think this reflects the status of the profession in the different countries present and, in particular, the ordered and bureaucratized French system within which the majority of French architects operate. While this evidently allows for quite a coherent and consistent quality in French architecture, it does seem to limit speculative work in a manner curiously at odds with their Dutch counterparts. In light of the dramatic technological changes in architecture at present, which demand a profound requalification of all aspects of practice, French architecture seems limited in its capacity to interrogate such change. This was the most surprising aspect of the conference: that the lack of critical or speculative discourse in French architecture and virtually no account of technical change led to a polarized discourse.

In terms of the debate during the Anymore Technology session, I was struck by the extent to which the CAD field is clarifying itself; quite distinct positions among the various practitioners are emerging. Anymore immediately followed the ArchiLab conference, which itself was a reconvening of the participants of the Morphe conference of 1997 (in many ways an announcement of a new technical field in architecture). The intervening two years saw a clarification and deepening understanding of the electronic creative environment and have prompted a reflection on the nature of technology per se. What seems apparent is that there are those who regard this new environment as an extension of existing modes of thought and practice, and those who consider it a radical new departure. Rosalind Krauss's comment that Lars Spuybroek's work "made the Guggenheim Bilbao look like the Parthenon" serves to underscore that all that is "technical" is not necessarily of the same nature, and I think one might begin to separate out the formalists (technicists) from the technologists – a quite subtle and surprising distinction, I think.

At the ArchiLab conference Lars Spuybroek recounted the story of a monkey with a stick, which he articulated at length. The monkey discovered that when it forced the stick into an anthill it came out covered in ants. Lars's point was to articulate the extraordinary extent to which we are able to fuse through the use of prosthetic devices: the stick – technology – is a prosthesis. The monkey rapidly becomes quite skilled at manipulating it effectively. It becomes an extension of its body. Lars then extended that to suggest a proprioceptive architecture enabled by a new technology; an ever-evolving man-machine symbiosis that allows hitherto unimaginable proprioceptive configurations.

But I was intrigued much more by how Spuybroek's account actually illustrates the nature of technology per se; that "man creates a tool, tool changes man" (McLuhan), thus shifting patterns of thought and cultural desire. In fact, it is difficult to separate the two. Prosthesis technology, for McLuhan, is not merely an external device but one that actively infiltrates retrospectively back within the organism, changing patterns of thought and cultural desire. The image of technology, which we are apt to dwell on, is a stick (plus, I guess, a ruined anthill, a fat monkey, and well, we might stop there). But in fact the fat monkey comes later, only after the real effect of this technology has taken hold. That effect being the desire for ants, which such technology engenders and which is a cognitive or psychological shift: the monkey, in fact, becomes ant-mad!

It may well be that the monkey does not appreciate this and simply plunders anthills with an increased determinism; the pattern of technological deployment remains essentially the same. But when the system is appreciated for its psychological and not merely technical consequence – that such desire for ants has been released – then creative thought may operate, propagating what? Deforestation? Monkeys breaking branches?

Perhaps we might then characterize the various players in this new terrain in such terms. Bernard Cache, intent on analyzing the moment the monkey took up the stick, anticipating what might be done with it (but he himself not into ants, I guess); Greg Lynn, going further, quite systematically plundering anthills, becoming replete simply by exploiting the technical capacity of the stick; Lars Spuybroek then going beyond the apparent technology to begin to colonize ants(!), actively pursuing the changed psychology in a positive sense, desire being called into play creatively. And dECOi? Well, as an Englishman, I reckon we will do little more than organize the table manners, articulating the anticipated feast!

During the question period, the issue of the difference between technique and technology was raised, which is a subtle distinction, but which might well serve to separate the manner of the various approaches. Lynn and Cache, it seems to me, whose interest seems to be in the formal (technicist) aspects of a new technology, continue a modern rationalist attitude that technology (per se) offers liberating potential – but which is in any case pursued narrowly as an interest in surface effects and the extent to which new technologies violate current disciplinary practices. dECOi and Nox concern themselves in a much broader sense, with the psychological effects of our latest technologies, adopting much more open-ended and ambiguous processes, less concerned with a reaction to historic precedent. For the latter two, technology may offer liberating potential in architecture, but this must occur through a rich and sustained pursuit via conditions of the social, the environmental, and the technical.

Crude as such distinctions may be, they might serve to re-orient or clarify technological debate as a new terrain begins to establish itself. If nothing else, Anymore made clear that there is quite a distinct platform emerging, which profoundly requali-fies extant modes of practice. The closure of Any next year may well mark an (or several) opening(s) of sorts.

Yours, with great appreciation for your efforts behind the scenes,

MARK GOULTHORPE
PARIS

DEAR ANY,

Anymore's strength was its ability to engage a dazzling array of subjects within a critical framework. However, it was at this same juncture that the conference was disconcerting. A critical approach is essential to the development of any discipline, but in order to be effective, criticism must be deployed with intellec-tual rigor.

To a large extent, recent attacks on "French" or "critical" theory have been due to the lack of intellectual rigor in the use of theory. Consequently, it is claimed that advocates of French theory deliberately obscure scientific and theoretical under-standings, and amount to no more than "intellectual impostors." At the core of this debate, now called the "science wars," is the question of the nature of "truth." Some maintain that entering into the argument valorizes a narrowly positivist understanding of truth, and that the best strategy is simply not to engage the debate.

I believe this response is flawed. There is more at stake here than intellectual notoriety. The proponents of the science wars are arguing that public funding to these so-called impostors should be cut off. And indeed, this has started to happen. In the United States, academics have recently been refused prominent posts as a result of mere association with those accused of work-ing within a critical framework.

Yet at Anymore, architects routinely made loose references to concepts such as chaos, which are central to debates in the science wars. It was disturbingly evident that such terms were being deployed without any of the caution that theorists, doing their best to ward off attacks and preserve their status within academia, currently seem to advocate.

I am not arguing against the use of critical ideas, nor for an exclusive, academically privileged, deployment of them. On the contrary, I feel it is imperative that practitioners engage their dis-cipline critically. And for this effort, architects should be applauded. However, when the majority of the theory being used by archi-tects is under constant attack, which in turn causes theorists themselves to modify their positions, one would hope that the users of such ideas be aware of the changing dimensions of debate. Apart from the social scientists present at Anymore, this did not seem to be the case.

To date, architecture has been immune to the science wars. Perhaps this has resulted in a freedom of inquiry that has made Any the successful series that it is. However, for all the talk of "context" and "after" at Anymore, perhaps it will be in the inter-est of future architecture to situate its theory within the context of a wider contemporary debate.

MICHAEL NUROK
PARIS

In my opinion, the Anymore conference in Paris was of the highest interest. I was very glad to be there and I do hope to join the next one in NYC. I wish there were more opportunities like this in the architecture world.

I would just like to add a couple of quick thoughts that I did not get a chance to express during the conference.

1. During his talk, Peter Eisenman mentioned various ghosts. The first was the ghost of Bilbao. The Guggenheim is more and more some kind of *convité de pierre* that we expect to appear from below, in front of us at any moment, as if via some kind of underworld. It works in this way and will continue to do so for a while. The same thing happened a few years ago at a meeting at the NAi in Rotterdam on the future of museums. Gehry was not physically there (many others were: Libeskind, Hollein, Jencks, Fuchs, etc.) but the Guggenheim ghost was hovering in the room. Nothing to be afraid of. Bilbao is just a masterpiece at the end of the 20th century. It is not "Mickey Mouse" and it does not need Lars Spuybroek's work or any other recent experimentation to cause it to be upgraded and eventually become like the Parthenon, as Rosalind Krauss suggested. But Bilbao is also a cul de sac: you cannot go any further in that direction. Peter's Staten Island is a very different project. When built, it may – hopefully will – become the masterpiece at the beginning of the 21st century. It is an amazing piece of architecture.

2. There is another interesting aspect. A kind of generational gap seemed to materialize, in some way, inside the auditorium of the Palais de Chaillot and probably outside it as well. It seemed difficult to me – and to others with whom I happened to talk – to establish a real dialogue between the generation of architects who are now in their fifties and sixties, and those who are in their thirties and early forties. The work of Lars Spuybroek, Greg Lynn, or Mark Goulthorpe, for example, though as important and experimental as any other work, is not yet mature enough. I recently visited Greg's church in Queens, New York. It is a tough building, very impressive. You may not like it (I did), but you can't feel neutral looking at it. And Lars's Water Pavilion in Holland is a wild interior, an amazingly original architectural space. This kind of computer age neo-expressionism seems to constitute today what minimalism and transparency did yesterday. It is probably the most meaningful arena in contemporary experimentation. Is there any way of quickly filling this generational gap?

3. A last question: The other experimental area of the contemporary agenda is the so-called "transcultural dimension" in architecture. Is there anymore interest in it?

Thank you very much.

LIVIO SACCHI
ROME

1. According to Borges, the Chinese think that;
"Every new thing there is on earth projects its archetype in the sky."
This also goes for Any.[1]
2. Any: word with a bifurcated meaning, motionless yet ever moving, masked by freedom but concealing its own rules.[2]
3. Like a cabal, Any encloses and protects the sign.[3]
4. On the banks of the Seine, Any pretended to sleepily stare at the water but was fascinated by the still, tall, dark shadow.[4]

[1] This comment by J.L. Borges, taken from "Atlas," in the *Tutte le opere* [Complete Works], vol. II, has, in this instance, both a geographical and a literary meaning. The first clearly refers to the trend, pioneered by Borges in Argentine literature, from the picturesque to the more aesthetic, from which emerges the second meaning, that is, from the local to the universal. Analogously, Any has looked to carry its architectural language from an autonomous individuality to a universal autonomy, repositioning the newly mediated architecture onto a theoretical/aesthetic/real level. Indeed, for Peter Eisenman the problem seems to be that of "writing" a new and different "metaphysics" that would surpass the classical, anthropologically centered Graeco-Roman tradition, even if it doesn't really clarify its relationship with nihilism.
[2] We could say "composed word," but this would inevitably diminish its meaning; Any-one, Any-more, Any-body, etc.: multiples of an echo of meaning that have to be at the same time continuously "fastened," "anchored," and included inside the oxymoron of the initial pronoun *any*. In other words, the theoretical obligation, or obsession, of Peter Eisenman is that of finding the principles and laws for an architectonic language. Paradoxically, Eisenman is searching for rules simulating their uselessness.
[3] From *Oppositions* to *Any*, we cannot fail to recognize the Jewish heritage of its founder, Peter Eisenman, who has created, with great success, a cultural and mediated strategy unique in contemporary criticism. But to most, the depth and originality of such "theory" is but a fleeting moment.
[4] The Anymore conference was held at the Cinémathèque in the Palais de Chaillot, against which, in the morning light, was silhouetted the long vertical shadows of the Eiffel Tower. In this expansive scenario of parterre, of memories and of pretense, the many words of the orators flowed fluidly, yet were indifferent to each other – reflecting the same indifference as the water that flows in the Seine. But nobody but Eisenman realized that this event was merely the repetition of that eternal spectacle of the sign.

RENATO RIZZI
ROVERETO, ITALY

DEAR ANY,

It has been six years, you tell me, since I last attended an Any conference. While I have missed actively participating in the discussions, in retrospect, I appreciate the value of the break. Gaps as well as pauses can be productive. Returning to the debate after this interval, it quickly became apparent that my absence afforded an opportunity for a critical distance, which otherwise would have been unavailable to me. In Paris, everything seemed both familiar and strange. It was not just a question of the continuity and discontinuity of the participants – old friends and new faces; something else, something far less easy to identify was shifting. It was fitting for the penultimate Any conference to be held in Paris. Though the first conference had taken place in LA, the intellectual "origin" of Any was always Paris. The theoretical controversies that erupted on the world stage in Paris in 1968 have governed critical debate in the arts and humanities for thirty years. Throughout the decade, the questions posed in Paris during the 1960s have continued to frame – directly and indirectly – most of the important issues considered in the Any conferences. What became clear – sometimes painfully clear – in Paris in 1999 was that the critical trajectory from which Any had taken its initial orientation had actually run its course before the decade of the 1990s began. Paris – and all it has come to represent during the last half of the 20th century – has become a specter haunting reflection, which is no longer capable of inspiring creative thinking and practice.

The decade of Any has been marked by three closely interrelated developments: 1. The worldwide triumph of market capitalism; 2. Rapidly accelerating processes of globalization; and 3. The exponential growth of information and communications technologies. When Any began in 1990, it should have been obvious that the collapse of the Berlin Wall marked a seismic shift, which would reverberate throughout the social, economic, and political landscape in ways that would transform the conditions of cultural production. Yet few anticipated the remarkable developments of the past ten years. In the face of a world that looks very different from the world in which Any began, the theories, questions, and preoccupations of the 1970s–1980s now seem strangely dated.

What most impressed me – other than the size of Sam – about Anymore was the palpable tension pervading the conference. This was, in part, a function of a generational shift – with all its inevitable oedipal overtones. Young architects and theorists I had never met were visibly disturbed by an avant-garde, which, for them, had become a repressive old-garde. Needless to say, those who have set the terms of debate for more than a decade were far from ready to yield ground quickly. Far from a failure, this tension was a mark of Anymore's success. And yet,

in spite of well-intended efforts, the conference failed to create an atmosphere in which these tensions and conflicts could find clear and explicit articulation. This failure, not surprisingly, was a result of an inequitable distribution of power.

It would, however, be a mistake to attribute these potentially productive tensions merely to traditional psycho-social conflicts. More importantly, they also reflect very different orientations to the new situation emerging at the turn of the millennium. Without succumbing to apocalyptic excesses, it is undeniable that we are in the midst of an extraordinary socio-cultural transition. In attempting to identify what is occurring in our midst, I have been led to analyze what I describe as emerging *network culture*. Network culture is not merely the function of rapid technological innovation but involves changes that pervade *all* aspects of contemporary experience. Firmly entrenched in the ways of modernism, the older generation of theorists and practitioners remains resolutely committed to a tradition of criticism marked by repeated resistance to the situation at hand. The younger generation, by contrast, appears to be far less interested in theory, criticism, and resistance and much more inclined to accept given conditions. This acceptance does not, of course, imply a rejection of change; on the contrary, change is actively embraced, even celebrated. The quest for change, however, is no longer inspired by criticism; rather, change is an end in itself and, thus, is affirmed *as such*. The "Yes" echoing in this affirmation is the "Yes" of Nietzsche's *Gay Science* – with all of the nihilistic implications it inevitably implies. When history loses both its moorings and direction, temporal process becomes, in the words of Michael Lewis, the ceaseless search for "the new new thing."

The affirmation of change as such both reflects and reinforces a world in which the highest good is the increasing acceleration of flows of capital. Capital becomes, as Marx anticipated, "a *perpetuum mobile*" whose value increases with the rate of exchange. In such an economy, speed becomes the highest economic value. If you are not making it new, you are not making it. There has always been a covert complicity between modernism, speed, and capitalism. Even when attempting to escape capitalism's machinations, modernism's preoccupation with innovation has served to reinforce the economic need for rapid obsolescence. What is now occurring in network culture explicitly displays the aesthetics of this economic process as well as the economics of this aesthetic.

Nowhere is this display more evident than in New York. Anticipating a future that seemed to be moving toward the so-called near and far East, Any began in LA. In the intervening years, we discovered that we were too far south and were looking toward the wrong East. The most significant changes of the past decade have come from Silicon Valley and increasingly have been supported by northeastern financial investors and institutions. Global capitalism would no more have been possible without Silicon Valley's technological revolution than Silicon Valley would have been possible without Wall Street's financial revolution. Throughout the course of the decade, there has been a gradual drift of power from West to East. If global capitalism had a capital, it would be New York City. There is no better place to ponder the coming millennium than New York. The trajectory of the A-NY project was prescient in ways that never could have been imagined a decade ago. The challenge when we meet once again, and for the last time, will be to determine what all of this means – if, indeed, it means anything.

MARK TAYLOR
WILLIAMSTOWN, MA

June 25, 1999

Akira Asada [21]
Eric Briat [11]
Christine Buci-Glucksman [23]
Bernard Cache [7]
Jean-Louis Cohen [16]
Marie-Hélène Contal [10]
Hubert Damisch [18]
Cynthia Davidson [19]
Mark Goulthorpe [25]
Elizabeth Grosz [17]
Paul Henninger [28]
Dominique Jakob [8]
Tom Kovac [2]
Phyllis Lambert [26]
Brendan MacFarlane [12]
Fiona Meadows [13]
Frédéric Migayrou [3]
Marc Mimram [22]
Frédéric Nantois [1]
Molly Nesbit [6]
Franco Purini [15]
Kazuyo Sejima [14]
Lars Spuybroek [4]
Mark C. Taylor [9]
Bernard Tschumi [24]
Yannis Tsiomis [27]
Anthony Vidler [20]
Mirko Zardini [5]

Anyone Corporation and its 11-year program of
Any books and conferences are made possible b
a gift from Shimizu Corporation. Based in Japan
Shimizu Corporation is an international design,
engineering, and construction firm that takes
pride in supporting leading-edge research and
development to better the human environment.